MYTH AND SYMBOL IN ANCIENT EGYPT

MYTH AND SYMBOL IN ANCIENT EGYPT

R. T. RUNDLE CLARK

WITH 18 PLATES
40 LINE DRAWINGS
A CHART OF RELIGIOUS SYMBOLS
AND A MAP

THAMES AND HUDSON

© 1959 Thames and Hudson Ltd, London
First paperback edition 1978
Reprinted 1978

Originally published in the United States of America
in 1960 by The Grove Press

Library of Congress Catalog card number: 77–92262

Printed in Great Britain

CONTENTS

6 *Contents*

ILLUSTRATIONS

Plates

Line Drawings

TO MY WIFE

PREFACE

THE EGYPTIANS lived apart from the rest of the ancient world. The Nile valley was separated from Asia by sea and tracts of desert. There are signs of relations with the developing civilization of Mesopotamia at the very beginning of Egyptian history but after that very little was borrowed from abroad until Asiatic invaders overwhelmed the country about 1700 B.C. It is this cultural isolation which makes Egyptian ideas so difficult to appreciate.

The myths, symbols and social concepts of the Babylonians, Syrians and Jews were passed on from people to people to become part of the Western heritage, whereas those of the Egyptians were never transmitted and so seem completely alien. Furthermore, whilst the cuneiform script of the Mesopotamians became the means of communication between the peoples of the Near East, Egyptian hieroglyphs never became popular beyond the borders of Egypt itself.[1] Hence, even when Egyptian art forms were taken up by Asiatics the ideas which they expressed were left behind. So the idea grew up that the Egyptians were somehow different from the rest of mankind and that the values of their civilization were impenetrable.

Basically this cannot be true. In recent years psychologists and anthropologists have been showing with increasingly convincing evidence that the major psychic, religious and social problems are common to all mankind. If, then, the thinking of any people makes no sense to us it must be that we have not yet understood the unfamiliar terms in which it is presented. In Egypt the terminology is mythological, but not quite in the way we usually understand myths. Our ideas about myths are derived from the stories of the Greeks and the Norsemen. It is only in the last few years that we have come to realize that these are late and sophisticated versions of more primitive originals. They have lost their connection with ritual and make their appeal as stories whose significance is in themselves rather than in what they may hint at beyond themselves. They are about human beings, not gods, whatever names the characters may have.

But there is another kind of mythology. Egyptian myths are not closely integrated stories. They concern gods who are not blown-up human beings but forces of nature. There is a close relation between the things done in the myths and temple or popular ritual, but this is less obtrusive than the symbolism. The Egyptians lived before the birth of philosophy as an independent way of thinking. They used their myths to convey their insights into the workings of nature and the ultimately indescribable realities of the soul. This is why their legends cannot be understood without constant reference to the supporting theology. Egyptian gods are nearer the stark archetypes of the unconscious mind than the Greek ones and, in a sense, they are more intellectual too, for they are expressing ideas. Egyptian myths cannot be retold, for then they become meaningless or trivial; they can only be appreciated through the actual texts, and these are to be read not for their linguistic interest but for their religious and metaphysical penetration. It will then be seen that the matter is not so strange after all. The Ancient Egyptians were an immensely able and deeply God-conscious people, concerned with the same great themes that are familiar to us in Greek and Christian literature.

The study of Egyptian religion is still in its infancy. In the last few years there has been a notable tendency to treat the texts with greater respect for their contents than was usual a generation ago. The religious literature cannot be understood without some sympathy for the outlook of its authors. But this is exactly what modern scholars have found most difficult. The moving rhetoric of the hymns and prayers cannot be conveyed in flat literal translation because Egyptian means of expression were very different from our own. But the rhetoric and under-lying excitement may be the most important thing that should be expressed, at least to the non-specialist reader. Hence there is a need to paraphrase in some places; in others, excessive caution leads to complete misunderstanding. It is in interpre-tation, however, that courage is really needed. The Pyramid and Coffin Texts, for example, are the supreme achievements of their time and are to be explained as such and not as a chance collection of heterogeneous tags put together to justify the pretensions of rival priesthoods. The more they are studied the greater appear their literary quality and intellectual content. It is in this spirit that the present work has been written. The author is convinced that the Egyptians are themselves their best interpreters. Where possible, therefore, the myths have been told in the words of the original. The references in the hymns are often so oblique that they have to be coaxed to reveal their true or significant meaning. But the Egyptians did this them-selves, as we know from the explanatory glosses which they interspersed in their most important theological works. It is only fair to warn the reader that this is a personal interpretation of the material; it could be no other in the present state of our knowledge. The rationalistic and slightly contemptuous objectivity of the traditional Orientalist can no longer be upheld in this field.

Too much time and energy has been spent studying the origins of the Egyptian gods. It is vain, for example, to seek for the prehistory of Osiris until one knows what sort of god he was in his heyday. This work therefore omits all reference to origins; it concentrates on the creative and classical phases of Egyptian history. That is, it deals with the myths known to have been current between 2700 and 1700 B.C. This is not to say that after the latter date there was no creative spirit left in the religion. However, the subsequent developments did not add significantly to the repertoire of myths.

The selection of myths may seem somewhat arbitrary, but this cannot be avoided in such a vast subject. The Egyptians had many myths not mentioned here, but it is hoped that the main themes have been described. The chief sources are the Pyramid Texts, which were inscribed in the walls of the inner rooms of pharaohs and queens of the Sixth Dynasty (2350–2250 B.C.), and the Coffin Texts which belong to the succeeding period; the latter provide a new source of material not available to the general public in translation and give a unique insight into the workings of the Egyptian mind. They are the earliest and most intelligible version of many sections of the famous Book of the Dead.

A chapter has been added on the visual symbolism because it has such close connections with the literature—in fact, one cannot be understood without the other. Where possible the illustrations have been chosen from coffins of the late New Empire in the British Museum, a relatively unfamiliar but accessible source of material.

The author is indebted to the following for permission to reproduce objects in their charge: Mr I. E. S. Edwards, Keeper of Egyptian Antiquities and the Trustees of the British Museum (Pl. 1, 3–5, 7–12, 14–17), the City of Birmingham Museum and Art Gallery (Pl. 6, 13), the Director and Trustees of the Fitzwilliam Museum, Cambridge (Pl. 18). He has received invaluable help from Dr J. Gwyn Griffiths of University College, Swansea, who has read most of the work in MS. and saved him from many errors. He is grateful to the Rev. Professor S. G. F. Brandon of the University of Manchester for many suggestions and advice. Mr T. G. H. James and Mr A. F. Shore of the British Museum were of great service in helping to choose the illustrations and made many valuable suggestions and corrections. He wishes to thank Professor Otto of Heidelberg, and Professor Brunner of Tübingen, for invaluable and stimulating letters on the cosmology and the Coffin Texts. Dr Erik Hornung kindly allowed the author access to his doctoral thesis on Egyptian ideas of darkness and night. He has benefited much from his talks with colleagues at the University of Birmingham, notably Professor George Thomson, Dr F. J. Tritsch and Mr R. Willetts. He has to thank Mr F. Rushton, the university's photographer, for several fine pictures, and Mrs D. Godwin and Mrs J. Cattell who have typed his MS.

R.T.R.C.

CHRONOLOGICAL TABLE
(TO THE END OF THE NEW KINGDOM)

Following the example of Manetho, who wrote a history of Egypt in Greek in the second century B.C., it is customary to arrange the kings in dynasties. The First and Second Dynasties cover the Early Dynastic Period. Then follows the Old Kingdom: the Third to Sixth Dynasties. This is succeeded by what is now known as the First Intermediate Period, followed by the Middle Kingdom, then the Second Intermediate Period and the New Kingdom, which ends with the collapse of the Twenty-first Dynasty.

EARLY DYNASTIC PERIOD

Dynasty 1
c. 3000 B.C.

Union of Upper and Lower Egypt into one nation, with capital at Memphis.
Beginnings of writing.
Formative period of ritual and calendar.
High God—Horus as a falcon.

Dynasty 2
c. 2850 B.C.

South and north fall apart.
Southern kingdom takes Seth as its emblem.

OLD KINGDOM

Dynasty 3
c. 2780 B.C.

Reassertion of united kingdom.
Construction of earlier phase of Heliopolitan theology.
Presumed time of the development of the Osiris legends.
Kings buried in step-pyramid complexes.
High God—Atum.

Dynasty 4
c. 2600 B.C.

Great Pyramid Age, absolute concentration of power in the hands of the royal family.
Supreme achievements of art and architecture.
High God—Atum or Rê.

Dynasties 5 and 6   High priests of Heliopolis increase power.
c. 2500 B.C.   Decline of royal power and the beginnings of feudalism.
Spread of Osiris cult. Pyramid Texts.

FIRST INTERMEDIATE PERIOD
Dynasties 7 to 10   Anarchy, followed by the rise of a kingdom at
c. 2250 B.C.   Herakleopolis and a rival power at Thebes.
Intense literary activity.
Early Coffin Texts.

MIDDLE KINGDOM
Dynasties 11 to 13   Theban power victorious. State reunited.
c. 2050 B.C.   Reorganization of monarchy. End of feudalism.
Developing relations with Asia and Crete.
High God—Amun.

SECOND INTERMEDIATE PERIOD
Dynasties 14 to 17   Egypt invaded by Asiatic invaders, the 'Hyksos'.
c. 1750 B.C.   Introduction of horses and chariots, bronze and improved methods of irrigation.

NEW KINGDOM
Dynasty 18   Hyksos driven out. Restoration of native rule.
c. 1580 B.C.   Egypt takes the warpath and becomes an imperial power, and the richest State in the civilized world.
Priesthood of Amun at the height of its power and influence.
Development of theology of Amun as Universal Spirit.
Rebellion against Amunism by Akhenaton in favour of a monotheistic concept of the visible sun.
Dynasties 19 to 21   Restoration of Amunism.
c. 1320 B.C.   Second period of imperial wars. Egypt's drive to the north cut off by the Hittites.
Israelites attested in Palestine.
Invasions of sea peoples repelled.
Literary activity—tales and love poetry.
Merging of the church of Amun with the State.

THE GODS

1 THE SYSTEM OF HELIOPOLIS

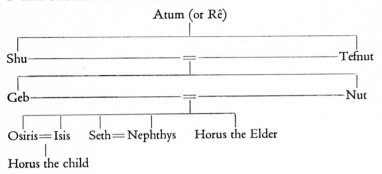

Atum (or Rê)

Shu ════════ Tefnut

Geb ════════ Nut

Osiris═Isis   Seth═Nephthys   Horus the Elder

Horus the child

2 THE GODS OF MEMPHIS

Ptah—Creator and supreme lord (cf. Atum)
Nefertem—the Primeval Lotus
Sakhmet—the Terrible Lioness
Sokar—the God of the Dead (cf. Osiris)

3 THE GODS OF HERMOPOLIS

Nothing, Endlessness, Inertness, Darkness—the negatives of the
Primeval Waters (given consorts they form 'the Eight')
Thoth—Ibis or baboon. Intelligence, writing and Moon God. Master
of Ceremonies at the Divine Court

4 THE GREAT GODDESS

She had different names:
Hathor—at Dendera
Neith—at Sais
Mut—at Thebes
Ejo (the Cobra)—at Buto
Nekhabit (the Vulture)—at El Kab

5 THE GODS OF THEBES

Amun—'the Invisible One'—created by the spirits of Hermopolis and
the Sun God Rê at the same time
Mut—Amun's consort
Khonsu—the Moon Child of Amun and Mut

6 THE GOD OF EDFU

Horus as the Winged Sun Disk. Falcon and human hero

7 THE GODS OF DENDERA

Hathor—woman, cow, sky. Mother of all things
Ihy—Hathor's child, worshipped as Child or Primeval Serpent

(The systems of Edfu and Dendera were interrelated)

N.B. The system of Heliopolis was the orthodoxy, but it was not
regarded as exclusively correct, except in Heliopolis itself.

MYTHOLOGICAL SCHEME

The Universe was organized in stages. All Egyptian myths are episodes in a developing scheme from the beginning to the establishment of Horus as king of the present world. It was roughly as follows:

In the Primeval Waters	Original Spirit moved and begat the first Twain and dispatched his original Eye *or* Original Spirit created the patterns of future creation *or* Negative Qualities came together to form the Cosmic Egg
The Emergence	Spirit appeared as Primeval Mound *or* as Flower, as rearing Serpent, as Child, as Pillar *or* a series of these transformations *or* Spirit recalled the first Twain *or* Spirit flew up as Primeval Bird
The Order	The Spirit (now High God) embraced his daughter *or* recalled his Eye The taming of the Eye The tears of the Eye become mankind The reign of Rê—a Golden Age
The Departure of the High God	The High God retreated from his creation The reign of Shu—birth of Geb and Nut (Earth and Sky)
The Separation of Earth and Sky	Shu separated his children Nut gave birth to the stars Nut gave birth to her five great children

	or Geb assumed serpent-form and swallowed seven cobras, thus forming the ring of the world. Rule of Geb
The Reign of Osiris	Osiris' claims were disputed by Seth Osiris taught mankind the arts of civilization Another (and alternative) Golden Age
The Passion of Osiris	Osiris murdered by Seth. Isis sought his body and cared for it The procreation of Horus The vigil over the body of Osiris
The Reign of Seth	Seth ruled the world—confusion and terror Isis went into hiding and gave birth to Horus The childhood adventures of Horus Horus set out to avenge his father (Perhaps here?) Seth defeated a sea monster
The Great Quarrel	Horus and Seth fought for the supremacy The adventures of the Eye of Horus and the testicles of Thoth Thoth persuaded the two contestants to take their dispute to the Council of the Gods
The Judgment	Horus was awarded the supremacy and crowned king Seth became the God of Storm and was put into the boat of the Sun God
The Salvation of Osiris	Horus (or his representative) went down to the Underworld to see Osiris Osiris was given the Eye or the good news that Horus was king The soul of Osiris was liberated The reign of Horus—the beginning of the earthly monarchy

CHIEF CULT CENTRES OF
ANCIENT EGYPT

The principal deities worshipped in the temples marked on the map opposite were:

BUTO: Originally two temples, one on each bank of the river. The western one was sacred to Ejo, the cobra-goddess, the eastern to a heron and later to Horus the son of Isis

SAIS: Neith

TANIS: Seth—at least in the later period

BUSIRIS: Osiris

LETOPOLIS: Horus who controls his two eyes—a form of Horus the Elder

HELIOPOLIS: Atum or Rê

MEMPHIS: Ptah and Sakhmet

HERAKLEOPOLIS: Herishef

HERMOPOLIS: Thoth and the 'Eight'—the primordial creatures of the Abyss

SIUT: Wepwat, the 'Opener of the Ways'

THINIS: Onuris

ABYDOS: a jackal called 'Controller of the Westerners' and, later, Osiris

DENDERA: Hathor and her child Ihy

KOPTOS: Min

OMBOS: Seth

THEBES: Amun

EL KAB: Nekhabit

HIERAKONPOLIS: Horus the Elder

EDFU: Horus as the High God

ELEPHANTINE: Khnum

Hathor was the goddess of mountainous or desert foreign countries—especially Syria, Sinai or the Eastern Desert
Libya, the Western Desert, belonged to Seth or to Ha, the patron of the Western Mountains

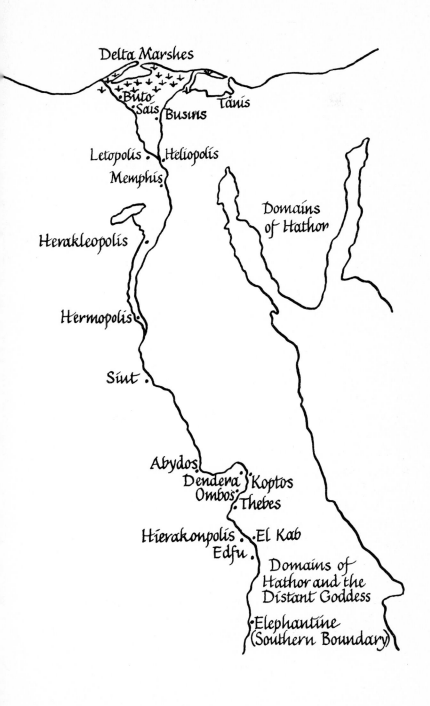

Delta Marshes

Buto
Sais
Busiris
Tanis

Letopolis
Heliopolis

Memphis

Domains
of Hathor

Herakleopolis

Hermopolis

Siut

Abydos
Dendera
Koptos
Ombos
Thebes

Hierakonpolis
El Kab
Edfu

Domains of
Hathor and the
Distant Goddess

Elephantine
(Southern Boundary)

INTRODUCTION

ABOUT 3000 B.C. the Egyptians of the Nile valley invaded and conquered the Delta. This was the beginning of the 'Two Lands', the first great nation State. Since the system of picture/ writing known as Hieroglyphs was being evolved at the same time, the union of Egypt marks the beginning of history. During the following five centuries the Egyptians made very rapid advances in material culture, social organization and government. This was paralleled by equally vigorous activity in the more intellectual spheres of literature and religion. By the end of the so/called Old Kingdom, about 2300 B.C., the pat/ tern of Egyptian civilization was complete. Much happened in the following two millennia, but there was no fundamental change until the conversion to Christianity in the fourth and fifth centuries A.D. An Egyptian of the early dynasties would have been at home in the Egypt of the Roman Empire; he would have recognized the gods, the art, the methods of agriculture and, with a little help, he would have been able to read the public inscriptions.

The apparently fixed pattern of Ancient Egyptian civilization is usually explained in terms of the unchanging system of irrigational agriculture, which has remained almost the same from the beginning of history until the present time. Now it is true that the modern *fellah* spends his time performing practi/ cally the same tasks as his predecessor did four thousand years ago, and with very much the same tools. As a consequence the peasant of today must resemble his remote ancestor in many ways. In fact, this is true in all sorts of things—music, humour, folk/tales, birth customs, diet, festivals and attitudes towards the aged and children. But what may be valid for the peasantry has certainly not been the case with the leading sections of the people. The upper classes have been profoundly affected by political events, while conversion to Christianity, and then to Islam, completely changed the lives and outlooks of the educated. When we speak of Ancient Egypt we are not thinking of the unchanging world of the peasant but the great world of the pharaohs and the priests, scribes and artists who supported it. And this world, in spite of foreign invasions and political domination by Greeks and then by Romans, remained more or less intact until the third century A.D. It was Christianity that killed it, in all its aspects. The inevitable conclusion is that Egyptian religion was the heart of the civilization. When that lost its nerve or was superseded the rest fell apart.

Any religion is a complex thing; Egyptian religion was especially so, partly because of the rich diversity of the civiliza-tion but even more because it penetrated and informed every aspect of life. The Greeks were the first to discover spheres of activity which were independent of religious conditions or to be expressed in non-religious terms. Since then—but only intermittently—Western man has been accustomed to set experience into two divisions, Church and State, clerical and lay, religion and science. The Egyptians belonged to the pre-Greek era; for them there was no dichotomy. The gods were everywhere, the king was the essential priest and all acts were played out against a background of divine patterns. Gods, men, animals, plants and physical phenomena all belonged to the same great order. There were no distinct realms of being. Conception, germination, sickness or chemical change were just as much god-directed as the motions of the stars or the beginnings of the world. The first and most characteristic mark of the religion was the ritual. This was built around a few basic ceremonies—a dedication rite known as 'Opening the Mouth'; the treatment of images in their shrines; the offering of Mayet, the Goddess of the World Order, at the end of certain rites; the liturgy of offerings; the enthronement rites of the king; and the *Proyet* or public procession of the god. The various rites determined the calendar, primarily an arrangement of festivals, which was arranged with reference to the phases of the moon and governed by reference to the observation of Sirius, the dog star. The dispositions of the celebrants in these rites were the governing factor in the design of temples and tombs. And the ritual alphabet, so to speak, remained almost unchanged for several thousand years. However complex the services became, they were compounded of the same elements. One is reminded of how the Christian Church has been a place for the celebration of Holy Communion and how this determined the layout of every building and provided the element of architectural continuity.

Religious ritual is not just a series of actions performed for their own sake. These acts are symbolic; that is, they refer to things other than themselves, and this reference is always to something in the world of the gods. In Egyptian religion there is a theology wound around the ritual, so that one cannot be considered without the other. The shrine of the god, for instance, was 'the Horizon', the land of glorious light beyond the dawn horizon where the gods dwelt. The temple was an image of the universe as it now exists and, at the same time, the land on which it stood was the Primeval Mound which arose from the waters of the Primordial Ocean at creation. When, again, at the close of the daily temple service, the priest raised a small figure of Mayet in front of the divine image, this act was meant to assert that rightness and order had been re-established, but it was also a repetition of an event that took place at the beginning of the world. It is vital to the spirit of Egyptian religion that the symbolism should be twofold. The rite was celebrated to ensure that divine grace should flow out into the affairs of mankind, but it also stood for the repetition of some mythical happening in the time of the gods. A ceremony was meaningless without its mythical and theological references, and these were provided in the prayers, litanies and hymns that accompanied the actions. Things done and things said were complementary. This is why there were two priestly roles in any service, the Celebrant and the Reader. The former was called the 'Semty' and wore a leopard-skin draped over his back, the latter was 'the Holder of the Roll' and was distin-guished by a strip of linen passing over one shoulder like a deacon's stole.

All the universal religions look back to some founder or particular revelation. This implies that they are deliberately different from the earlier cults and outlooks of the countries where they originated. Egyptian religion belonged to the older dispensation. It grew directly out of the customs of prehistoric farmers and herdsmen.

In spite of much speculation, nothing definite is known about this early religion. It was obviously a collective business, concerned with the prosperity of the community in terms of fertility and success in war and hunting. It was also devoted to the cult of the dead or ancestor worship and had an especial regard for the moon and stars. In one respect the Egyptians remained throughout their long history addicted to these primitive attitudes. It is likely that the main cult of the pre-historic people was that of a Mother Goddess who was also the sky. This goddess-worship seems to have been kept alive among the common people throughout the ages, reappearing in pro-vincial centres and whenever the official religion lost its grip, until finally it almost ousted all the other gods in the great expansion of Isis mysteries at the second and third centuries A.D. Most of the ritual was a legacy from the prehistoric past, when it had been performed by semi-divine chieftains to ensure the continuation of the powers of nature. During the formative period of the first five dynasties, however, these ceremonies were transformed and reinterpreted to suit the requirements of new religious ideas. There is no doubt that the priests of Heliopolis and Memphis were the leaders in this practice and that the centralizing kings of the time gradually forced the ceremonies of Heliopolis on the rest of the country. The process can be seen at work in the texts on the pyramids of the Old Kingdom, where the temple hymns have been taken from their contexts to provide the services of the then new funerary cult. It can be seen, too, very clearly in the rite of 'Opening the Mouth' and the 'Liturgy of Offerings' which have been revised to fit the doctrines of Osiris. In other places one can see myths being composed to fit or justify the old ritual.[1] The ritual was fixed but the myth was elastic. Therefore the myths went on being revised and elaborated, particularly during the time of the kings of the Ninth Dynasty, but to some extent all through Egyptian history.

In recent years it has come to be realized that Egyptian art is nearly all symbolism. The architectural arrangements and decoration were a kind of mythical landscape. This was worked out down to the last detail of the furnishing; everything had a meaning or could be made to have one. Columns, capitals, walls, windowlattices, drainage outlets, gateways, screens and shrines all had significant traditional shapes with decoration indicative of mythical or theological schemes. The great temple halls, for example, with their papyrusshaped columns simulated a Delta swamp in which the god's boat floated when it was carried out of the inner shrine in procession. The papyrus swamp, however, was not quite the earthly one but the 'Reed Marshes',[2] the faery Land of the Rising Sun just beyond the eastern horizon. If we say that the architecture provided a background for the ritual, that is to make the one subordinate to the other; but in fact the visual arts, mythology and ritual were facets of one reality. An Egyptian temple appealed to the eye and the imagination at the same time. The full sensuous impact of a great ceremony must have been very impressive indeed. In addition to what can be directly known there must have been the music, the stately language of the prayers and the prevailing atmosphere. But all had a deeper meaning, part mystical, part reasonable.

Even so, the religion would not have persisted so long had it not been for the many ways in which it satisfied and enriched intellectual curiosity. The texts are full of explanatory asides and added notes, the accretions of generations of speculating or inquiring scribes. Many Egyptians were deeply aware that their myths and symbols expressed intuitions about the nature of God, man and the universe and that there could only be partial answers to the major metaphysical and spiritual problems. The difficult and perhaps insoluble questions that have bedevilled Christian theology are to be encountered in the literature of Ancient Egypt: the rival claims of the immanent and transcendent concepts of God, for example; the paradox about the uncreated Creator; the origin of evil; the male and female sides of the divine; or whether God exists in time. Such problems were already worrying the minds of men two thousand years before Christ. They were more noticeable in the formative periods discussed in this book, but the rational spirit never died out, as can be seen from the enigmatic script of the Ptolemaic temples.

In two ways Egyptian religion is unique—in the elaborate theory which it wove around the monarchy and in its pre-occupation with the after-life. Essentially the pharaonic kingship was concerned with the same things as kingship everywhere. It grew out of the ideas and customs of the prehistoric chieftains of the Neolithic world. The real spirit, however, was created during the third millennium B.C., in historical times. The pharaoh had a complex relationship with the divine world. He was the manifestation of the Godhead on earth, the son of God as the sun, begotten through divine intervention. The ritual of the Osiris cycle connected him with the powers of nature. On the earthly plane he was the supreme man, heroic warrior and hunter, champion of right, uniquely vigorous and virtuous. All beneficial power flowed into the world through him, so he was the only true priest and all ceremonies were conducted in his name.[3] Egypt was a union of two distinct regions, the Delta in the north and the Nile valley in the south, and the king was the reconciler of the two. According to one symbol he was the son of an earthly mother and a heavenly father, while according to another he was born —or reborn—the child of the great Mother Goddess. All this was acted out in elaborate ceremonies and expressed in the five names which each pharaoh bore. The king belonged half to the world of myth. Egyptian legends described the transformations of godly power from the first stirrings in the Primeval Waters until the final establishment of Horus, the first king and the pattern of rule and authority.

The cult of the dead has been responsible, one way or another, for preserving most of the remains of Egyptian civilization that we have. It penetrated into nearly every sphere of life. It largely dictated the system of land tenure, its need for permanent buildings was the stimulus for the erection of the first buildings in dressed stone and, more than the royal religion, it linked men with the powers of the unseen world. But in spite of all this, Egyptian ideas about the next world were not very precise. There were two quite distinct fates. According to one, the deceased joined his ancestors who were already lodged in the cemetery on the edge of the desert and with them lived a carefree existence on the model of that on earth—or would do so if his tomb was properly attended to. The other belief was that the soul soared up to join the stars and the sun and moon in their eternal round. The difficulty is that both fates were believed in at the same time. The second idea was expanded considerably during the early Middle Kingdom. In order to reach the heights of the sky the soul had to undergo those transformations which the High God had gone through as he developed from a spirit in the Primeval Waters to his final position as Sun God, or into some of the assistants at these great events. It was this idea that made the cult of the dead an opportunity for creative speculation and gave scope for the elaboration of mythical detail in the funerary literature. Looked at sceptically all this excessive preoccupation with the fate of the dead is foolishness and wishful thinking. The imposing façade of Egyptian culture seems to be nothing but an elaborate excuse for refusing to face up to the inevitable; and some Egyptians themselves felt this. On the other hand, the subtler texts are hardly about death at all but are really about the nature of the human soul and nature and God. Under pressure from

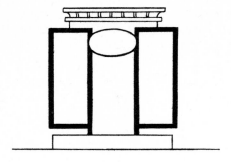

Fig. 1. Representations of sunrise

crude minds the scribes of the Middle Kingdom provided a
Paradise and several Hells, but the majority of the texts provide
alternative symbols of redemption rather than graphic descriptions of ultimate fate. However childish and magic-ridden the
cult of the dead may have been, it was the way the Egyptians
rose above collective religion into the realm of personal piety.

The mythology had therefore to serve two purposes. It was
to give the steps whereby the universe was arranged, leading up
to the final triumph of Horus and the coming of the pharaonic
monarchy. The other purpose—only gradually understood—

was to provide a series of symbols to describe the origin and development of consciousness. The theory of divine kingship was the stimulus of the one, the cult of the soul was the stimulus of the other. This sounds like the verdict of a modern psychologist, but it was already realized by the Egyptians themselves, although not in modern terms. When they mythologized they knew what they were doing.

CHAPTER I

The High God in the Old Kingdom

THE BASIC PRINCIPLE of Egyptian cosmology is the
Primeval Waters. It is common to all the accounts of the
origin of the universe, however much they may differ in detail.
Every creation myth assumes that before the beginning of
things the Primordial Abyss of waters was everywhere, stretching endlessly in all directions. It was not like a sea, for that has
a surface, whereas the original waters extended above as well
as below. There was no region of air or visibility; all was dark
and formless. The present cosmos is a vast cavity, rather like an
air-bubble, amid the limitless expanse. Hence the waters are
still to be met everywhere at the limits of the known—below
the earth, above the sky, and at the ends of the world. Seas,
rivers, rains, wells and floods are parts of the eternal ocean. For
the Egyptians as for the Hebrews, the sky was a 'firmament'
which 'divides the waters from the waters'.

The universe is the abode of light, surrounded by infinite
'thick darkness', a bubble of clarity and order enveloped by the
eternal night of the Primordial Ocean. Before creation 'darkness was upon the face of the deep' and the present world, the
dominion of the Sun God, is only a partial rolling back of the
eternal night. When the gods give dominion to an Egyptian
monarch they

> 'cause your boundaries to extend beneath the whole reach
> of the sky, to the limits of the eternal darkness'[1]

while in a late myth the cosmic sun-bird who illumines the
world says:

> 'I can see right through to the limits of the darkness, I can
> behold everything right through to the Primeval Waters.'[2]

All the legends of origins are, therefore, explanations of how
the positive region of light and form was generated amid the
indefinite watery nothingness of the timeless night.
Water is formless, it has no positive features and of itself
assumes no shape. The Primeval Waters being infinite, all
dimensions, directions or spatial qualities of any kind are
irrelevant. Nevertheless the waters are not nothing. They are
the basic matter of the universe and, in one way or another, all
living things depend upon them. Without the rain and the
river floods plants and animals could not live and the return of
the season of inundation or winter showers marks the start of a
new year of life and growth. The waters are, then, 'the waters of
life' and the Primordial Ocean, known to the Egyptians as
Nun, is 'the father of the gods'.

The emergence from the waters has four aspects: it signifies
the coming of light, life, land and consciousness. The legends
of how things began—the cosmogonies—differ according to
which elements are stressed. The first appearance of light gives
the separation of earth and sky—the myth of Shu, or the first
dawn, when the sun arose out of the waters—often symbolized
by a Divine Child with its finger in its mouth. Life means
spontaneous movement—essentially movement upwards—and
this can be conceived in terms of a rearing serpent or a flower
rising from the waters and opening its petals to reveal the first
light. Land means the emergence of the Primeval Mound, the
'First Place' or 'the Primeval Throne', and with it the establishment of order and direction. The world of life implies mind
or will and mastery over a self. In this sense the origins can be
understood through the original 'Word' and the multitude of
phenomena derived from semi-personified abstractions such as
'Command' or 'Will', and 'Understanding'. There is no
recorded cosmogony where only one of these four elements is
considered in isolation; every account is a compound of several
symbols. Moreover, a canonical or official cosmogony never
existed in Ancient Egypt; there seems to have been a feeling that
the creation of the universe was too mysterious and complex to

be explained always in the same terms. It has been the custom of Egyptologists to believe that the symbols of the creation legends derive from distinct myth cycles associated with the major temples, such as Heliopolis, Hermopolis, Memphis or Thebes. But doubts have recently been expressed whether this is, in fact, correct. There was no standard creation myth, even in the most important cult centres. Rê, the High God of Heliopolis, appears as the original spirit in quite early texts from Hermopolis—where the chief god was Thoth, whereas at Herakleopolis the presiding deity, a ram-headed figure known as Arsaphes ('he who presides over his pool'), only receives acclaim as the Creator of the universe during the late period, when he was no more than the god of a provincial town.[3]

Heliopolis, now a suburb on the northern side of Cairo, is the site of the greatest theological centre in Ancient Egypt. Here was the chief temple of Rê, the High God as the sun, or, as he was called in early times, Atum—'the Complete One'. From the time of Zoser in the twenty-eighth century B.C. the doctrines of Heliopolis were developed to become the nearest approach to an orthodoxy known in Egypt—at least until the rise of Amun at Thebes. The Pyramid Texts, which are the largest single collection of religious compositions yet recovered from the early period, were obviously composed in the main by Heliopolitan priests. They contain the oldest references to cosmogony in terms of Atum. Utterance 600 is a prayer which puts the whole complex of buildings around the pyramid under the protection of the major gods; it begins with a call to the High God:

> 'O Atum! When you came into being you rose up as a High Hill,
> You shone as the Benben Stone in the Temple of the Phoenix in Heliopolis.'

Atum is therefore the Primeval Hill itself. This is still clearer from Utterance 587 which begins:

'Hail to you, O Atum!
Hail to you, O Becoming One who came into being of
   himself!
You rose up in this your name of High Hill,
You came into being in this your name of "Becoming
   One".'

There was no fixed form for the Primeval Hill. In the
Pyramid Text just quoted it is engraved as a simple hill slope.
Such an idea could be easily derived from the mounds which
emerged each year from the waters as the Nile flood receded.
Soon the muddy hillocks would sprout with weeds and begin
to teem with insect and animal life. The earth itself would
seem to be the source of myriads of new creatures. This,
enlarged to cosmic dimensions, is the idea of Atum—the complete and all-containing one—the world-mound rising out of
the Primeval Ocean containing within it the promise of all
that was to come. The mound was soon formalized into an
eminence with sloping or battered sides or a platform surrounded by steps on each side. This became the most usual
symbol. It is probably what the step pyramids represent. In
Pyramid Utterance 600, Atum is the 'High Hill' at Heliopolis on which the temples were built. As such it was said to
be the site of the emergence out of the Abyss—the 'mound of
the first time'. A later text, when describing the condition of
the High God before the creation of the world, makes him
say:

'. . . when I was still alone in the waters, in a state of
   inertness,
before I found anywhere to stand or sit,
before Heliopolis had been founded that I might be
   therein.'[4]

So Heliopolis was itself the Primeval Mound, the first part of
the land world to appear from the depths of the waters and the
dwelling-place of the High God as light. But there is an inconsistency here. If the Great Spirit emerged, this assumes that

the waters had a surface—'the face of the deep'. On the other hand, the Primeval Waters stretched in all directions and emergence would have been impossible. This, however, is a modern quibble; the Egyptians do not seem to have been bothered by such a contradiction in their ideas.

Fig. 2. Primeval Mound symbols

The appearance of Atum as, or, in later versions, on the Primeval Mound was not the only way of expressing the first event, even in Heliopolis. Since the waters were in absolute darkness the emergence of God meant the coming of light, the first morning. For the Heliopolitans morning was marked by the shining of light on an erect pillar or pyramidion on a support which could reflect the rays of the rising sun. At the beginning a light-bird, the Phoenix, had alighted on the sacred stand, known as the Benben, to initiate the great age of the visible God. The rising of the mound and the appearance of the Phoenix are not consecutive events but parallel state-ments, two aspects of the supreme creative moment. But the original appearance was not unique. In a sense it is repeated every day at dawn and every month with the coming of the new moon, perhaps at every recurrent festival. Creation was also repeated in the rebirth of the soul after death and it pro-vided the basic theme in the installation ceremonies of the kings. In fact most solemn religious rites derived their power or authority from the pretence that they were in some way a return to the original events of creation. The temple which enclosed the Benben stone was the centre of calendrical rites as well as the scene of the rising of the High God. It was the place where the mysteries of creation were ceremonially repeated. Hence, in Chapter 140 of the Book of the Dead the damaged parts of the Eye are restored in the temple of the Benbenet[5] at full moon in the second month of winter:

'and His Majesty shines forth as he shone on the first
   occasion
when the Divine Eye (sun and moon) was first upon his
   head.'

Another Heliopolitan form of the emerging deity was Khoprer
—'the Becoming One'—a word which was pronounced like
the word for a scarabaeus beetle, an insect which has the habit

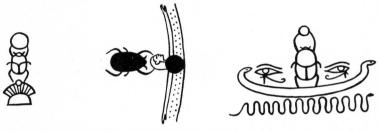

Fig. 3. Pictures of Khopri: (*left*) rising from Primeval Mound; (*centre*) pushing
out the sun from the Underworld; (*right*) sailing over the Monster of the Waters

of pushing its egg out of the sand enclosed in a ball of its own
dung. The beetle therefore became the symbol of God as he
came into existence and of the rising sun, the daily recapitula‚
tion of creation. Chapter 85 of the Book of the Dead—a text
of the period which succeeded the Old Kingdom (*i.e.* just
before 2000 B.C.)—makes the Creator say:

'I came into being of myself in the midst of the Primeval
   Waters in this my name of Khopri.'

Khoprer lost the final 'r' in Middle Egyptian to become
Khopri, the rising sun, half‚way between a person and an
abstract idea. As a human being with a beetle for a head
he takes his place among the attendant gods in the solar
barque.

   The Primeval Mound has many aspects. When the deceased,
impersonated by his statue, was crowned during the final
ceremony inside the pyramid he was invested with the red

crown of Lower Egypt.[6] A heap of sand was put on the floor
and the statue placed upon it while a long prayer was recited,
beginning:

> 'Rise upon it, this land which came forth as Atum, the
> spittle which came forth as Khoprer,
> assume your form upon it, rise high upon it,
> that your father may see you, that Rê may see you.'[7]

Fig. 4. Symbolic ways of writing *To-*land: (a) land; (b) God's Land; (c) the
World; (d) the Two Lands (Egypt)

The sand represents the Primeval Mound. When the king
stands upon it in full regalia he will be 'recognized' by his
father, the High God. The land is an exhalation—literally a
'spitting forth'—from the waters. It is the manifestation of God
as he 'came into being'—that is, as Khoprer. Hence in the late
symbolic hieroglyphic script the word 'To-land'—can be
written as a beetle or as a spitting serpent, signifying outflow or exhalation. Both ideas are present in this text. The
instruction to the king is to ascend the mound and be greeted
by the sun. This implies that the mound can become the
world mountain whereon the king ascends to meet God in his
present form—the sun. Atum is the aboriginal deity and
ultimate but hidden godhead; Khoprer is God as he appears
in visible form, whether at the beginning or every day; Rê is
God now in the sky. Atum is essentially invisible, so he later
becomes the night sun as it journeys through the underworld or
the arbiter of destiny perched on top of the world pole.

Atum was at first alone in the universe. He was not only God
but all things to come. The writers of the texts speak of him as
a male but he was really bisexual—'that great He-She'.[8] In
Utterance 571 of the Pyramid Texts the king (in this case

Pepi I of the Sixth Dynasty) is reborn as the aboriginal off-spring of the High God in his primary state in the waters:

> 'O Actor as the mother wherein was Pepi! O Dweller in
> the nether sky!
> This Pepi was born by his father Atum
> before the appearance of the sky, before the appearance of
> the earth,
> before the appearance of men, before the birth of the gods,
> before the appearance of death. . . .'[9]

But why should God have produced an offspring? Being all alone he desired a companion. A Coffin Text alludes to an old myth:

> 'O you that arose in your [first] arising,
> O you that came into being in this your name of Khopri,
> You are he that did say, "Would that I had a son
> to cleanse me when I appear in my might
> and bring me acclaim in the pure land."'[10]

So Atum proceeded to create the first creatures, Shu and Tefnut, male and female. Pyramid Utterance 527 says:

> 'Atum was creative in that he proceeded to masturbate
> with himself in Heliopolis; he put his penis in his hand
> that he might obtain the pleasure of emission thereby and
> there were born brother and sister—that is Shu and
> Tefnut.'

This, to us, excessively crude motif of masturbation was to remain the most popular creation motif throughout Egyptian history. It emphasizes the bisexual character of Atum or, what is the same thing at a more sophisticated level, the self-sufficiency of the High God who 'divided his contentment in the condition of the Primeval Waters'.[11] The masturba-tion is usually said to have taken place in the waters, but here

Fig. 5. Offering Mayet, the World Order

Heliopolis is the location. This looks like an interpolation and it may well be that Heliopolis was not the source of the mastur-bation legend.[12] As time went on the gods grew more personal. Atum became more of a man and less of an abstract principle. He became exclusively male and his hand, which had performed the creative act, became his consort. This strange misunderstanding is certainly as old as the pyramids; it may even be implied in the name of King Wedimu, one of the earliest pharaohs.[13] This hand-goddess was called Iusas— 'she comes and is mighty'—and had a special shrine in the sacred enclosure at Heliopolis.

Another myth accounted for Shu and Tefnut by having them spat forth from the Creator's mouth. Thus, Utterance 600 of the Pyramid Texts, after the section quoted above, goes on:

'You spat forth as Shu, you expectorated as Tefnut,
you put your arms around them in an act of Ka-giving,
so that your Ka might be in them.'

There are two puns here. Shu has a sound similar to *ishesh*— 'to spit', while Tefnut resembles *tef*—another word with the same meaning as *ishesh*. The mythical motif is built around the verbal assonance. The masturbation tale belongs to a primitive naturalistic view of the world which can only account for creation in terms of physical generation, whereas the spitting motif expresses creation through the Divine Word or the entry of the breath of life. Although they were now in existence Shu and Tefnut were still protected by their father, for we are told that he held them in his embrace, shielding them from harm and imparting to them his *Ka*, *i.e.* his vital essence.

The Egyptians lived under an absolute and benevolent autocracy. There was one source of authority on earth, so it was natural that they should have believed in a single creator and originator of divine power. The merit of the Heliopolitans is that they accounted for the development of the cosmos from the stirring of the original spirit down to their own times in terms which pay regard not only to the single divine purpose but to the infinite diversity of phenomena in the created world. The masturbation motif stresses the reproductive aspect of life, but behind lies the mystery of life itself, the breath of the Divine Soul. Hence the generation of Shu and Tefnut has to be described in terms of both the masturbation and the spitting myths—they are, in fact, complementary, not alternative. This is not clear from the texts of the Old Kingdom, but the early Coffin Text quoted above[14] is quite definite on this point. (Shu speaks to Atum-Rê):

'This was the manner of your engendering:
you conceived with your mouth
and you gave birth from your hand in the pleasure of
emission.
I am that star which came forth from the two . . .[15] of Rê,
I am that space which came about in the waters,
I came into being in them, I grew in them,
but I was not consigned to the abode of darkness.'

Conception and birth provide the author with the frame-work into which he can fit both spitting and masturbation.

From the two acts came Shu, the 'space', the light cavity in the midst of the primordial darkness. Shu is both light and air, and as the offspring of God he is manifest life. As light he separates the earth from the sky and as air he upholds the sky vault. The Primeval Waters are here stretching endlessly in all directions, whereas the earlier cosmogonies had assumed that a mound emerged out of the ocean.

Between the Old and the Middle Kingdoms the Heliopolitan cosmogony became more comprehensive. Shu, who had originally been the air and the separator of earth and sky, became 'the Eternal One'—Life itself and the mediator between the One, the High God, and the multiplicity of subsequent creatures. At the same time Tefnut, a colourless deity in the Pyramid Texts, became Mayet, the World Order. Spell 80 of the Coffin Texts contains a complete mythological composition in dramatic form. It will be given here because it throws light on the Heliopolitan cosmogonies of the Old Kingdom.

(Shu, the spirit of life and eternity speaks):

'I am Eternity, the creator of the millions,
who repeats the spitting of Atum—that which came from
   his mouth—
He put forth his hand [to create] the matter he desired
before he let it fall to the ground.'
And Atum said:
'That is my daughter, the living female one, Tefnut,
who shall be with her brother Shu.
Life is his name, Order is her name.
[At first] I lived with my two children, my little ones,
the one before me, the other behind me.
Life reposed with my daughter Order,
the one within me, the other without me.
I rose over them, but their arms were around me.'

(The text then alludes to Geb, the earth, and Nut, the sky):

'As for Geb, as for my grandson,
after the appearance of my Eye, which I dispatched
while I was still alone in the waters in a state of inertness,
before I had found anywhere to stand or sit,
before Heliopolis had been founded that I might be there,
before a perch had been formed for me to sit on,
before I had created Nut that she might be above my head,
before the first corporation had been born,
before the Primeval Companies of the Gods had come
    into being.
[In this primordial epoch] Atum said to the Abyss:
I am in a relaxed state, whereof I am very weary,
my humanity are inert,[16]
If earth were alive it would cheer my heart and enliven my
    bosom.
Let my limbs be assembled for (*i.e.* to form) him,
and let this great weariness be settled for us.
And the Abyss said to Atum:
Kiss your daughter Order,[17] put her to your nose,
so will your heart live.
Never let her leave you, let Order, who is your daughter,
be with your son Shu, whose name is Life.
You will eat (*sic* MSS.) with your daughter Order,
while your son Shu will lift you up.'
(At this point Shu intervenes to say):
'I am Life, the son of Atum,
he has borne me from his nose.
Let him place me on his neck that he may greet me with
    my sister Order
when he shines every day as he appears from his egg.
The birth of the god is the appearance of daylight,
and he is acclaimed by his scions on the horizon.'

At the beginning the great spirit Atum lay helpless and inert
in the waters of the Abyss. The god had already procreated
Shu and Tefnut, but they and he were still together in the

waters in one body—or, as the text explains it, embracing one another. Initially God seems to have had only one Eye—a mysterious entity which is separable from its owner and which is sent out as an envoy to seek Shu and Tefnut, who have become separated from Atum and are lost in the immensity of the Abyss. The Eye finds them and brings them back to their father who proceeds to regenerate them as the life and order of the universe. Atum is distressed because he has no resting-place. He asks the Abyss how the firm earth can be created. He is told to kiss his daughter, the World Order—or as the Egyptians would express it—to put her to his nose, while he makes Shu hold him up. The basic arrangement of the universe is, then, a combination of Atum as Primary Spirit, Life and the World Order. Every morning the creative process is repeated when the sun—symbolized as a bird bursting forth from its egg—soars up into the air of Shu upon the ways of the Order. Heliopolis is mentioned as the first location of the High God and essential home of God on earth. There are allusions to the separation of earth (Geb) and sky (Nut)—which is the next act in the cosmic drama. Mayet, the World Order, had been worshipped from at least the Third Dynasty, but she had been distinct from Tefnut. In combining the two goddesses and reinterpreting the Heliopolitan creation legends in this light the author of the text has recognized that the universe depends upon the life-force controlled by the laws of what we should now call nature. How things began was not, with the Egyptians, the matter of a traditional tale but a challenge to their imagination and understanding of the world. They manipulated the symbols of their myths to express their growing and earnest concern with the major problems of life—the working of God as spirit and intelligence, the source of time and motion, the moral and natural order—metaphysical questions that have perplexed men throughout history. Their cosmogony is, then, a serious business, it is philosophic rather than imaginative and concerned with inquiries into the nature of a divine power of whom they were passionately aware.

Atum was unhappy in the Primeval Waters because he was, in the words of this text, 'in a relaxed state, very weary and inert'. This existence in the waters was painful; Atum was in travail until he could settle his limbs in a definite place. From the emerging deity's point of view the waters are bad, they represent the conditions of helplessness and chaos which have to be transcended. On the other hand they can be regarded as 'pure' and as 'the waters of life' for the soul who wishes to return to their state of negation. Immersion in them means going back to primeval innocence. This ambivalence of the waters will be noted in other contexts.

In the Heliopolitan legends Shu and Tefnut produced the next pair—Geb, the earth, and Nut, the sky. The Pyramid Texts have echoes of lost tales about the gestation of Nut and how she freed herself violently from her mother's womb. But the essential event connected with Geb and Nut is their separation. The belief that earth and sky were originally one and were rent apart is one of the basic myths of many races. In Egypt there is no narrative of this myth; it has to be inferred from textual allusions and pictures on the coffins of the late New Kingdom, where it is a favourite theme. The earliest reference occurs in the Pyramid Texts in a recitation which accompanied the lowering of the lid upon the sarcophagus containing the body of the dead king. The sarcophagus represents the earth and its lid stands for the sky.[18]

(Priest speaks):

> 'O Nut, spread yourself over your son Osiris,
> and hide him from Seth. Protect him, O Nut!
> Have you come to hide your son? . . .'

(Words to be spoken by Geb):[19]

> 'O Nut! You became a spirit,
> you waxed mighty in the belly of your mother Tefnut
> before you were born.
> How mighty is your heart!

Fig. 6. Shu, helped by wind spirits, separates Nut and Geb

You stirred in the belly of your mother in your name of
  Nut,
you are indeed a daughter more powerful than her
  mother . . .
O Great One who has become the sky!
You have the mastery, you have filled every place with
  your beauty,
the whole earth lies beneath you, you have taken possession
  thereof,
you have enclosed the whole earth and everything therein
  within your arms. . . .
As Geb shall I impregnate you in your name of sky,
I shall join the whole earth to you in every place.
O high above the earth! You are supported upon your
  father Shu,
but you have power over him,
he so loved you that he placed himself—and all things
  beside—beneath you
so that you took up into you every god with his heavenly
  barque,
and as "a thousand souls is she" did you teach them
that they should not leave you—as the stars.'

Myth and ritual are closely interwoven in this hymn. The deceased is Osiris, who lies within the earth, still in great danger from Seth, the demon of death and decay. As the lid is set down on the sarcophagus the sky makes union with the earth. The symbolism is based on a legend that originally earth and sky were together in total and sexual union. So, when the sky descends ritually upon the earth, Nut is impregnated by Geb. We are then told why the sky was lifted away from the earth. Shu, Nut's father, 'so loved her' that he separated her from her mate Geb and, as the air, held her aloft with his arms. Nut was then able to give birth to the stars and to 'take them up'—allow them to sail across her belly, the sky. Presumably this means that Shu was enamoured of Nut and in jealousy broke up her union with Geb. There is also an allusion to a lost legend that Nut rebelled against her mother 'while still in the womb'.

There was a myth about a primeval serpent, but it is impossible to be precise about it because no text or picture yet discovered gives a detailed description of the origin of the world in terms of this symbol. The inscriptions of the later periods abound in references to 'the Serpent in the Primeval Darkness'.[20] In Thebes it was called Kematef—'he who completed his time'; in Dendera it was 'Horus the combiner of the Two Lands'. It was generally referred to as Sito, 'Son of Earth', or Iru-To, 'Creator of Earth'—a monstrous serpent who 'took form as Iru-To, arising out of the darkness of the Primeval Waters before any definite thing yet existed.'[21] This manifestation of the High God in his emergent form was, however, already known to the Pyramid Texts, for par. 1146 makes the Creator-spirit say:

'I am the outflow of the Primeval Flood,
he who emerged from the waters.
I am the "Provider of Attributes" serpent with its many coils,
I am the Scribe of the Divine Book
which says what has been and effects what is yet to be.'

Here the serpent is the creator of multiplicity, God as the spirit who assigns to everything its essence—its *Ka*. The serpent is therefore a symbol for creation by word, the belief that the universe in its variety is based on the realization of the commands of a designing and conscious mind. In a hymn from the Coffin Texts the serpent exclaims:

> 'I extended everywhere, in accordance with what was to
> come into existence,
> I knew, as the One, alone, majestic, the Indwelling Soul,
> the most potent of the gods.
> He [the Indwelling Soul] it was who made the universe
> in that he copulated with his fist and took the pleasure of
> emission.
> I bent right around myself, I was encircled in my coils,
> one who made a place for himself in the midst of his coils.
> His utterance was what came forth from his own mouth.'²²

The Primeval Serpent came into being in the midst of the dark waters of the Abyss. In one sense he is the Atum figure of Heliopolis performing creation by masturbation. In another he is the serpent whose coils delimit the creation—the outer coils of the serpent are the limits of the world. God is the serpent but he is also in the centre of the coils, where he devises the Logos, the creative Word which lays down the laws of what is to be made. Hence the serpent in the Pyramid Text merges into the scribe of the divine book, while in the Coffin Text the 'utterance' comes from the serpent's mouth. In another recitation of the First Intermediate Period the 'Universal Master' explains to the minor gods how he came to deliver the four basic laws of creation:

> 'while I was still in the midst of the serpent coil.'²³

The combination of the masturbating motif with the serpent is significant. The beginning of the world is so mysterious and so complex that the best expression is a series of fleeting images, each merging into the next.

The serpent is an image of God at the beginning, but God is not now manifest in this form, for it has been superseded. The serpent belongs to the mythological past. Chapter 175 of the Book of the Dead prophesies that at the end of time the world will revert to the primary state of undifferentiated chaos and Atum will become a serpent once more. This must have been a common belief, for it provided a figure of speech; rulers of Siut in the First Intermediate Period claimed to be as pre-eminent as

> 'that great surviving serpent, when all mankind has reverted to the slime.'

God the Serpent therefore exists at both ends of time, when the world emerged from the waters and when, at the end of the present dispensation,[24] it is engulfed in them once more. In the Pyramid Texts the 'Provider of Attributes' serpent is sometimes the supreme deity but in one of the spells he is the enemy of Atum. A ritual object is described as:

> 'this is the claw of Atum which was upon the neck of the Provider of Attributes serpent and which put an end to the uproar in Hermopolis.'[25]

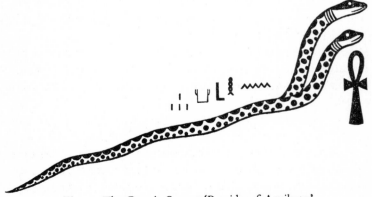

Fig. 7. The Cosmic Serpent 'Provider of Attributes'

Fig. 8. The Cosmic Serpent encircles
Hermopolis

There are later representations of Atum as a mongoose, a
snake-destroying animal. This can only make sense if Atum in
a new form as mongoose became the killer of his earlier form.
The uproar in Hermopolis must mean the old age of confusion, the time of the Primeval Waters. Atum put an end to
the time of the serpent and instituted a new age. Hermopolis is
here the original state of the world rather than the actual city in
Middle Egypt. This remained a lively tradition for a thousand
years after the composition of the Pyramid Texts; in some
coffin pictures of the Twenty-first Dynasty the serpent encircles
the district of Hermopolis.

The original serpent was known to the people of the Old
Empire under a variety of names. 'Provider of Attributes'—
Neheb-kau—was associated with Hermopolis and with the
belief in the doctrine of the Divine Word. There were, however, other aspects. The serpent came before the appearance of
light, so it was sometimes called Amun, the 'Hidden' or
'Invisible One'. At Heliopolis there was also a primordial
serpent enemy called Imy-Uhaf—which seems to mean something like 'Slippery One'. The High Priest at Heliopolis wore
a side lock to commemorate:

'what happened when Rê had an altercation with the Slippery Serpent about the inheritance of Heliopolis. His mouth was hurt. . . . Then he said, "I will take my harpoon that I may inherit this city," and Rê said, "I will stir up my brethren against him to drive him away." Now it happened that . . . the Slippery One surprised him before he could raise his arm against him,[26] ensnaring him in the form of a curly-haired maiden. And thus came "he with the lock of hair" in Heliopolis.'[27]

Since Rê is both the Master of the World and the Lord of Heliopolis, the serpent's challenge over 'the inheritance of Heliopolis' was really a contest for universal supremacy. In the first phase the enemy must be a water monster, for the god has to take a harpoon against it. Apparently the serpent then resorted to a ruse, taking the shape of a beautiful woman. One senses an echo of a legend quite different from the serious, hieratic creation myths. Who was the seductive maiden with the curly hair? Kees thinks she is the Moon Goddess, but whatever her cosmic connotations she is the prototype of the temptresses who are the most dangerous forms of the dragon of chaos—from Circe to the Wagnerian Venus, the representatives of an earlier dispensation who must be overcome by the High God in his heroic form.

Primordial Ocean, Primeval Waters, Abyss—there is no agreement whether the original state should be described as one or many. In Heliopolis the waters are one—Nun—and this is the general Egyptian tradition. At Hermopolis, however, a city in Middle Egypt, there was a doctrine that the idea of the abyss could be best conveyed by saying what it was not, by enumerating a list of negative characteristics. The Shu Texts of the First Intermediate Period, which are strongly influenced by Hermopolitan ideas, have preserved a phrase:

'in the infinity, the nothingness, the nowhere and the dark,'[28]

which is repeated like a refrain to emphasize that something happened in the Primeval Waters before the coming of

Fig. 9. The Primeval Goose

positive, visible, created things in time. In a contemporary
spell, when the soul has to cross the heavenly ocean its path lies
amid the waters

'where the Universal Lord dwelt when he was in the
infinity, the nothingness and the listlessness.'[29]

In another text the characteristics are personified:

'when the Waters spoke to Infinity, Nothingness, Nowhere and Darkness.'[30]

Whenever the ancients had to divide a cosmic unity into parts
they imagined a division into three, four or seven—or into
multiples of these numbers. At Hermopolis the sacred number
was four.[31] Accordingly in the local cosmogony the waters
became, or produced out of themselves, four beings—Nothing,
Inertness, Infinity and Invisibility or Darkness. To emphasize
their creative role they were given female counterparts. These
eight genii gave the name Shmunu, 'Eight Town', to Hermopolis. They were worshipped there as genii with the heads of
frogs and serpents—creatures of mud and slime. These eight
swam together and formed the primeval egg

'in the darkness of Father Nun.'[32]

The egg was invisible, for it took shape before the appearance of light. In fact, the bird of light burst forth from the egg.

'I am the Soul, the creation of the Primeval Waters . . .
my nest was unseen, my egg was unbroken,'[33]

for the generation of the egg took place in the time of non/being.

There was another version of the myth in which the egg was laid by a goose, the Great Primeval Spirit. This bird was 'the Great Cackler' whose voice broke the silence—'while the world was still flooded in silence'.[34]

The egg contained the bird of light, but other sources make it clear that it was filled with air. The authors of the Coffin Texts realized that it was the first created thing—although invisible—and therefore the equivalent of Shu in the myth of Heliopolis:

'Hail, Atum (I am the Double Lion), give me the pleasant
breeze that is in your nose, for I am that egg that was in
the Great Primeval One,
I am the keeper of that great support that separates Geb
from Nut. . . .
I breathe the breezes it breathes,
I am he who both joins and separates.
for I go all around the egg, the master of yesterday.'[35]

The egg in the waters is therefore the air and so 'that great support'—the separator of earth and sky which, as we are told, both holds apart and unites the two halves of the world. Time is regulated by the motion around the egg, so it is 'the master of yesterday'. In another sense the egg contains the breath of life and so marks the victory over 'yesterday'—the old time of the inert waters.[36]

The earliest allusion to the creation genii of Hermopolis occurs in a Pyramid Text where the king makes an offering to the creatures of the Primeval Waters—here equated with the

lower world—so that they should not hinder him from ascend-
ing to the High God in his present form as the spirit who
presides over the universe at the apex of the sky:

> 'The accustomed offering cake is still yours, O Niu and
> Naunet!
>> O you that were the source of the gods and kept them
>> in your protective shade!
> The accustomed offering cake is still yours, O Amun and
> Amaunet!
>> O you that were the source of the gods, etc.
> The accustomed offering cake is still yours, O Atum and
> Double Lion!
>> You two that have created your own divine selves and
>> powers!
>> that is, Shu and Tefnut, the pair who engendered the
>> gods and put them in their proper places.
>> (apparently added as a gloss)
> Tell your father that I have given you your accustomed
> offering cakes. . . .
> Do not hinder me as I proceed to HIM.'[37]

The endowments founded at the beginning of history for the
Primeval Gods have been continued by the king during his
lifetime, so he hopes they will allow him to ascend to the sky
where he will meet HIM, the transcendent deity of the world
order, the master of destiny in his present form. Niu and
Naunet are members of the Hermopolitan eight. So, in some
versions, are Amun and Amaunet, the personifications of
invisibility. Atum and the Double Lion are the corresponding
Heliopolitan figures. The Double Lion is, we are told by an
ancient editor, a manifestation of Shu and Tefnut. Burial in the
sarcophagus was a return to the waters or into the earth of the
Primeval Mound. The soul had to break free from the con-
strictions of the primeval epoch to ascend to the present divine
world of light. The powers of the old mythical past might
restrain it, so they have to be placated or cajoled. In its use of

creation myths to realize the rebirth of the soul this text is typical of the pyramids. The doctrines of Heliopolis and Hermopolis are woven together to form a background for a transcendent God who presides over the cosmic circuit of stars from the top of the heavenly pole. The primeval deities are described as sources, springs set in shady groves—a surprising poetical touch. The theological subtlety and literary artifice of these early hymns and litanies is very impressive. There must have been a vigorous intellectual movement in the late Old Kingdom when all the rest of the world—Mesopotamia excepted—was still engulfed in illiterate barbarism.

The Egyptians arranged the stars in patterns representing the figures of their mythology. There was a crocodile climbing on the back of a hippopotamus; there were wrestlers, lions, serpents, a god stretching a cord, a hawk perching on a papyrus, Orion as a striding man for ever looking behind him, and many more. Nevertheless, the stars were the most striking example of order, the evidence of a supreme controller. No other ancient people was so deeply affected by the eternal circuit of the stars around a point in the northern sky. Here must be the node of the universe, the centre of regulation, able to be located but invisible—for in antiquity the Pole Star was not in its present position. The celestial pole is 'that place' or 'the great city'. Sometimes the pole is regarded as a tree with the circumpolar stars—as souls—perching on its branches; at others, it is a tower or a pole with guide-ropes. The various designations show how deeply it impressed the Egyptian imagination. If God is the governor of the universe and it revolves around an axis, then God must preside over that axis:

'I know his name, Eternity is his name,
"Eternity, the master of years" is his name,
exalted over the vault of the sky,
bringing the sun to life every day.'[38]

More explicitly, four Coffin Texts have incorporated an ancient statement:

'The Great God lives,
fixed in the middle of the sky upon his support;
the guide-ropes are adjusted for that great hidden one,
the dweller in the city.'[39]

'The Living One' and 'Eternity, the master of years' are names for Ptah, the form in which the High God was worshipped at Memphis, the capital of the Old Kingdom. He is God as master of destiny, both cosmic and personal. The personal names of the time show how intimate was the relation felt between man and the 'Living One': *Ny-ka-onkh*—'I belong to the grace of the Living One'; *Onkh-haf*—'The Living One is all around him'; *Meres-onkh*—'She loves the Living One';[40] *Onkh-khui*—'The Living One is my protector'. God, the regulator of the circuit of the heavenly bodies is also the protector and friend of individual men and women. But he is hidden, the invisible source of life and movement at the heart of the universe. A Pyramid Text calls him 'the greatest of those who are in the northern sky', while a Coffin Text lets him say:

'I am that Creator who sits in the supreme place in the sky. Every god (*i.e.* star) who does not now come down beside me, I have put him off until later.'[41]

In the popular imagination the lord of destiny is 'high above on his reed float, he who dwells apart'.[42] He floats across the sky-ocean looking down upon his creation. Every now and then in the myths a mysterious voice calls out with authority, commanding things to be put right when the order of the world is threatened. This is the intervention of the commanding deity in the present world.

There is a gap in our knowledge of the creation legends. No Old Kingdom text reveals how God, when he rose out of the waters, removed himself to the heights of the sky where he now lives, far away from the earth he made. But

'I am that living soul with outstretched face
who pushed out its head, who freed itself, who brought itself away

> when the doing of that which was to be done was [still] in
>   confusion,
> when the doing and the commanding of that which was
>   to be done was [still] asleep.
> I create and I command for him who commands the good;
> My lips are the Twin Companies,
> I am the great Word,
> I am a redeemer—so shall I be redeemed, and I shall be
>   redeemed from all evil.'⁴³

It is impossible to discover what was the exact image in the
mind of the author of this fragment. The 'living soul' struggles
to free itself from the sleep and retarding power of the primordial chaos—the Primeval Waters are obviously meant but they
have been reduced to abstractions. The myth is seen—more
clearly than anywhere else in the Pyramid Texts—in the terms
of its metaphysical basis. Strictly, this is a spell to identify one-
self with the Creator-spirit rather than a monody of the spirit
itself. Hence the speaker says he will deliver the 'good' Word
just as the Creator did. This is standard Egyptian theology;
the Word is all that is good and fair (*nofret*), evil does not
belong to creation at all. In raising itself from the sleep and
chaos of inaction the spirit is the redeemer from evil, which
belongs to the realm of non-being; so, in becoming one with
that spirit the soul will be able to shed its earthly dross.

In the lips of the High God, Schott has recognized a
reference to the Memphite Theology, perhaps the highest
achievement of Egyptian thought. At some time during the
Old Kingdom the theologians of Memphis produced a document which ascribed the origin of things to their great god
Ptah. Echoes of this doctrine can be traced in the texts of all
periods, but fortunately what seems to be the original text was
copied during the reign of Shabako (*c.* 700 B.C.). It accepts the
gods of Heliopolis and Hermopolis but subordinates them to
Ptah, of whom they are said to be forms. First is 'Ptah who is
upon the great (*i.e.* primeval) place'—the original ultimate

spirit. Then comes Ptah-Niu, as the waters, 'who was the father of Atum' and Ptah-Naunet, the female counterpart of the spirit of the Abyss, 'the Primeval Mother who gave birth to Atum'. This is followed by 'Ptah, the very great [or ancient] one, who is the heart and tongue of the Divine Company.' Instead of the anthropomorphic Shu and Tefnut the Creator brings forth 'heart' which was, for the Egyptians, the seat of the intelligence, and 'tongue', the organ of speech. In all, eight primitive forms of God were brought into the scheme but the names of the others, except the last, Nefertum, the lotus, have been lost. Thus all the major Egyptian myths of creation are brought together under the aegis of Ptah.

In the Heliopolitan myth the High God Atum was a human being, even if his sex was indeterminate. The Memphite Theology rejects this crude anthropomorphism. Not only is God a spirit but the fundamental principles of the world's organization seem to the author of this document to be ideas rather than persons.

> 'In the form of Atum there came into being heart and there came into being tongue. But the supreme god is Ptah, who has endowed all the gods and their *Ka's* through that heart [of his] which appeared in the form of Horus and through that tongue [of his] which appeared in the form of Thoth, both of which were forms of Ptah.'

This is, quite clearly, an attempt to impose Ptah over Atum as the highest god. Atum has become a mere symbol for the aspect of God as the begetter of the first pair. All the actors in the primeval drama are aspects of Ptah, the supreme power. He is not only the creator of the gods but the provider of their peculiar power to be divine and eternal—their *Ka's*. The essence of Ptah is heart, the organ of thought and tongue, that of command. At this point there is an allusion to another old myth. At an early period the chief deity had been a mysterious hawk whose eyes were the sun and moon. Therefore, instead of Shu and Tefnut the original pair are first the organs of command and intelligence and then Horus, the Sun God and personification of royal command, and Thoth, the Moon God and patron of learning and intelligence. Two older cosmo-gonies are reinterpreted in terms of a new concept of God as a pervading spirit whose creation is brought about by the exercise of mind and will.

The underlying thought is explained in purely mundane terms in another part of the text, which Spiegel[44] has shown is to be taken as a development of the above section:

> 'Now heart and tongue have power over all the limbs, because the former is to be found in every body and the latter is to be found in every mouth—in all gods, all men, all animals, all worms—in all that lives. The heart thinks what it will and the tongue commands what it will.'

We know from their medical treatises that the Egyptians understood how blood-vessels led out from the heart to all the limbs. From this they concluded that the limbs moved because the heart sent messages along the blood telling them to do so. Hence the heart was the organ of thought, the seat of the mind. The Memphite Theology shows that the same blood system had been observed in all mammals, so it was concluded that the world was arranged in the same way. Just as the heart and the voice-organ determine the actions of men and animals or, as the text says, 'have primacy' over them, so God is the heart and tongue of his Creation.

The section about the High God proceeds:

> 'His Divine Company is part of him as his teeth and lips, which correspond to the seed and hands of Atum. [In that myth] the Divine Company arose through the action of his seed and fingers. But the Divine Company is [really] the teeth and lips in that great mouth which gave all things their names; [that mouth] from which Shu and Tefnut proceeded was [really] the creation of the Divine Company.'

Further details of the doctrine of Heliopolis are explained as variants of the abstract concepts of Memphis. The real creator was the Word—the primeval speech which came from God wherein all things got their names. Since the name is also the nature of a thing, in the view of ancient man the naming of manifold creation means the demarcation of individual characteristics. This is the method related in the Bible, when God created the animals:

> 'And out of the ground the Lord God formed every beast of the field and every fowl of the air; and brought them unto Adam to see what he would call them: and whatso/ ever Adam called every living thing, that was the name thereof.'[45]

Still more to the point are the opening lines of the Babylonian epic of Creation describing the state of affairs before the appearance of the positive gods:

> 'When the heaven above had not yet been named
> and the earth below had not yet been called by a name . . .
> when none of the gods had yet been brought into being,
> when they had not yet been called by their names . . .
> Lakhmy and Lakhamu came into being, they were called by their names.'

Atum has lost not only the primacy but his human character as well. He has become the intermediary between God's thought and the multitude of created things. He only exists in the Memphite Theology to possess the organs which pre/ meditated and delivered the creative Word. In the older legend Shu and Tefnut had been spat forth as male and female to become the original parents. We are told that this crude anthropomorphism is merely a way of referring to a process which was really not to be comprehended in materialistic terms at all:

> 'And thus were all the gods made and the whole company created. And thus happens every word of God from what the heart has thought out and the tongue commanded.

Just as all the gods were made and the whole Divine Company created, so happens every word of God from what the heart has thought out and the tongue commands. So were the *Ka's* made and the Fates determined—which produce all food and nourishment through that same Word which also declares what is to be loved and what is to be hated. And so life is given to the peaceful and death to the criminal.'

The world exists, at the beginning and always, as the manifestation of God's will. The events at the Creation were brought about in the same way as is every change in nature. The *Ka's* and Fates (*Hemsut*) are here the genii of growth and reproduction. Life proceeds according to God's word. In considering how the will of the Creator-spirit could be translated into actuality the Memphite author has built his theory on the analogy of the mind controlling the motions of the body. This is the unique contribution of this text to cosmology. Whereas later philosophers—from the Ionians down to Hegel—retreated into tautologies before the problem of how the Word or the Idea actualized itself, the Egyptian constructed his theory on the model of mind and body, the closest analogy he knew. He specifically recognized that the problem of the origin of the world in the remote past is the same as, or is only part of, the problem of how life is sustained now.

Even this does not exhaust the originality of this text, for it goes on to declare that God's word is not only concerned with the physical order but with human conduct as well. It is part of the great Word that life, God's essential activity, is furthered by peacefulness and that all wrong-doing is 'an abomination to the *Ka*', hindering the flow of divine power and grace. The identification of an ethical code with God's purpose is the underlying theme of the sages of the Old Kingdom. Ptah-hotep says:

'Great is Mayet, lasting and penetrating, it has not been disturbed since the time of him who made it. He who transgresses its laws is to be punished. . . .

That it should be lasting is the nature of Mayet. . . .
What is truly effective is the command of God, hence it
follows that life is to be lived in gentleness. . . .
Let not frivolity be repeated, for, as the common saying
goes: "A great man of little matter is an abomination to
the *Ka*."
The great-hearted is one of God's chosen but he who
listens to his instincts is his own enemy.'[46]

The analogy between God's action in creation and the working
of the mind and senses is worked out in the Memphite Theology in some detail:

'The seeing of the eyes and the breathing of the nose bring
messages to the heart. The seeing of the eyes, the hearing
of the ears and the breathing of the nose bring messages
to the heart. It is the latter which causes all decisions to be
made, but it is the tongue which reports what the heart
has thought out. Thus is all action, whether simple or
complex, carried out—the manipulation of the hands, the
movement of the legs and the functioning of every limb.
All is in accord with the command which the heart has
devised and which has appeared upon the tongue. Thus
is determined the peculiar nature of everything.'

Rightly or not, the Memphite thinker had arrived at an
idealist metaphysic. The conclusion is inevitable:

'And so the making of everything and the creation of the
gods should be assigned to Ptah. He is Tatenen[47] who
produced the gods, from whom everything has come,
whether food, divine sustenance or any other good thing.
So it has been found and understood that his power is
greater than that of the other gods.
And then Ptah rested[48] after he had created every thing
and every Divine Word.'

Fig. 10. The half-formed Self Creator and
the Cosmic Flower (Abydos)

Tatenen is the Memphite name for the god of the Primeval
Mound. We are therefore back to the original theme at
Heliopolis but with much deeper understanding. Ptah, the
great mind and word, is also the originator of the physical
world. He is the same spirit through all his creative manifestations and in the world of men. When Kant looked upon
the movements of the starry sky and then into the moral order
within himself and recognized the two as the signs of one and
the same God, he was closely following the thought of an
anonymous Memphite more than four thousand years before.

In spite of the immense prestige of Atum and Ptah there are
traces of other ideas, even during the Old Kingdom. Of these
one of the most interesting is the cosmic lotus. In this myth, the
waters do not extend in all directions but are to be imagined as

a limitless dark sea. From the surface emerges an immense lotus bud. It is luminous even as it rises—as an early hieroglyph shows,[49] but with the opening of the bud there emerges the light of the world and the sweet perfume of the morning air. This is 'the redolent flower, the soul of Rê'[50] worshipped at Memphis as Nefertum, 'the lotus at the nostril of Rê'. Strictly, the god is not the flower itself but 'that great god who is within the lotus bud of gold'. Hence what rises from the opening flower is the world soul which is the light, life and air and sun. In the pyramid of Wenis what appears to be a bundle of flowers is offered to the High God:

> 'and it is Wenis, the flowers that have sprung from the pure earth . . .
> and it is Wenis at the nose of the Great and Mighty One.
> Wenis gleams as Nefertum, as the lotus at the nostril of Rê, when he appears daily on the horizon and the gods are purified at his sight.'[51]

But a myth has been lost. In the Pyramid Text the king is said to have 'put Order in the place of Chaos' as his qualification for appearing as the lotus, and in the Coffin Texts (335) the redolent flower is the spirit who is in 'the battle of the gods'. The lotus is thus the symbol for the final defeat of the powers of the Abyss. In the pictorial symbolism the flower opens to reveal the head of the emerging soul, the Divine Child (see p. 239) or, in the case of Nefertum, two feathers. In Buddhism the flower became the most pervasive symbol of all, but in Egypt it remained an attractive but minor thing, a poetical rather than a speculative mystery.

CHAPTER II

The High God in the Age of the Coffin Texts

DURING THE OLD KINGDOM the good and ordered had been aspects of the divine command. God's creation was essentially good, the expression of his benevolent will in nature, the state and the mind of man. At the end of the Sixth Dynasty, however, about 2250 B.C., the royal authority broke down and for some generations there was political confusion and great distress. The various districts became virtually independent principalities, Asiatic invaders appeared in the Delta, and, perhaps most significant of all, the social tensions which had been checked during the Pyramid Age, now broke out into open violence between the people and the old aristocracy. The basic optimistic assumptions of the old order were shattered. Ipu, a prophet of the time, has graphically described the disillusion and despair:[1]

'It used to be said that he was every man's shepherd, that there was no evil in his heart, that however insignificant his flock he would spend the whole day in caring for them. . . . Ah! Had he understood the character of men in the first generation he would have launched his curse and raised his arm against them. He would have destroyed their heirs, although they were his own seed. But he wished that birth should continue . . . it could not come to an end as long as these gods (the righteous kings of the past) were there. Progeny still comes forth from the wombs of the women of Egypt but one does not find it [playing?] in the road. It is rapine and violence against the weak that these gods (the recent kings) have wrought.

There has been no true pilot in their time. Where is he? Does he sleep perchance? Behold, one sees no sign of his almighty power!'

In his distress Ipu has no thought for minor deities, he even calls upon God by name. In the last resort the director of the universe is 'he', and it is just this that makes this outburst so moving. It reveals the underlying monotheism of the Egyptian mind and the tragic situation that results when this imposing conception has been shaken to the very roots. God as the loving shepherd of his flock has always been the most moving expression of the ultimate goodness of the world and its governance. But it seemed irrelevant in chaotic times when every man's arm was raised against his neighbour. Seeking for a fitting metaphor to convey his ebbing faith in the divinely instituted kingship, Ipu has recourse to the picture of the sleeping helmsman on a stormy sea.

What is, in effect, a direct answer to this pessimistic outburst occurs in the Instructions of Kheti to Merikare:

'A [whole] generation of men will pass by while God, who knows the real nature of things, [will seem] to have hidden himself. In that time there is no withstanding the man of violence and none but the evilly disposed can be seen with the eyes (*i.e.* wherever one looks). None the less God should be revered as upon his way. Whether [his image] be made of precious stone or cast in copper, these are like the mud banks which are continually shifting; the river will not allow itself to be hidden for ever but it breaks the dam which conceals it.'[2]

However chaotic the state of things may seem, God is still 'on his way'—active in the world—and will manifest himself again sooner or later. As in Job, the travails and disasters of human life are set in the framework of a God-appointed universe; expressly made for human needs and happiness.

'Consider mankind as the flocks of God. He made the sky for the enjoyment of their hearts, he repelled the greed of the waters, he created the breath of life for their noses; his images are they, the products of his flesh. He rises in the sky for their heart's desire, for them he has made the plants, animals, birds and fish—all for their delight. He slew his enemies and destroyed his children when they were plotting to make rebellion. He makes the dawn for their delight, he sails above to look upon them, he raised a shelter around their heads. When they weep he listens to them, he has made for them hereditary rulers (?) as supporters to support the backs of the weak. He made spells for them as weapons against accidents, and dreams by night and by day. How has he slain the froward-hearted?[3] Even as a man may smite his son for his brother's sake. For God [alone] knows the nature of every man.[4]

The real subtlety of the last two sentences—or so it seems to the present writer—lies in their assumption that pessimism about the nature of man in dark and anarchic times may be a subjective judgment. Ipu, after all, was probably a dis- possessed and disgruntled nobleman caught up in a social up- heaval in which he had all to lose. God, however, 'knows the nature of every man'. When he punishes the wicked they remain his kinsfolk; he does not withhold himself completely from them but treats them as errant members of his family. Fundamentally God is wholly good, but he is also omniscient and his judgment is not that of frail and committed men.

The personal relation between man and God had been expressed during the days of old by the symbol of the divine shepherd, but in evil times the Egyptians found this a problem rather than a comfort. While still thinking within their traditional mythological framework they began to analyse and refine their notions of God and his ways with his creation. Otto has recently suggested that Chapter 17 of the Book of the Dead contains a garbled quotation from a lost myth of the time:[5]

'Understanding said of him (*i.e.* God), "He is like that which he creates."'

God and man partake of the same nature; to cavil with the basic disposition of men is to misunderstand the divine nature. But the new scepticism could not be quietened by bland assertions of the divine omnipotence. A new form of mythical literature began to be written, in which God is questioned or even reproached for the seeming unreasonableness or injustice of the world, or in which he seems to be anticipating such questions.[6]

As the sun, God sailed across the sky in his boat, governing the world as well as bringing it light and life. At death the Egyptian hoped, after many trials and mystic journeys, to reach the divine barque. This was the final beatitude, for it meant immortality in the eternal circuit of the heavenly bodies. In the new spirit of inquiry, however, being in the presence of God was reinterpreted:

> 'Indeed he who is yonder will be a living god,
>   punishing anyone who commits a sin,
> Indeed he who is yonder will stand in the boat
>   causing the choicest offerings in it to be given to the
>   temples,
> Indeed he who is yonder will become a sage
>   who will not be hindered from appealing to God when-
>   ever he speaks.'[7]

When, at last, the soul reaches the solar barque, all its questions will be answered. The boat is the seat of judgment and the allocation of material prosperity. More important, the soul will be able to question God freely concerning the reasons for the apparent disharmonies of existence.

It is in the light of the power of the soul to ask God the great and humanly insoluble questions that one can understand a speech of 'the Universal Lord' in another fragment which has been preserved in a magical work of the First Intermediate Period called 'The Book of the Two Ways'.[8]

> 'The Universal Lord spoke to the gods, now at rest after
>   the tumult [of life?] in the voyage of the Divine Band:

All is well, be of good cheer!
I will repeat to you the four good deeds which mine own
     heart contrived when I was still in the midst of the
     serpent coils, in order that evil should be silenced;
I performed four good deeds within the portals of the
     Horizon.
I made the four winds that every man might breathe
     thereof, wherever he might be;
that was one deed.
I made the mighty inundation waters that the poor should
     have rights therein like the powerful;
that was one deed.
I made every man like his fellow—it was not my decree
     that they (*i.e.* men) should do evil, but it was their
     hearts which violated what I said;
that was one deed.
I made their hearts not to be forgetful of the West, that
     offerings should be made to the gods and their estates;
that was one deed.
The gods I created from my sweat,
     but mankind is from the tears of mine eye.'

The word 'sep', translated above as 'deed', was used by
Ptah-hotep, a wise man of the Old Kingdom, to signify the
teaching of the ancestors which was the guiding principle of
generations to come. 'If you take to heart what I have told you,
your conduct will in all respects correspond to that of the
ancestors. Their "sep" of righteousness was the best thing that
they did, its memory is repeated in the mouths of men on
account of the goodness of their teaching.'9 The idea, then,
that guiding rules were laid down at the beginning is a general
tradition, but in the case of the fourfold law it is not the
ancestors but God himself who is the author. To underline the
importance of these principles as prior and basic to the whole
creative scheme they are said to have been declared before God
had arisen in visible form, when he was still a serpent in the

waters. 'Within the portals of the Horizon' means beyond the accessible world, in the place whence power and authority come. The law was delivered in sacred time and space.

These principles are like the programme of a revolutionary party, simple but far-reaching in their significance. The fundamental needs of life and some mitigations of its worst hazards are, by God's will, the right of every man. God made men, not equals in the modern democratic sense, but equal in value, as brothers and members of one family. The idea is allied to that in the passage from Merikare (p. 69); it emphasizes the close link between man and man and between man and God. But the blame for injustice is laid squarely on the shoulders of men. Their 'hearts' are the cause of evil. This is the earliest unequivocal statement that wrong lies in the will (Egyptian 'heart') rather than in the deed itself.

The final command is concerned with religion. 'To remember the West' has a wider meaning than the mere care for the tomb of the departed. The provision of offerings and the estates from which they came underlay the whole system of land tenure in Ancient Egypt. Moreover, whereas the temple ceremonies were the business of priests, everyone was under the obligation to care for the tombs of his parents; so the funerary cult meant the practice of religion for most people.

In the last two sentences two creation myths are juxtaposed. The gods are the exhalations of God himself or, as the text says, they come from his sweat, but mankind comes from the tears of his eye. This essential difference between the two kinds of beings, gods and men, is not mentioned elsewhere. The second myth, about the origin of mankind, is founded on assonance between the words for tears and mankind—'remeyet' and 'romech'.

If the universe is regarded as essentially visible, its origin can be described in terms of what the Egyptians called 'the appearance'—the first manifestation of the High God as light. They were not, however, satisfied with this but tried to penetrate beneath the outward semblance of phenomena. At a simple level this took the form of a number of mythical events before the establishment of the High God as supreme master. The texts of the Old Kingdom contain echoes of a mass slaughter of the denizens of the Abyss[10] or of the defeat of a monster of chaos.[11] The Memphite Theology hints at this problem by declaring that Ptah has undergone a series of avatars from the first spirit in the Primeval Waters to the emergent lotus bud. But in the Coffin Texts there are hints that during the Herakleopolitan Period the evolution of the divine spirit began to be considered in a more abstract way. The myth almost falls away to reveal the metaphysical assumptions that underly it. Thus, in Coffin Text 714 the High God says:

> 'I was [the spirit in ?] the Primeval Waters,
> he who had no companion when my name came into existence.
> The most ancient form in which I came into existence was as a drowned one.
> I was [also] he who came into existence as a circle,
> he who was the dweller in his egg.
> I was the one who began [everything], the dweller in the Primeval Waters.
> First Hahu emerged for me
> and then I began to move.
> I created my limbs in my "glory".[12]
> I was the maker of myself, in that I formed myself according to my desire and in accord with my heart.'

The first form of God was as a spirit, alone and—so to speak —held in solution in the waters. Then, but still in the waters, God was 'a circle', which, in turn, was replaced by the symbol of the cosmic egg. These are primordial images expressing the evolution of the divine life before it became fully conscious and began to move. The second, dynamic stage is initiated by Hahu, which a late inscription defines as 'the wind, which began the separation and raised the sky vault as its hall'. The act of Hahu is the separation of the waters, the creation of the space-bubble in the midst of the Abyss that is the theatre of

God's development, the space in which he can 'move'. Finally God creates his limbs in his 'glory', fully conscious at last. This is a variant of the theology of the Word, exemplified in the Hermopolitan and Memphite doctrines. The new precision is the division of the divine act into heart and will.

Heart and Will are replaced in another version of the same period by Command and Intelligence:[13]

> 'I am he . . . whose speech was what had come forth from his heart.
> His cycle with Shu was the circling of Command and Intelligence,
> asking his (Intelligence's) advice;
> and Command and Intelligence said to him—
> "Come, then, let us go and create the names of this coil[14] according to what has come forth from his heart."
> And that was the cycle with Shu, the son whom he himself had borne.'

Shu, the son of the Creator in the old legend, is equated with Command and Intelligence who 'go around' the circle of total being, giving everything its name, *i.e.* its distinct characteristic. At the end there is a reaffirmation that this is the same episode which is connected with Shu. The writer of this difficult and subtle monologue understood that the creation legends were symbols and that divergent legends might be different ways of saying the same thing. The generation of Shu is the act which produced the multiplicity, the primary division of the original unity. Into this context is brought the giving of names. The cosmogony is basically idealist. In the earlier part (quoted on p. 51) it emphasizes that the thinking of the High God is the first reality and this can be divided at a later stage into Will, or Command, its expression, and Intelligence. The mythological framework is almost but not quite transcended.

The Creative Word could be understood in several ways. In one contemporary text it is 'Command' alone, without Intelligence.

'An eye of Atum appeared on the Babet Tree,
an eye of Atum appeared on the Date Palm
   (He gave Command to the Primeval Waters that he
     might have power thereby)
and that was his appearance at the beginning.
A powerful one, whose might subdued the powers [of
   the Abyss],
it curbed the eye when it raged and burnt,
it introduced the primeval gods,
it was supreme over the deities,
it created Time—
   (Which was when Shu was there to raise the sky; it
     curbed the demon of darkness)
that was Shu, that it might bring heart to the Tousled
and cheer their bulls.
What it said, the same was performed,
that it might cause a light, like the sun, in the night.
   (variant: that the gods should likewise have form by
     night)
Now I am Command,
what I said was good, and what came forth from my
   mouth was good,
and what I now say, the same shall be performed, for I am
   Command. . . .'[15]

The opening lines refer to two mythical trees about which nothing is known. The text is distinctive by its allusions to the powers of chaos that threatened the rise of the ordered world. The chief of these was the eye of God himself which rebelled and had to be curbed by the Divine Command. The most important clarification, however, is in the lines which say that the creation of time is the same thing as the raising of the sky and the coming of light. Before that the gods had been 'tousled', in a state of confusion and dismay. Now their males can take heart. Does this mean that the separation of earth and sky, the beginning of calendrical time, marks the transference to male supremacy? The following phrases tell of the creation of the moon as the second great sign of Divine Command. But the variant text seems to refer to the stars in general as the forms of the gods during the night-time. This is related to the Egyptian concept of the soul as it developed during the Middle Kingdom. The stars were the 'souls' of the gods, their *alter egos* while darkness reigned on earth. In the last lines the soul of the deceased claims identity with the Command. There is an assurance that the good and the Command are the same—a doctrine which is affirmed still more strongly in another mono-logue of the time:[16]

> 'I am the Eternal Spirit,
> I am the sun that rose from the Primeval Waters.
> My soul is God, I am the creator of the Word.
> Evil is my abomination, I see it not.
> I am the Creator of the Order wherein I live,
> I am the Word, which will never be annihilated
> in this my name of "Soul".'

To become one with the Word was, then, to be removed from all evil. The Word is good and is manifest in the Order of the world. God, as goodness, obeys his own laws, for the Order and the good are identical. We have seen that this optimistic theology was challenged at the breakdown of the old society of the Pyramid Age; it is reaffirmed here to help in the deification of the individual soul.

On its journey after death the soul reached the horizon, where dwelt the 'ancestral gods'—the beings who were superseded after the enthronement of Rê in the sky. The soul claims to be Hikê, the Divine Word as 'Magic':

> 'Hail, O Noble Ones! O Predecessors of the Universal Master!
> I am he who created for the One God
> before the twin affairs appeared in the world
> when he sent forth his single eye,
> while he was still alone, at the enunciation of his mouth,

when his *Ka* became a millionfold to protect his subjects,
when he spoke with Khopri, but was mightier than he,
when he put Command upon his mouth.
Now I am indeed that son of the all-mother,
born before any mother existed,
that I might be the safeguard of the Command of the One
   Master.
I am he who enlivened the companies of the gods,
I am he who did whatever he wished, the father of the
   gods. . . .
All things were mine, before you came into being, O
   Gods!
You only came afterwards, for I am Hikê.'[17]

Once again, we learn about the time of the primal unity.
While in the waters, God dispatched his single eye. This time
the multiplicity is described, not as names but as *Ka's*. In the
early Heliopolitan cosmogony Atum had imparted his single
Ka to Shu and Tefnut, but now the *Ka* has become a plura-
lity. Each 'subject' of God is protected in that he shares in the
divine essence. The theology is personalized, as might be
expected when the aristocratic society of the Old Kingdom had
disappeared and been replaced by one where everybody could
claim direct relation with God. The appearance of the sun is
a showing of the Word, but even the mighty light of the dawn
is a lesser power than the all-pervading command of the High
God. A double paradox is used to convey the mystery of the
generation of the Word from the bisexual Atum. Hikê is, like
Shu, the son of Atum. In other words, Shu, Hikê, Command
and Intelligence are all really the same principle or god, the
Demiurge, first-born child of the original spirit.

   The most popular religious text in Ancient Egypt was
Chapter 17 of the Book of the Dead. It seems to have been
written down at Herakleopolis during the Ninth Dynasty as a
compendium of stages through which the soul had to pass
from the time it was liberated during the lustrations at the

funeral to the time when it emerged from the Underworld to join the sun.[18] It opens with a monologue by the High God which is quite distinct from the rest of the composition:

'The Word came into being.
All things were mine when I was alone.
I was Rê in [all] his first manifestations:
I was the great one who came into being of himself,
who created all his names as the Companies of the [lesser] gods,
he who is irresistible among the gods.
The battleship[19] of the gods was made according to what I said.
Now I know the name of the great god who was therein.
(An early gloss adds, 'Perfume of Rê is his name'.)
I was that great Phoenix who is in Heliopolis,
who looks after the decision of all that is.'
(An early gloss adds, 'That is Osiris, while as to all that is, that is eternity and everlastingness.')

The Word is the beginning and, probably, the cause of every-thing. In the primordial state all things were in God, who persists essentially the same throughout his 'manifestations'. As the self-creator he pronounced the names—his names, or, as a later gloss explains, the names of his limbs. These are parts of him, but they are also the lesser divinities. Then comes a dark hint of lost legends about the defeat of cosmic enemies in the ages of strife and confusion. There follows the classic reference to the Phoenix, the bird who comes to Heliopolis to herald a new age and functions as a determiner of destiny. This is most likely to mean the institution of regulated time-cycles, with which event the evolution of the world was complete. The glosses show that some Egyptians were aware that really there was only one God—at least only one great positive figure —and that even Osiris was but a partial form of him. There is nothing here that is not already in the Memphite Theology, but it is explained in more cogent language. Perhaps it lacks the metaphysical overtones of other statements of the period, but it is clear and unambiguous. It is a challenge thrown out to Egyptian polytheism. Unfortunately the challenge was taken up, for it serves as an introduction to the most bewildering polytheistic effusion in the whole of Egyptian literature.

One of the distinctive characteristics of Egyptian cosmogony is its feeling for space:

> 'I am Atum, the creator of the Eldest Gods,[20]
> I am he who gave birth to Shu,
> I am that great He-She,
> I am he who did what seemed good to him,
> I took my space[21] in the place of my will,
> Mine is the space of those who move along
> like those two serpentine circles.'[22]

God needed space in the waters to carry out what seemed good to him; this is the meaning here of the creation of Shu. It is the space for the stars, those who move along the heavenly roads. This space is—at least pictorially—to be conceived as bounded above and below by two encircling serpents. This is not the usual idea. The Egyptians, like other early peoples, occasion-ally thought of the world as surrounded by a serpent with its tail in its mouth, a symbol for the Cosmic Ocean.[23] On the in-most shrine of Tutankhamun there is a strange mummy-like figure erect and ringed above and below by two encircling serpents. They must be the two serpentine circles of the Coffin Text, delimiters of space when it is imagined as extending upwards.

The bisexual nature of Atum is asserted, not only by calling him 'that great He-She' but by saying that he 'gave birth' to Shu. A variant MS.[24] has laid even greater stress on this by saying that Atum is 'he who conceived Shu', who is space personified.

The most advanced theological movement of the time was connected with Shu. It transcended local cosmogonies for it was philosophic rather than mythical. Most of the relevant

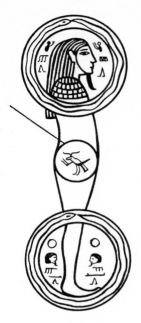

Fig. 11. Two serpents enclose
the Cosmic Form
(the potential inert form
occupying the whole Universe
bounded by the serpents
of Earth and Sky).
From the second shrine
of Tutankhamun

texts were collected by de Buck and form Spells 75 to 81 in his
edition of the Coffin Texts. In them Shu is the mediator
between God—and these texts use the word God advisedly—
and 'his multiplicity'. He is also the breath of life, in fact life
itself and the creator in detail, the Demiurge in the sense of
Plato's *Timaeus*. In order to clarify their ideas the authors of
the Shu Texts create myths which are parables rather than
relations of events. The general form is that of a dramatic
monologue but dialogue is freely used.

Spell 75 begins:

'I am the soul of Shu, the self-created,
I am the soul of Shu, the moulder of form,
I am coextensive with God,
I came into being with him.'

So, for the apologists of Shu, God is not removed from the universe. He is everywhere and Shu is everywhere with him. The temporal assumptions of mythology are denied. In the older legends Shu came 'after' his father Atum, but in this version they come into being together. Creation is not a series of events in time but a speculation about the principles of life and the arrangement of the cosmos.

'I am the announcer of him that comes forth from the horizon,
I am he that spreads respect for him in those who seek his name.
I am indwelling in the millions [of creatures],
who is heard in a million words.
I am he who brings the words of the Self-Creator to his multiplicity.
I am the captain of his crew,
I am the strongest and most vigorous of the Divine Band.'

Shu is the dawn breeze which announces the coming of the sun. As breath he is the speech of all the worshippers of the High God when he is worshipped at the moment that the full light breaks upon the waiting world. As the sun rises into the sky, Shu as the wind takes command of the solar boat. In what follows there is a strange denigration of Nun, the Primeval Waters:

'The ancestral gods (*i.e.* the crew of the boat) enquired about my form from Nun for they saw how strong and vigorous I was in the boat which conveys the Self-Creator,
I stood up among them that I might exercise power as

befitted my form, and when I spoke the company fell
silent, the gods were afraid. I said:
"I will tell you, I came into existence in my own form.
Do not ask Nun about my form.
He [could only] look at me as I came into existence,
    but I knew his name and the place where I should come
    into being.
He could not see my form with his face
for I came into being in the limbs of the Self-Creator,
he formed me in his heart and created me in his glory.[25]
I am he who breathed out form. I stretched forth—
this noble god who fills the sky with his beauty
and whose name the gods do not know." '[26]

There is an echo of long-forgotten controversy in this
passage. As on p. 72, the High God is the sun delivering his
judgments from the divine sky-boat, the seat of ultimate
authority from which he governs the world. It is used here to
strengthen a controversial statement; any declaration which
comes from the Sun God's boat must be definitive. From the
Old Kingdom there had been a tendency to personify Nun, the
Primeval Waters, as 'the Father of the Gods'. In the productions of the Heracleopolitan period he becomes vocal as the
oldest being and so tends to oust Rê and Shu from their
positions as primeval beings. This, however, was to forget that
the waters are unconscious and pre-personal, and so incapable
of any positive role. Shu, on the other hand, is consciousness
itself, invisible and coextensive with the Creator, the active
thought as distinct from the inert world-stuff. The creation of
light makes forms visible and 'fills the sky with beauty'—
perhaps the earliest recognition that aesthetic values are an
essential part of the world.

In Spell 76 the generation of Shu is told in careful but
recondite terms:

'I am Shu, whom Atum created on the day that he himself
    appeared.

He did not form me in a womb nor shape me in an egg,
I was not conceived by any manner of conception,
but my father Atum spat me forth with the spittle of his
    mouth,
me and my sister Tefnut.
She emerged behind me[27] when I was enveloped in the
    breath of life
that came from the throat of the Phoenix,
on the day that Atum appeared
in the infinity, the nothing, the darkness and shapelessness.
I am Shu, Father of the gods—
which was when Atum sent out his single eye to seek me
    and my sister Tefnut.
I am he who made the darkness light for her
when she found me as a man upholding.'

Shu belongs to the appearance; he is, in fact, the means of
visibility, whereas Atum is the essential godhead persisting
through all his forms. The old Heliopolitan cosmogony is not
a myth here but a group of parallel symbols.

The appearance of the primary pair is equated with the call
of the Phoenix who delivers the message of life. This is also the
symbol of Atum breathing form from the chaos of the eternal
Abyss. Now, as appeared in Pyramid Text 1660 (see p. 37),
the coming of the sacred bird upon the stone at Heliopolis is a
symbol for the shining of the first light. When the Phoenix
opens its beak and utters its call this

'declares everything that is and is not yet'[28]

and is the call to life. In a Nile hymn the annual inundation of
the Nile is said to be:

'The flood of the eye of Atum
    when the water rises and the overflow appears,'[29]

from which it seems that the eye of Atum makes the waters
active. After their mystic generation in the Abyss, Atum sent
out Shu and Tefnut and then dispatched his eye into the

waters to find them. The eye found Shu in his traditional shape as a man with his arms above his head, creating an empty space.

Orthodox Egyptian cosmology assigned four supports to the sky, but the Shu texts double this number. Eight 'supporters' —figures in the traditional role of Shu—hold the sky above them. They are part of the original scheme, for Shu says he

> 'gave their names according to the words of creation of the
>   Primeval Waters
> with Atum, on the day that Atum arose within his limit,
> before he saw Geb beneath his legs.
> Shu was coextensive [with Atum?]
>   (variant: 'Shu was still within the waters, nor had the
>   earth been created)'
> before the creation of the Heavenly Ocean for Atum
> that he might float upon it.'[30]

The sky supports are part of the initial scheme of things, and their names, *i.e.* their nature and function, were involved in the Creative Word[31] spoken by Atum in the midst of the waters. This, again, is an idealist trait. Only their 'names', not the supports themselves, existed in the Primeval Abyss. They were part of the original 'Word' which was enumerated, before the separation, when earth and sky were still together. There is a reminder that creation is a limited activity. Atum is 'within his limit' and Shu is 'coextensive' with him. This harks back to the old Heliopolitan idea that the High God in assuming his form gives the limits to the world. 'He extended everywhere, in accordance with what was to come into existence.' But wherever Atum is, there Shu is also. The two are aspects of the great power which creates and sustains the universe; both are involved in the Primeval Word and were so even when God was still 'within the Waters'.

In another text Shu says:

> 'I am Life, the Lord of years, living for ever, Lord of
>   eternity,[32]

the eldest one that Atum made in his "glory",
in giving birth to Shu and Tefnut in Heliopolis,
when he was one and became three,
when he separated Geb from Nut,
before the birth of the first corporation,[33]
before the coming of the twin companies.
They were with me in his nose,
and he conceived me with his nose.
I emerged from his nostrils,
he put me on his neck and would not let me leave him.'

When Atum breathed forth Shu he sent forth not only the god
but life itself and all the living things that were to come thereafter. Shu—in becoming both life and eternity—has lost his
individuality. The Demiurge has almost become identified
with his creation; but not quite, for the Egyptians had a lively
appreciation of the wonder of his light:

'The Eldest Gods exult, the Ancestors are well pleased,
the quarrelling and the fighting cease in Heliopolis
when they behold Shu bearing the light.
He brings appearance to him who has willed [it],
he gives happiness to the Double Company.
The gods come babbling to him
as he divides the hours with the twilight,
as he satisfies the sun with Mayet.
When Shu arises, Father of the Gods,
the river around him is ablaze with light.
So may my strength be the strength of Shu
as I carry yonder sky that I may steady her brightness.
I have commanded males to forget females
as Nut raises every god before me.
The multitudes are moved, the millions are well pleased
as they give me full salutation.
I am Shu for all the gods, heaven and earth are mine,
mine are all that are therein, mine are the ends of the earth,
I am the Ruler as I am he in the midst of all.'[34]

Shu is the dazzling light of an Oriental morning. But in this paean of joy there is a memory of the dawn of time. In classical mythology the Nereids and Tritons, who are creatures of the times before the rise of Zeus, gaze in rapture at the appearance of the sun as it rises from the baths of Ocean. Similarly in this old Egyptian song the gods of old are stupefied and 'satisfied'. Night, the time of confusion and terror, is called the time of fighting in Heliopolis. Myth is here passing into metaphor. The age of myth is the time before the coming of the light of day. In terms of legend this means the essential period of confusion when Horus and Seth were contending for the inheritance of Osiris. Heliopolis is the scene of this epic contest, as is confirmed by the text quoted on p. 110. The light reaching the upper sky is a repetition of the separation of earth and sky by Shu, for it was by this act that light was first brought into the world. Lovers must cease their caresses, wrapt in wonder at the glorious morning, whose light penetrates to the ends of the earth.

So far the High God and the Primeval Waters have been considered as masculine or bisexual. There was, however, another tradition, about a Mother Goddess, which was probably ignored or suppressed during the Old Kingdom but emerged in the Coffin Texts, when the weakening of the central control allowed provincial cults to appear in the texts. The heavenly ocean was imagined as a 'great flood'—worshipped in several places as a cow whose star-specked belly formed the sky. This strange and unlikely conjunction of ideas emerges from time to time in Egyptian symbolism, an intruder into the speculative theology of the priests from the world of popular devotion. Dendera, a town about forty miles north of Thebes, was the centre of the cult of Hathor, the most attractive form of the great goddess for the Egyptians. Hathor is the face of the sky, the deep and the lady who dwells in a grove at the end of the world. Her son is Ihy,[35] the child who emerges from his mother every day at dawn as the new sun—in which case his mother is the sky—but who is also the Primeval Ocean as the all-mother, whether as Hathor, Nut, or

Isis—the three great forms of the Mother Goddess. A creation myth has been preserved in a text from Gebelein:

> 'My majesty precedes me as Ihy, the son of Hathor.
> I am the male of masculinity,
> I slid forth from the outflow between her thighs
> in this my name of Jackal of the Light.[36]
> I broke forth from the egg, I oozed out of her essence,
> I escaped in her blood. I am the master of the redness.
> I am the Bull of the Confusion, my mother Isis generated
>   me
> though she was ignorant of herself beneath the fingers of
>   the Lord of the gods.
> I broke free from her on that day that the deep was uplifted
>   as the . . .
> for the Lord of the gods on the day of confusion;
> [this happened] before necks had been fixed, before the
>   heads of the gods had
> been severed, before the disk had been fastened on the
>   horns, before
> the face of the Sistrum[37] had been moulded—
> I took shape, I grew, I crawled about, I crept around, I
>   grew big,
> I became tall like my father[38] when he rose to his full
>   height . . .
> The flood it was that raised me up while the waters gave
>   me . . .
> My mother Isis suckled me, I tasted of her sweetness . . .
> I am the babe in the Primeval Waters . . .
> I sought an abiding place in this my name of Hahu[39]
> and I found it in Punt. I built a house there on the hillside
>   where my mother resides beneath her sycamores.'

Ihy is the light-child, a symbol for the first emergence in its freshness and potentiality. He is 'the bull of the confusion', the first male to rise out of the chaos of the waters. Like Shu, he has only one progenitor, for he is the offspring of the primordial

Fig. 12. Forms of Hathor Head

God, in his case the Mother Goddess. The rosy hue of the dawn sky, whether on the first morning or every day, is the blood emitted by Hathor or Isis—the names are interchangeable—when she bears her son. 'The Lord of the gods', although mentioned, does not have a place in this theology; it looks as if he is a polemical figure to be dismissed from consideration. Ihy is the master.

There is a list of mythical events about which nothing is known. Were the heads of the chaotic monsters of the deep cut off and then rearranged on more fitting bodies? There must have been a legend relating how the sun's disk came to be fixed between the horns of Hathor. The sistrum face is the flattened form of a female face with cow's ears which, for some reason, symbolized the Mother Goddess Hathor as the sky. As Hahu the child claims identity with Shu, for the word means 'the upholder', *i.e.* the air/light god who supports the sky. Punt is the land far to the south of Egypt where the child goes to join his mother, who is the goddess of the distant regions of the world.[40]

The Bremner Rhind Papyrus is a document of the fourth century B.C. containing a long series of curses against Apopis, the cosmic dragon. Embedded in it are two versions of the

Heliopolitan creation myth. The language is archaic for the age of the papyrus, and the prototype was probably a work in Middle Egyptian, dating from the period of most of the texts discussed in this chapter. Atum, while still formless in the waters, delivered an utterance and from this had come the 'myriads of forms'; that is, the patterns of all that was to take shape in the visible world already existed in the mind of the Creator while he was still—as the Coffin Texts say—'a drowned one'. It is tempting to think that this basically idealist concept was borrowed from the Greeks—Plato died only a few years before the extant copy of the work was written—but on internal evidence the Bremner Rhind cosmogonies are purely Egyptian and a product of the speculations of the Middle Kingdom or earlier.

The masturbation and spitting motifs are combined into one act, the dispatch of Shu and Tefnut into the waters. God sent his single Eye to fetch them back. The return means a resump/ tion of the primordial unity of the divine power. Atum, over/ whelmed by joy at the reunion, put his arms around Shu and Tefnut, weeping tears which were to become the ancestors of mankind. Meanwhile the Eye had become enraged when it saw that Atum had put another eye in its place. According to the strange conventions of Egyptian symbolism the enraged Eye became a rearing cobra with swollen neck, the uraeus snake. Atum pacified the Eye by binding it—now a snake— around his forehead as the uraeus that guards the crown. Since as early as the Pyramid Texts the eye could represent the crown, this proceeding means that the pacification of the Eye is the establishment of monarchy. Finally—and the papyrus pur/ posely omits any reference to the times of Shu and Geb—earth and sky produce their five children—'the children of Nut'—the deities of the Osirian cycle and the patrons of the five days which precede the New Year.[41]

'The multitudes came from my utterance[42]
   before the appearance of Heaven and Earth,

before the snakes and worms had been moulded in that
place,[43]
but I created some of them while I was still in the Primeval
Waters in a state of inertness, without anywhere to stand.
It occurred to my heart, I devised with my face (*sic*)
that I should make every form, while I was still alone,
before I had spat forth as Shu, before I had expectorated as
Tefnut,
before another had come into being that he might create
with me.
I devised in my own heart that myriads of forms should
come into being
and the forms of their children and then theirs again.
I am he who rubbed with his fist, I emitted into my own
hand and then
I spat forth from my own mouth.
I spat forth Shu, I expectorated Tefnut,
while my father, the Primeval Waters, supported them.
My Eye followed them for many ages,
they departed from me—so that instead of my being one
god, there were now three.
Then I appeared in the world and Shu and Tefnut
rejoiced thereat
while they were still in a state of inertness,
and they brought back my Eye with them.
Whereupon I rejoined my limbs. I wept over them
—and thus mankind came into existence from the tears
that sprang from my Eye.
Then it became enraged against me, when it returned and
saw
that I had put another in its place,
replacing it with a brighter one;[44]
so I promoted it to the front of my face
so that it could rule the whole world.
Then their (*sic*) wrath died away in that I had replaced
what had been taken away,

> I emerged from the . . . and created all the serpents and
> every form of them.
> Then Shu and Tefnut produced Geb and Nut, and these
> produced
> Osiris, Horus the Sightless,[45] Seth, Isis and Nephthys—
> all in one Company, one after the other,
> and they produced the myriads in the world.'

The second version gives further details about the creation
within the waters:

> 'I fulfilled all my desires when I was alone,
> before there had appeared a second to be with me in this
> place;
> I assumed form as that great soul wherein I started being
> creative
> while still in the Primeval Waters in a state of inertness,
> before I had found anywhere to stand.
> I considered in my heart, I planned in my head how I
> should make every shape
> —this was while I was still alone—I planned in my heart
> how I should create
> other beings—the myriad forms of Khopri—and that there
> should come into being their children and theirs.
> So it was I who spat forth Shu and expectorated Tefnut[46]
> so that where there had been one god there were now three
> as well as myself[47]
> and there were now a male and a female in the world.
> Shu and Tefnut rejoiced thereat in the Primeval Waters
> in which they were.
> After an age my Eye brought them to me and they
> approached me and joined my body, that they might
> issue from me.
> When I rubbed with my fist my heart came into my
> mouth in that I spat forth Shu and expectorated Tefnut.
> But, as my father was relaxed . . . for ages . . . serpents . . .

Fig. 13. The Eye as an independent god

I wept tears . . . the form of my Eye; and that is how mankind came into existence.

I replaced it with a shining one (the sun) and it became enraged with me when it came back and found another growing in its place.'

Until the publication of the Coffin Texts this creation myth could reasonably be attributed to a very late period, but it must —in its general principles—be as early as the Middle Kingdom, for several mythical episodes in the Coffin Texts can be explained in the light of Bremner Rhind. Thus a 'Chapter of becoming Hathor' (Spell 331) describes how the High God dispatched his eye 'before he had repeated himself'. The original procreation of Shu and Tefnut—here developed as a spitting—took place in the Primeval Waters. The first pair were not therefore really existent until the Eye could return them to their creator. The Eye is personified might, the essential violence that is used to protect the gods and kings against disintegration in the waters or spirit enemies in the created world. Shu and Tefnut, as mere exhalations or even thoughts of the High God, were helpless in the waters; hence the Eye's mission to defend them on their dark journey and to bring them back to their maker. Reunited with him they were safe in his embrace, in his original act of *Ka*-giving. The idealistic overtones of Bremner Rhind are absent from the Coffin Text, although the sending out of the Eye is equated with the Divine Word in the text quoted on p. 77 (Spell 261).

'. . . I am that Eye of Horus[48]
the messenger of the Lord, when he was alone, before he
    had repeated himself.
I am he that created his name, I grew a growing
before the sky had been created that it might give me
    acclaim,
before the earth had been laid out that it might extol me,
when I went seeking what you had spat out and what you
    had expectorated (that is, Shu and Tefnut).[49]
I went groping and I went seeking and behold I have
    brought [them] back!
[The High God says]
"Come, then, upon my forehead that you may exalt my
    beauty!
come, then, in front of me, that I have made you
    elevated!" '[50]

In this version the Eye is elevated as the defensive cobra which
—on the pattern of the earthly pharaohs—encircled the brows
of the High God. For Bremner Rhind this motif is an act of
amnesty on Rê's part, to soothe the anger of the Eye when it
returned to its creator, only to find that another had taken its
place in the god's face. Here, however, the transformation of
the Eye into a cobra is, apparently, a reward for its labours in
seeking Shu and Tefnut in the waters. In either case the return
of the Eye marks the assumption of kingship by the High God
and the end of the age of inchoate chaos. The task of the first
Eye was to rescue the formless, indeterminate creations of God
from the sightless negativities of the Abyss. The eye is the power
of life to defend itself inviolate against dissolution and the spirits
of non-being.

What God said to the Eye when he installed it as the cobra
on his brow has been preserved in a splendidly rhetorical piece
from Siut:[51]

'. . . of whom Rê said:
"Great will be your majesty and mighty your influence,

great will be your power and mighty your magic over the
  bodies of your enemies;
they will fall howling on their faces,
all mankind will be curbed beneath your power;
fear will be yours when they behold you in this vigorous
  form
which the Lord of the Primeval Gods has given you."
Thus did he speak, the Lord of the Primeval Company,
  even to me.'

In his original condition the High God had one eye—that is
clear although such a Polyphemus figure does not occur on the
monuments.[52] An eye of God was the medium of creation on
two occasions: when he was alone in the waters he produced a
brood of creatures from his eye and then, 'ages after', says
Bremner Rhind, mankind sprang from his tears.

At first the primeval brood had the forms of serpents, but they
were later transformed into the attendant deities of the Sun God.
A messenger of Horus known as a 'Divine Falcon' relates:[53]

'I am one of those whom Atum created,
who came into being from the root of his eye,
whom Atum formed and whom he glorified,[54]
whom he shaped and whose faces he distinguished,
that they might be with him when he was alone in the
  Primeval Waters;
who [now] foretell his appearance on the horizon . . .
I am one of those serpents whom he made in his eye
before Isis, the mother of Horus, came into being.'

So these original 'worms' or 'serpents' in the waters are also the
original forms of the morning stars. Another text hints at a
myth about their creation:

'I [released ?] the worms in the Eye of Atum, for I am the
  sun . . .
I have come to repeat his tears for him.
I am Rê (or, the sun) who wept for himself in his single eye

that I might cool the flame in my eye, cooling the ways
with my tears;
I am Rê who wept for himself in his single eye to quench
the flame in his eye.'[55]

The Eye must have begun to 'burn' and God cooled it with
his tears. These tears flowed out into the Primeval Waters as
worms or serpents. These might be the original forms of minor
deities, but the imaginative author of another Coffin Text
identifies them with the great principles, Command and
Intelligence:

'Verily I know the ways through the darkness [of the
Primeval Waters][56]
into which Command and Intelligence entered as worms
with darkness behind them and the light before them;
I enter between them upon the invisible path within the
forehead of Atum.'

To call Command and Intelligence 'worms' violates the
modern Western feeling for symbolic propriety. It is, however,
an attempt to reconcile the visually conceived symbolism of the
Eye myth with a cosmogony in abstract terms. The underlying idealism of Egyptian cosmogony has elevated ideas into
mythical figures. The Primeval Waters are fundamental to all
creation; so, too, are the principles of the divine mind. In the
invisible path within the forehead of the High God there is an
echo of the old sky-god whose eyes were sun and moon. It is a
journey from sun to moon which is also a way through the
dark waters of eternity and a way across the night sky. God in
the Primeval Waters is half understood as a vast face—an idea
difficult to realize but strangely powerful.

Bremner Rhind, therefore, with its assertions that God had
thought out the ideas of all the creatures in the universe before
creation began, when he was still motionless in the waters, fits
naturally into the Egyptian tradition. Like the Memphite
Theology it explicitly states the metaphysical ideas that are
implicit in all the accounts of creation.

CHAPTER III

Osiris—Original Scheme

OSIRIS is the most vivid achievement of the Egyptian imagination. He is also the most complex. Although not the Lord of
the universe, he is not therefore a subordinate deity. The High
God, creator and determiner of fate, is a theological concept,
the supreme personification of power, will and wisdom,
eternal and ineffable—to some extent beyond the power of the
imagination to understand, to be apprehended in symbolic
terms. Osiris is quite different, he demands sympathy. He is the
completely helpless one, the essential victim. Yet he is avenged
and his passion has an end at last, when justice and order are
re-established on earth. The other gods are transcendent,
distinct from their worshippers. Osiris, however, is immanent.
He is the sufferer with all mortality but at the same time he is
all the power of revival and fertility in the world. He is the
power of growth in plants and of reproduction in animals and
human beings. He is both dead and the source of all living.
Hence to become Osiris is to become one with the cosmic
cycles of death and rebirth.

It is not to be expected that so universal and complicated a
god would have remained absolutely unchanged throughout
three thousand years of worship. Osiris is closely related to the
dying and reborn divinities of the Near East, such as the
Sumerian Dumuzi, the West Semitic Adonis, the Syrian
Baal, the Hittite Telepinush or the Phrygian Attis. In Egypt,
Osiris absorbed the nature or attributes of many cyclic or
fertility figures such as Anedjety of the Eastern Delta (whose
insignia he borrowed), Sokar of Giza, the 'Lord of the
Westerners' at Abydos and others now forgotten. The exact
parcelling-out of the various aspects which came from this
place or that does not help to elucidate Osiris' real nature, for he

transcends his origins. Once synthesized, he lived on for nearly three thousand years in the hearts of the people as the symbol of the great human drama, the union of nature with the hope for survival after death.

There is no definite evidence as yet that Osiris was wor-shipped in the prehistoric period. Even if he were, that would not imply that the primitive figure had much in common with the highly developed god we encounter in historical times. A symbol of Osiris has recently been found that dates from the beginning of historical times, about 3000 B.C.,[1] otherwise there is no specific proof of his existence until he appears in the Pyramid Texts which were inscribed between 2400 and 2200 B.C. In these texts he is already fully developed, not only already provided with a complete mythology but a carefully thought-out theology as well. Moreover, the power and pre-tensions of the god increase as time goes on. Many have sup-posed that Osiris was the god of the common people as opposed to the more aristocratic Rê, the Sun God of the pharaohs. This may be partially true, for there are signs of religious controversy between the devotees of the two gods. Theologians tried on several occasions to reconcile their claims but without complete success. During the New Kingdom, Amun—the successor of Rê as the official High God—acquired an almost monotheistic character, rendering other gods un-necessary. This, however, failed to have lasting effect. During the last millennium B.C. the popularity of Osiris grew steadily until, under the Ptolemies who ruled Egypt from 323 B.C. to the Roman conquest, he became Serapis, the Lord of the universe in all its aspects.

Throughout Egyptian history, then, there was a con-troversy about the position of Osiris. There was no doubt about the existence of the god but his relative position in the pan-theon changed from time to time. There was always strong pressure to expand his worship at the expense of local or less attractive gods. No doubt, politics—the claims of rival temples or priesthoods and social pressure from the illiterate—had much to do with it. Yet it would be wrong to see Osiris in this materialist light. Osiris appealed to the emotions; Rê, Atum and the rest (except Amun) were there to account for the origin and maintenance of the world and to provide a rationale for political leadership.

The drama of Osiris may have begun as the theme of a cycle of fertility rites. It always retained agricultural traits but these were subordinated to the pathetic element, for the cult of Osiris was distinguished above all others in Ancient Egypt by its expenditure of emotion. At times the theme is more concerned with kingship than with the life of the fields, and the atmosphere is almost political. But here, too, the feeling is more important than the narrative content, which seems too trivial to sustain or justify the unrestrained outpouring of emotion. Fertility and the kingship are integral parts of the cycle but they are overshadowed by the pathos. The main problem is not to discover the origins of the drama's meaning but to account for the profound sorrow and subsequent elation of the Osirian literature. This is as true of the hymns and litanies of the third millennium B.C. as it is of the late Ptolemaic texts from Dendera or Philae.

Oriental man, and the Egyptians and Sumerians in particular, experienced the climatic changes of the seasons in a more dramatic form than did the peoples of Western Europe. In the West one can speak of a 'dead season' but with us the expression is a mild one, almost a harmless metaphor. The agricultural year is a round of tasks, each suitable in its proper season, and there is an unspoken confidence that there will be no absolute failure in the order of natural events. In the East, however, the heat and drought of summer reduce the country to something indistinguishable from the surrounding desert. The vegetation is almost completely burnt up, the animals grow listless from heat and lack of water. The desert has always been, to Eastern peasants, the place of death, the abode of wild animals, evil spirits, terror and chaos. During the high summer the difference between the valley lands of life and order, and the desert with

its terrors, has ceased to exist. It is what an inscription of
c. 2100 B.C. calls 'the carnage of the year'.[2] Moreover, there was
the constant fear that the river floods would not return at all, or
in insufficient quantity, and the land would be faced with
famine and the consequent social disintegration. Nor was this
fear groundless. Throughout Egyptian history there are graphic
references to famines which find an echo in the story of Joseph.
On the causeway leading up to the pyramid of King Wenis at
Sakkarah there is a particularly vivid scene in which the
starving peasants are depicted with stark realism. These figures
were obviously designed by artists who had had personal
acquaintance with such things in all their horror. Such disasters were not a remote possibility but an all too frequent
occurrence. Consequently there was none of the Western confidence in the inevitable return of the seasons. 'If winter comes,
can spring be far behind?' On the contrary, anxiety bit deep
into the ancient mind. This is the reason for the extremely vivid
imagery used to express the feeling when the flood waters
return or the rain comes to the highlands:

'Greetings to you, O Waters that Shu (*i.e.* the air) has
   brought
 or the Twin Caverns have gushed forth
 in which the earth (Geb) will bathe his limbs!
Now hearts can lose their fear and bosoms their terror.'[3]

The coming of the new waters was more than a change of
season, it meant the end of fear and terror, the rebirth of life in
the hearts of men. Osiris is not the inundation itself but the
life-force in plants and the reproductive power in animals and
human beings, which are stimulated when the waters come.
As a Coffin Text tersely explains:

'Osiris appears whenever there is an outflow [of water].'[4]

When the waters pour out over the earth they cause the seed
to grow in the soil and this sprouting of the vegetation is the
uprising of Osiris' soul. This is clearly seen in a relief from
Philae.

Fig. 14. The Inundation makes the vegetation grow (Philae)

A cow-headed goddess pours water from a vase into what is the symbol for a black (*i.e.* earth-filled) irrigation channel. This is the sign for irrigated land in general. Out of the top of the channel corn is sprouting. Above the corn and obviously rising from it is a soul-bird with a human head. The cow-goddess is Isis-Hathor-Sothis—the great Mother Goddess in her star form as Sothis, the Dog Star, whose rising in the east just before dawn heralded the annual inundation. The water let loose by the coming of the flood fills the irrigation channels and so reaches the land where the corn has been sown. The moisture stimulates the growth of the seed into corn-stalks which rise up from the earth. It is this 'rising up' that is the liberation of the 'soul'-form of Osiris. In a Coffin Text the Nile Spirit says:

'I am he who performs the service of gifts (*i.e.* the harvest)
    for Osiris at the great inundation,
I raise up my Divine Command
    at the rising of the Great God (*i.e.* Osiris),
I nourish the plants, I make green what was dried up.'[5]

The harvest is the peculiar property of Osiris. The Divine
Command, the Logos which determines the life-principle in the
world is reasserted annually in the flood. When Osiris rises in
his 'soul'-form the plants begin to grow. In fact, they are really
the same thing.

The anxiety and fear of the people during the dry summer
heat and the compensating joy when at last the river begins to
rise are vividly portrayed in the Pyramid Texts where the Nile
Spirit declares:[6]

'I am the messenger of the year, for Osiris,
    here I come with the news of your father, Geb,[7]
The state of the year is good, how good it is!
The state of the year is fair, how fair it is!
I have come down with the Twin Companies of the gods
    upon the flood;[8]
I am the creator for the Twin Companies,
provider of the fields with plenty;[9]
I have found the gods standing, clothed in their linen,
    their white sandals upon their feet.
They throw off their sandals upon the ground,
they divest themselves of their fine linen;
"There was no happiness until you came down!" they say.
"What is told you will abide with you!
Canal of happiness will be the name of this canal
    as it floods the fields with plenty."'

The passage has been slightly altered by the editors of the
Pyramid Texts to suit the requirements of a ferryman-spell for
passing over to the next world. If, however, men are understood in the place of gods, we have a picture of the people
hailing the arrival of the new Nile flood with its promise of

'fields of plenty', putting on their best raiment to greet the spirit of a year of prosperity and then stripping to bathe in the river —a custom we know to have been common at flood-time.

Mythologically the main aspects of Osiris are as follows:

(1) He belonged to the fourth generation of gods. First, according to the doctrine of Heliopolis, was Atum or Rê, the sun. He produced Shu, the air, and Tefnut, the moisture, or, as was later held, the world order. These were the primeval pair, who in turn brought forth Geb, the earth, and Nut, the sky. From them there came two males—Osiris and Seth, and two females—Isis and Nephthys. Isis became the wife of Osiris and Nephthys that of Seth.

(2) Osiris was a king who ruled over Egypt and who taught the arts of civilization to his subjects. As a New Kingdom hymn says:[10]

> 'He . . . established justice throughout both banks [of the Nile],
> he put the son in his father's place . . .
> overthrowing the adversary with might and power . . .
> [Earth] saw how excellent he was and entrusted the kingship to him to lead the Two Lands into prosperity.'

In typical Oriental hyperbole the encomium ends with:

> 'His crown clove the sky and consorted with the stars.'[11]

The reign of Osiris was, then, a golden age, the model for subsequent generations. Throughout their history the Egyptians believed in a time of perfection at the beginning of the world. Originally it was probably attributed to Rê, but Osiris had become its patron by the Middle Kingdom.

(3) The idyllic 'order' of Osiris was destroyed by Seth, his younger brother. Plutarch, writing in the second century after Christ, tells how, during a feast, Seth tempted Osiris to lie in a chest to see if it would fit him. Having Osiris temporarily at his mercy, Seth and his confederates (and Seth always has confederates) threw the chest into the Nile. In the early

Pyramid Texts Osiris was killed at a place known either as Nedit (*i.e.* 'where he was cast down') or Gazelles' Mountain, perhaps the modern Komir, in southern Egypt. It is wrong to seek for exactness of location in these ancient myths. Osiris was killed or cast down wherever his rites were performed. Plutarch's version may be a memory of another tradition that Osiris was not killed but drowned. This motif is extremely ancient—it occurs in the so-called 'Memphite Theology', the earliest source for the cult of Osiris at Memphis, and can be compared with the fate of Tammuz, the Mesopotamian parallel to Osiris, who is also sometimes considered as 'drowned' in the waters of the river. The Memphite Theology describes the event in vivid terms:

> 'Nephthys and Isis came straightway
> for Osiris was drowning in the water.
> Isis and Nephthys looked out, caught sight of him and were terrified for him.
> Then Horus commanded Isis and Nephthys straightway to seize Osiris
> and prevent him from being drowned.
> Horus [said] to Isis and Nephthys: "Hasten, lay hold of him."
> Isis and Nephthys [cried] to Osiris: "We come to save you."
> They turned his head to the right, they brought him to land.'

There is a curious allusion in the Coffin Texts to a tradition that Seth changed himself into a 'flea' and crawled inside Osiris' sandal, biting and poisoning him. This looks as if Osiris was the first victim of bilharzia, the scourge of modern Egypt. However, whatever the variations of traditions, Osiris was always reduced to impotence, if not killed, by his wicked brother.

(4) Plutarch says that Osiris' body was washed up upon the Syrian shore at Byblos. The chest containing the body was cast

up into a tree which grew around it. The tree ultimately attained enormous size and attracted the notice of the king of that country, who had it felled to form the main column of his palace. Isis, meanwhile, had wandered everywhere seeking the body of her beloved. In some way Isis knew that Osiris' body was hidden within the tree-trunk. She ingratiated herself with the king and queen of Byblos, obtained possession of the tree column, extracted Osiris' body and brought it back to Egypt.

This episode seems to have been an attempt to reconcile the ritual and symbolic associations of Osiris with his legends. As a fertility god, Osiris—like Dionysos and Tammuz—was some-times regarded as a tree or as imprisoned within one. His soul perched on a tree which grew by his tomb. He could also be symbolized by a column whose erection was the visible mark of his revival.

(5) Although the details differ, all sources agree that Seth tore up Osiris' body and scattered the pieces. Plutarch believed that parts of the body had been flung all over Egypt. Some native sources, including the Pyramid Texts, localize the event the place of the 'casting down' in Nedit; others say that Seth threw the fragments of the body into the Nile. In every version, however, Isis is the seeker for her husband's body—a trait she shares with the Mesopotamian Ishtar, who seeks her beloved Tammuz who has been reft from her and is held a prisoner in the Underworld. According to Plutarch, Isis found every part of Osiris' body except the phallus, which had been swallowed by a fish. This is not attested by the native sources, although it is clear that the sexual organ is capable of revivification and is magically distinct from the other members. It is generally admitted that Isis, helped by Nephthys, collected the limbs together again, thus making the first and essential mummy. As a hymn from the New Kingdom has it:[12]

'Beneficent Isis, who protected her brother
   and sought for him, she would
take no rest until she had found him.'

(Isis seems to have assumed the shape of a bird at this point.)

> 'She shaded him with her feathers and gave him air with
> her wings.
> She cried out for joy and brought her brother to land.'

(6) Isis was unable to bring her beloved back to life in the full sense, but she contrived to revive him sufficiently to be able to conceive a son by him. This was Horus. In her fear of the vengeance of Seth the goddess hid in the swamps of the Delta, where she gave birth to Osiris' heir and where she brought him up in secret. As the above-mentioned hymn tells:[13]

> 'She revived the weariness of the Listless One and took his
> seed into her body,
> [thus] giving him an heir.
> She suckled the child in secret, the place where he was
> being unknown.'

A whole cycle of myths gathered around Isis in the Delta. These will be discussed later. They form a distinct group of their own and have little bearing on Osiris.

(7) In due time Horus grew up and, according to Plutarch, gathered together the supporters of his murdered father and, leaving his Delta fastness, attacked the usurper Seth. The civil war was suspended for a while by the attempted arbitration of Hermes (*i.e.* the Greek form of Thoth), but at last Horus took up the fight again and succeeded in finally overwhelming Seth and his confederates. The Egyptian sources do not so much contradict Plutarch as speak a different mythical language. For the native Egyptian Osiris was always helpless. He is never represented in movement, but as a swathed figure with black or green face—for he is both a mummy and the life-spirit of the earth and vegetation. He is, above all, passive, and only in the texts of the Ninth and Tenth Dynasties is he allowed to speak for himself. The texts assume that the murder has already taken place. Osiris is the spirit of the past; as Chapter 17 of the Book of the Dead explicitly declares, 'Osiris is yesterday and Rê is today.'

Fig. 15. Isis suckles Horus in the Delta Swamps

When one compares all the references to the mythical events connected with Osiris one is struck by the absence of a canonical version of the legends. In fact there is no legend at all in the modern sense. Such may once have existed, for even the early texts are full of allusions to lost myths, but instead of written legends we have a number of motifs which conform to a pattern.

The kingship in Egypt, like all forms of property, consisted of a duality—it was based on a relationship between the living and the dead. The king exercised the supreme power in the world. He was the intermediary whereby the divine energies of the universe were made available for men. This power he derived from his ancestors, in particular from his father who for this reason was considered as himself divine. The deceased father in his tomb was the source of the power, called by the Egyptians the *Ka*, but he was in need of the care of his successor, his 'beloved son', in order to achieve beatification and to function as a 'spirit'. The living king was Horus, the son and heir of Osiris. The dead king was Osiris, the dweller in the West, or, as the Pyramid Texts have it, *Ka hotep*—'the *Ka* at rest'. If the king carried out the required rites for his father, the latter could then become 'a soul', which meant that the powers

of life and growth would begin again in nature. Osiris was
nothing without Horus, just as the latter was no true king
unless he was able to guarantee the fertility of his land. This
mutual obligation between living son and dead father runs
through Egyptian religion. It also exemplifies the essential
difference between the cult of Osiris and that of the other
fertility gods of the Ancient East. Tammuz is carried away to
the Underworld by enemies and then brought back to earth
and life by his consort-mother Ishtar. Osiris suffers death or
discomfiture in the Underworld, but he is not brought back
to life. It is Horus who fulfils the destiny for the present, under-
taking the role played in other religions by the resurrected god.

Osiris sojourns in the Underworld. This was interpreted in
many ways. The ancients did not have our sense of definite
exclusive topography—that if a god is in one place he cannot
be in another. The Underworld could be thought of cosmo-
logically, as situated beneath the earth or beyond the western
horizon or in the waters under the earth. In early times Osiris
was worshipped in 'tombs' which consisted of a tumulus in the
midst of a grove. They were chambers in these mounds
reached by a winding passage.[14] The memory of such subterranean resting-places for Osiris lasted throughout Egyptian
history. The Osireion, which Sethos I erected at Abydos about
1310 B.C., and the crypts of the Ptolemaic temples at Dendera
and Diospolis Parva were, in essentials, the same as the mound
at Medamud. The Underworld existed ritually in the subterranean temple, but in imagination it was often a great palace
or city with ramparts and a hall in which Osiris lay or, alter-
natively, presided over the court of the dead. This identification
of the mythical and localized underworlds was deliberate, as it
also was in Sumer, where Eridu, the sacred city of En-ki, the
god of the lower world, was Ab-Zu—'the abyss of waters'. In
Egypt the names of many of the major centres of Osiris worship
were used for the Underworld; for example, Busiris (in
Egyptian Djedu), the original city of his cult in the Delta;
Rosetau, the modern Giza, the burial-place of Memphis and

the home of a form of Osiris known as Sokar; and Naref, the site of Osiris' temple in Herakleopolis. During the time when the Coffin Texts and the Book of the Dead were being written Osiris could be put into a never-never-land beyond human ken known as the Isle of Fire.

Although Seth had killed Osiris, this was not the end of his malevolence. He tore the body into pieces and left them lying on the ground or, in another version, threw them into the Nile. He remained a potential danger to Osiris until the latter was redeemed. Hence, in the rites Osiris had to be protected by Isis and her sister Nephthys until the coming of Horus. The goddesses found the fragments of his body either on the ground or fished them out of the Nile and then proceeded to put them together, mourning him all the while. They had to watch over him during the difficult time of his helplessness which was symbolized by the night watches. Isis and Nephthys fulfil a role rather than inspire a myth. They belong to the ritual. Meanwhile the events of the upper world are mythical.

The battle of Horus and Seth for the kingdom was a long and bitter business. Several texts hint that the other gods grew heartily tired of the disturbance which the two contestants made throughout the universe. Incidents connected with the quarrel were collected together some time during the New Kingdom to form a semi-humorous tale called (by modern scholars) *The Contendings of Horus and Seth*.[15] The 'Two Fellows', as they were called, remind us of the Lion and the Unicorn; their long-standing enmity became wearisome and everyone else longed for them to compose their differences. It was the time of 'the confusion', the symbol of the terror and strife that lay behind the order of the world. During the fight Horus wrenched out Seth's testicles while Seth tore out Horus' left eye. Finally, at least in the common recension, Thoth, as the personification of order, persuaded the two to submit their quarrel to arbitration before the great council of the gods at Heliopolis. The Book of the Dead makes the High God exclaim:[16]

'O Thoth! What has come to pass with the children of
   Nut?
They have created strife, they have stirred up confusion,
they have done evil, they have raised rebellion,
they have indeed made the great into little
and made a secret destruction in all that I have created.'

Both the contestants were descendants of Nut, the sky-goddess,
for Seth was her younger son while Horus, as Osiris' child,
was her grandson. The council had, therefore, to decide the
right of inheritance. The long-drawn-out strife had upset the
happy age of the Creator. Hence, the fundamental order of the
universe must be established by Thoth and the 'Two Fellows'
brought to arbitration. This is one of the most profound elements
of the legend and one whose importance the texts recognize
quite clearly. Spell 37 of the Coffin Texts stresses the role of
Thoth:

'The earth was hacked up where the Two Fellows had
   fought,
their feet had taken possession of the whole field of the god
   at Heliopolis.
The Master Atum-Rê had entrusted him with the great
   task that reposed upon him,
and now the contest was at an end, the strife was over,
the burning flame [of anger] was quenched, the smell of
   blood was swept away
before the Divine Court which sat down to judge in the
   presence of Geb.'

Reason and law have prevailed against the terrific forces of
violence. Horus is adjudged the rightful heir of his father, the
patrilineal principle is assured and peace is established with the
enthronement of the new king. As soon as he has been installed, Horus journeys down to visit his father in the Underworld or sends a representative to tell Osiris the glad news. This
will enable Osiris to awake or 'set his soul in motion'. Osiris

revives, to become the spirit of life and growth—the New Year has begun.

Meanwhile, Seth was reduced to a subordinate role. His confederates were slaughtered, but the great enemy himself was forced to become the bearer of Osiris. This was interpreted in the ritual as meaning that Seth was the boat which carried Osiris during the festal voyage on the Nile or temple lake. In mythological terms Seth's fate was probably connected with his power over the winds, an aspect of the god which he retained from his prehistoric past.

One of the earliest hymns that have been preserved from the Osiris rituals occurs—only slightly altered for funerary purposes—in the pyramid of Wenis:[17]

'Hail to you, O Knowing One!
Geb has created you anew,
the Divine Company has brought you forth anew!
Horus is satisfied for his father,
Atum is satisfied for his offspring.
The gods of East and West are satisfied with this great event
which has come to pass through the action of the Divine
Progeny.
Ah! Osiris! See! Behold!
Osiris! Hear! Attend!
Ah! Osiris! Lift yourself upon your side! Carry out what
I ordain!
O Hater of Sleep! O Torpid One!
Rise up, you that were cast down in Nedit!
Take your bread with happiness in Pê!
Receive your sceptre in Heliopolis!
This is Horus [speaking], he has ordained action for his
father,
he has shown himself master of the storm,
he has countered the blustering of Seth,
so that he (Seth) must bear you—
for it is he that must carry him who is [again] complete.'

The Divine Company has given a verdict in favour of Horus; this is 'the great event which has come to pass'. The forces of confusion—here represented as 'the blustering of Seth' —have been overcome in Horus' victory. The new master of the universe visits his father where he lies sleeping in the Under-world. Horus has the power to revive Osiris or, at least, to rouse him from his state of unconsciousness. Osiris is to be revived—*i.e.* re-created—as a soul, in other words, is the reviving powers of the new year. Hence, Osiris has been reborn, not in his old form, but as the vegetation and reproductive activity of the ensuing period. This is described allusively in the present text: the earth (Geb) has remade Osiris, in that Osiris as the son of Geb is reborn as a soul. The Divine Court has remade Osiris by giving its verdict in favour of Horus. The High God Atum is 'satisfied' that his descendant has recovered from his 'sleep' and 'torpidity'. The revival of Osiris affects all the powers of the earth, who are 'satisfied' by the new order instituted by Horus. Osiris is requested to accept the offerings which, now that Horus has re-established ordered government, can be made him on the altars of the major temples. Seth has been made to subserve the new order; the unregulated powers of the universe are now mastered and made to help in sustaining the revived god. This hymn is distinctive in that the passion of Osiris is symbolized as unconsciousness. The revival of the god is therefore a reawakening, which is equated with death and living again. The fertility element is not explicitly mentioned although, of course, it would have been known to every Egyptian. It is perhaps significant that Osiris' fate is already being interpreted in a psychological sense in this, which may well be the earliest hymn from the Osirian rituals to have survived.

Another fragment of an Osiris hymn occurs twice in the Pyramid Texts. The god is bewailed by his sisters Isis and Nephthys, whose voices summon a group of ecstatic dancers, known as the 'souls' or 'gods' of Pê, the ancient capital of the predynastic northern community. In the ritual we are to

1 THE SPIRIT OF THE ETERNAL WATERS protects the eye of the
High God (British Museum, Papyrus of Ani). See p. 230

2 SEMTY AND LECTOR PRIESTS (Newberry, *Beni Hassan IV*, pl. XIV).
See p. 29

3 SHU separates earth and sky (British Museum). See pp. 48 and 250

imagine a group of people who personify the spirits of long-
dead prehistoric chieftains. The text begins with the strange
rubric[18]:

> 'The gates of the sky are opened, the gates of the "Bows"
> are flung wide.'

This simply means that the sanctuary doors are opened. A
rout of dancers comes in with wild demeanour:

> 'The gods of Pê bestir themselves, they come to Osiris
> at the tearful voice of Isis, at the plaint of Nephthys,
> at the wailing of those two mighty spirits.
> The souls of Pê dance for you,
> they strike their flesh,
> they agitate their hands,
> they loosen their hair,
> they crouch down upon their knees,
> they say to you:
> "Osiris! You went away, but you have returned,
> you fell asleep, but you have awakened,
> you died, but you live again.
> Arise! Behold this! Arise! Hear this,
> what your son has done for you!
> He has struck down him who struck you down,
> he has bound him who bound you,
> he has put him under [the care of] his great daughter, who
> dwells in Kedem.
> Now is sorrow at an end in the Twin Sanctuaries."'

Although the 'souls' lacerate themselves and adopt the
gestures usually associated with mourning, they are in fact the
bearers of the good tidings. They are visitors from another
world, like the carnival revellers of Western Europe.

This text is singularly enlightening as to the fate of Osiris.
The passion of the god is described as 'he went away, he fell
asleep, he died', and his salvation in the complementary terms

—'he came back, he awakened, he lives again'. Used rationally these verbs are mutually exclusive, but that is to misunderstand the way the Egyptians thought. Departure, sleep and death are used metaphorically, but unlike a modern metaphor, they are all employed together to convey the feeling of the god's plight. Osiris is nature itself or, to speak more accurately, nature as experienced by the farmers and stock-breeders of the Ancient Near East. During the summer heat the desolate condition of the world can be expressed as if either the spirit of life had departed, or was listless and asleep, or that life itself was dead. Any single metaphor would be insufficient to describe the dire calamity of the world. Similarly, the fate of Seth, the enemy, can be death, bonds or ignominious submission. He cannot be altogether annihilated, for he is a power that can be restrained or canalized, but not absolutely destroyed. Take away the pathos of the Osirian cycle, and the metaphors fall apart so that each can generate its own myth in narrative form. This is what happens in the myth of the contendings of Horus and Seth, in the saga of the Two Brothers and the other popular tales, which deal with mythical motives as connected stories. They arose on the periphery of Osiris worship, far away from the deep emotions displayed in the genuine cult. Even the simple statement that sorrow is at an end in the Twin Sanctuaries declares that the joy at the salvation of Osiris is universal, for the Twin Sanctuaries refer to the temples of the two divisions of Egypt.

In the myth, Osiris did not realize the evil intentions of his brother and so fell unwittingly into the trap which his enemy had laid. That is implied in the texts of all periods. When Horus resuscitated his father, he gave him the power of 'knowing', which included comprehension of Seth's real nature:[19]

'Horus has seized Seth, he has put him beneath you so that he can lift you up. He will groan beneath you as an earthquake. . . .

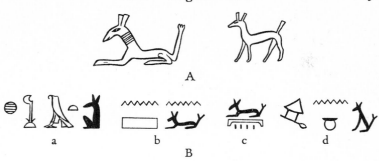

Fig. 16. A. Forms of the Seth animal
B. Seth animal determining illness (a), storms (b) and (c), confusion (d)

Horus has made you recognize him in his real nature, let
him not escape you;
he has made you hold him by your hand, let him not get
away from you.'

Seth is the essential enemy. He is the personification of blind
force and unregulated violence. Another Pyramid Text alludes
to a legend that he burst forth from his mother's womb:[20]

'You whom the pregnant goddess brought forth when you
clove the night in twain—
you are invested with the form of Seth, who broke out in
violence.'

Whenever there is a manifestation of blind force, Seth is in his
element. Hence, his animal form is used in the script to determine the words for storm, sickness and quarrelling.

In Spell 356, quoted above, Seth is an earthquake. He is the
god of storm and thunder. The lowering clouds are his, his
voice is the thunderclap and all untoward events in nature
belong to him. Hence he is the desert wind, dryness and death.
The later *Contendings of Horus and Seth* present him as a blustering bully. Usually the Osirian texts equate him with death
and the dissolution of the body, but tradition ascribes to him a
kind of low cunning. This must be why Osiris is warned to
be on his guard against possible tricks.

Osiris' passivity was unsatisfying to those who wanted their gods to be models of self-assertion. Some intriguing fragments of an old myth have survived in the Pyramid Texts which show that there were two trials: one when Seth was arraigned before the Court for the murder of Osiris and another when the gods had to decide between him and Horus. It is even suggested that Osiris should himself appear before the Court of the Gods and Seth's intransigence is cited as an example. The scene begins with the description of a storm:[21]

> 'The sky is darkened, the earth rocks,
> Horus comes, Thoth appears.
> They lift Osiris upon one side,
> they make him appear before the Divine Company.
> (Seth is now addressed):
> "Remember, Seth, put in your heart the charge which Geb
>   laid,
> the accusation which the gods made against you,
> in the House of the Elder (*i.e.* Atum the Primeval High
>   God) at Heliopolis,
> that you had cast Osiris down upon the ground,
> and how you declared, O Seth—'On the contrary, it was
>   he who provoked me.'
> . . . when you declared, O Seth, 'On the contrary, it was he
>   who attacked me.'
> . . . stretch out your leg[s], extend your paces to go beyond
>   the Southern Land."
> Raise yourself, Osiris, even as Seth raised himself when
>   he heard the accusation of the gods and the charge
>   upon the god's father.
> Give one arm to Isis, Osiris, and one hand to Nephthys,
> come between them.'

The theologians of the Old Kingdom made grandiose claims for Osiris. In Spell 600 of the Pyramid Texts he is equated with the whole pyramid complex:

'Ah! Horus! Osiris is this pyramid, Osiris is these buildings,
    come quickly to him, stay not away from him in his name of "Pyramid". . . .
Horus has brought you the gods, raising them for you in the pilasters
so that they greet you in the white (*i.e.* limestone) chapels.'

There was even a doctrine that Osiris was the whole earth, or the ocean which surrounded the known world. One hymn, which exists in several versions, implies that Isis and Nephthys found their beloved brother, not a mythical figure lying helpless on the bank where Seth had 'cast him down' but as:[22]

'the Great Black Thing, in your name of "Bitter Lakes",
the Great Green Thing, in your name of [Mediterranean?] Sea,
the Great Circle, in your name of "Great Surround",
an enveloping ring, in the "Ring that encircles the Outer-most Lands",
a Great Circle in the Great Round of the Surrounding Ocean.'

Another version of the hymn exclaims, 'You encircle every-thing within your arms,' while a slightly later variant from the Coffin Texts adds, 'Even what is not [? yet] in you has recognized you.' The intellectual claims of a pantheistic theology seem to be breaking through the hieratic terminology. Osiris as the power of growth is manifest in the earth—'the Great Black Thing', and in the water—'the Great Green Thing'. He is in the Red Sea, the Mediterranean and the cosmic ocean which surrounds the world.

Such thoughts were not a later development. They belong to one of the earliest hymns that have survived. Spiegel would put them back to the time of Zoser and the builders of his Step Pyramid, at the beginning of the classical Old Kingdom about 2750 B.C. They serve to emphasize the intellectual character of Egyptian religion, even at its formative stages. However emotional the cult of Osiris may have been, the Egyptians were not all simple *fellahin*, for some of them must have been people of high intellectual attainments. The men who planned the mighty pyramid complexes and organized the first great centralized nation-state would hardly have been content with a mere fertility cult, however elaborate its external trappings. The demands of reason and the rarer flights of the imagination had to be satisfied within the terms of the ritual and the myth. A minority must always have known that the gods were not completely to be comprehended in the material forms in which they were represented on the monuments or in the ceremonies. There could be no definitive form for Osiris. The intellectual and universal ideas of the god were reabsorbed into the popular symbolism by interpreting his surrounding ocean as a serpent or as a man bent round in a circle. On present evidence these symbols do not appear until the New Kingdom, but they certainly derive from the old universal aspects of the god.

Another manifestation is certainly primitive although it, too, is not attested until the Eighteenth Dynasty. It was then the custom to make a figure of Osiris as a mummy from a linen bag which was stuffed with corn. If this was watered, the corn sprouted through the meshes of the bag so that the god was seen to grow. Such a custom probably underlies a Coffin Text called 'Spell for becoming barley':[23]

> 'I am the plant of life
> which comes forth from Osiris,
> which grows upon the ribs of Osiris,
> which allows the people to live,
> which makes the gods divine,
> which spiritualizes the spirits,
> which sustains the masters of wealth and the masters of
>   substance,
> which makes the *pak* cakes for the spirits,
> which enlivens the living,
> which strengthens the limbs of the living.

I live as corn, the life of the living,
I . . . upon the rib of Geb (the earth),
but the love of me is in the sky, on earth, on the water and
   in the fields.
Now Isis is content for her [son] Horus, her god,
she is jubilant in him, her Horus, her god,
I am life appearing from Osiris.'

The early agricultural peoples combined fertility rites with
the cult of the dead. They were, in fact, two aspects of one
religion—expressions of the hopes and anxieties of the com/
munity. The world seemed full of power, everywhere would be
found signs of the life/force, manifest in all living creatures,
both animal and vegetable—in the heavens, in the waters and
in the mysterious events of disease, death and decay. These
forces could be temporarily localized in some person or place,
but ancient men were not sufficiently self/conscious to think of
them as residing in individuals as such. The community was
not merely composed of the living but of the ancestors as well.
Life on earth was a temporary exile from the true, undifferen/
tiated group—life somewhere beyond. The ancestors, the
custodians of the source of life, were the reservoir of power and
vitality, the source whence flowed all the forces of vigour,
sustenance and growth. Hence they were not only departed
souls but still active, the keepers of life and fortune. Whatever
happened, whether for good or evil, ultimately derived from
them. The sprouting of the corn, the increase of the herds,
potency in men, success in hunting or war, were all mani/
festations of their power and approval. Hence the place where
the ancestors dwelt was the most holy spot in the world. From
it flowed the well/being of the group. Without the tomb or the
cemetery, life on earth would be miserable, perhaps impossible.

The ancestors were not particularized. They were a collective
concept without individual names. To the ancient Persians
they were the 'Fravashis'. The Romans had their Manes, the
Chinese their Tzu's. The Egyptians knew them as 'the Souls',

the 'Glorious Ones', or 'the Gods', but chiefly as 'the *Ka's*'. The word *Ka* was written as two embracing arms, showing that the *Ka* was something which could be transmitted by an embrace, for to be transferred was of the essence of the *Ka*. As life-force, however, the *Ka's* were plural; they were not so much the ancestors themselves as their power—which is why the ancestors are not just *Ka's*, but 'the Lords of their *Ka's*'. The singular is related to the word for 'male', while the plural meant 'vitality', 'good fortune' or 'fertility'. To return to one's *Ka* meant to die. Moreover, the *Ka* was the ideal prototype of a person—a human being without any of the imperfections of earthly existence. It was responsible for fertility, sexual vigour, good fortune and group loyalty. In the world of the living, however, it was merely contingent. Not the terrestrial residence, but the tomb, was the house of the *Ka* and the mortuary priest was the 'servant of the *Ka*'. These ideas seem inconsistent to modern minds, but the Egyptians were living very close to their collective past and held on to such primitive patterns of belief with great persistence. The living did not worship their ancestors, but hoped that some of the power which resided among the ancestors could be transmitted for their own needs. The tomb was for the living as much as for the dead. Burial was partly collective. The tomb of an individual formed part of the group cemetery, known among the Egyptians as *brt ntr*— 'that which the God has'. The ancients, like modern primitives, were as collective in death as in life. The dead—the ancestors—lay close together in family or clan solidarity. This can be noted in all the major burial-grounds of the Near East. Junker[24] has recently shown that the pyramid field at Giza is a planned cemetery for the royal clan rather than a resting-place for the kings, and that group cohesion, the desire to lie close together and to preserve for ever the ties of family affection, was the chief motive in the arrangement of the mastabas around the great pyramids. The private tombs were invocations to the living and the outer rooms were intended to be visited by the surviving members of the family, above all on New Year's Day when, more than at any other time, power flowed into the world from the source—not so much beyond as in the grave.

Osiris developed in this context, but transcends it. He is a composite of royal theory and popular pressure during the Old Kingdom. There were other fertility gods, simpler figures closer to the immediate occupations of the peasantry, such as Ther‑muthis the Harvest, and her son Nepri the Corn, or Sekhête the Lady of the Marshes and her child 'Catch'. Min, the old fertility symbol at Koptos, and Sobek the crocodile, were also patrons of aspects of the life of the fields and river.

Osiris, however, was generalized; he was all forms of growth. He was also a king and so usually represented with the insignia of royalty. The king was the mediator between the community and the sources of divine power, obtaining it through the ritual and regularizing it through his government. In Egypt there were two sources of power—in the sky and in the tombs with the ancestors. The first location made the king the child of the Sun God; the second made him Horus, the son of Osiris, for the latter was the deceased monarch as well as the embodiment of fertility. He was not the ancestor in the old anonymous sense but the lord of the ancestors and unique inheritor of their power. As the old king he carried his royal function into the next world to become the Lord of the Dead, the president of a ghostly court. Osiris was both Hades and Dionysos.

The character of Osiris as a god of the dead is not readily understood, despite the copious material that is available. What follows must be understood as a tentative attempt to reconstruct the old theology. It is certainly an over‑simplification of a com‑plex subject, but is in general agreement with the discoveries of recent scholars such as Schott, Spiegel, Ricke, Jacobsohn and Drioton.

Osiris is dead. He is, in fact, the late king, mummified, who in dying has descended to the Underworld to become the inert, potential power of nature. He is helpless, and the power he embodies is inert, asleep or listless, and completely passive. But if, after death, the deceased king were to remain for ever in this

first Osiris form, the outlook for him and for the world would
be grim and hopeless. He only remains in this condition, however, until his son and successor, Horus, has vanquished his
enemies and ascended the throne. Horus, the new king, visits
his father to give him the news of what has happened; in other
words, to tell him that order has been re-established. During
the battle between Horus and Seth, the latter had wrenched out
one of Horus' eyes. This was rescued as a result of the victory of
the rightful heir and given to Osiris by his son as a symbol of
the confirmation of the new régime. There were other versions
of what Horus could do for his father, the chief of which was
that he could 'open his mouth'. This was performed by touching the mouth of Osiris with an adze which represented the
Great Bear—a constellation that belonged to Seth—and with
which, in a lost myth, he 'opened the mouths of the gods'. When
Osiris is specially considered as the spirit in the Nile flood,
Horus brings him the North Wind—the prevailing wind in
Egypt which cools the torrid parched land and heralds the
coming of the annual waters. Theologically, the result of
Horus' ministrations is that Osiris can 'send out his soul' or
'set himself in motion'. The god puts his soul into Osiris while
his body remains earthbound and inert:

'My body to the earth, my soul to the sky,'

as the old texts say. The rising of Orion in the southern sky after
the time of its invisibility is the sign for the beginning of a new
season of growth, the revival of nature in all aspects. Osiris has
been transformed into a 'living soul'. To achieve this, the
second form of Osiris, for the deceased, is the basic purpose of
the funeral rites. Just as the god *qua* fertility spirit annually
transcends his helplessness to become the life of the new year,
so as a new Osiris the dead king could, with due care by his
successor, become one with the soul of the original Osiris. This
is what is meant by becoming 'an Osiris'. Instead of being
addressed merely by his own name, the deceased is called
Osiris Teti, or Osiris Wenis, or whatever the name might be.

Hence to become Osiris X is not to be identified with Osiris as he is usually represented, but to share in the god's salvation and transformation into a 'soul'. Death and the indignities of embalmment represented, for earthly bodies, the passion of the god. Seth is the death that strikes one down; his confederates are the demons of decay and dissolution. The completion of the rites and the establishment of the ordered ritual at the tomb are the 'rescuing of the god'. The interim period between death and revival was one of great danger. Just as the pieces of Osiris' body had been put together, and his corpse watched all through the night of his passion by his sisters Isis and Nephthys, so priestesses personifying them play the role of mourners and protectors of his body from spirit enemies during the funerary rituals. They, in fact, are responsible for the safety of Osiris between his death and the coming of Horus. First they find the god and then they put his body together and mourn him.

CHAPTER IV

Osiris Universalized

THE PASSION of Osiris was, originally, a king's fate and not that of everyone. Nevertheless, there are signs that the cult of Osiris was becoming increasingly popular as the Old Kingdom drew towards its end. The rites originated in Busiris, 'the city of the *Djed* column' in the Nile Delta, which became a place of pilgrimage at a very early date. There the devotees took part in ceremonies connected with the death, vigil and restoration of the god. Contemporaneously with the spread of his popular devotion Osiris seems to have become or been transformed into the presiding deity of the royal funeral. Only the kings and their favourites could become an Osiris after death, because that depended on a costly tomb which required royal permission to erect, and on an endowment to continue the provision of offer-ings on all the major feast-days. The old society, however, crashed in ruins about 2250 B.C. after the death of Pepi II, the last effective pharaoh of the Sixth Dynasty. There followed a time of civil war and general confusion, marked not only by feudal anarchy but by a social upheaval as well. The scribal and military classes clamoured to share in the Osiris fate after death but without the materialist trappings of tomb endowments and funeral estates. Instead of a pyramid complex or mastaba, large wooden coffins were devised, generally in pairs, whose sides were painted to represent the essential parts of the old tombs. The false doors before which the offerings were presented, the pavilions in which the ceremonies of the opening of the mouth of the statues and the mummy had been conducted, together with pictures of the wealth of food offerings and furniture, were painted on the inside of the coffins. In addition, the insides of the coffins were covered with inscriptions based on those which had been recited on behalf of the great ones of the Old Kingdom.

In spite of the disorder, the time following the breakdown of the Old Kingdom was one of the great ages of the liberation of the human spirit. The collapse of the ordered society of the Pyramid Age shook confidence in everything. Doubts were expressed not only about the justice of the social order but about the possibility of survival after death, the nature of the gods and of the worshipper's relation to them. Partially concealed in the oblique, allusive language of the time are signs of an intense intellectual ferment. Fundamental problems about the nature of man and God, the problem of evil and—most insistently—the nature of the individual soul were raised for the first time in recorded history. It was a time of great literary activity—so much so that the end of this period, the so-called Herakleo-politan Period, was later regarded as the classical age of Egyptian writing. The new inquiring spirit is reflected in the Coffin Texts, wherein the old compositions of the Pyramid Age were remoulded and then partly discarded in favour of hymns which reflected the more personal attitude of the time.

Osiris is at the centre of the new ideas. For all their fervour and careful theology, the characters of the Osirian drama had been personified automata rather than distinct individuals. The new feeling is more personal. The rites are no longer the business of the kings or even of society as a collective unit; they reflect the inward feelings of ordinary men and women. Spell 74 of the Coffin Texts exhibits the spirit of the time:

'Ah Helpless One!
Ah Helpless One asleep!
Ah Helpless One in this place
    which you know not—yet I know it!
Behold, I have found you [lying] on your side—
    the great Listless One.
"Ah, Sister!" says Isis to Nephthys,
"This is our brother,
Come, let us lift up his head,
Come, let us [rejoin] his bones,

Come, let us reassemble his limbs,
Come, let us put an end to all his woe,
that, as far as we can help, he will weary no more.
May the moisture begin to mount for this spirit!
May the canals be filled through you!
May the names of the rivers be created through you!
Osiris, live!
Osiris, let the great Listless One arise!
I am Isis."
               "I am Nephthys.
It shall be that Horus will avenge you,
It shall be that Thoth will protect you
   —your two sons of the Great White Crown—
It shall be that you will act against him who acted against
   you,
It shall be that Geb will see,
It shall be that the Company will hear.
Then will your power be visible in the sky
and you will cause havoc among the [hostile] gods,
for Horus, your son, has seized the Great White Crown,
seizing it from him who acted against you.
Then will your father Atum call 'Come!'
Osiris, live!
Osiris, let the great Listless One arise!"'

Beginning of another speech (*sic*):

'"I am Isis, who meets the call [for help]."
               "I am Nephthys.
Awake, Rise up!
Lie on your side, O great Listless One!
Pour forth your water,
Set your flood in motion!
Defend your patrimony from the [hostile] gods
who will fall upon their faces
and cease from their attack.
Osiris, arise!

Osiris, live!
May the great Listless One rise upon his side.
I am Isis."
        "I am Nephthys.
Horus comes at your call, Osiris,
You will be placed upon his arms,
you will be safe in your power;
Horus [is] in the Underworld,
There will be a flood for you as far as Buto—
and all the gods will be flooded after you
—which will be given you by Atum.
The males will follow [your example],
the females will collect the formlessness that is in you,
through your seed, Osiris,
which will be vigorous as far as Buto.
Osiris, live!
May the great Listless One rise upon his side!
I am Isis!"
        "I am Nephthys.
Horus has come at your call;
through him you will be placed upon his (*i.e.* Seth's) back,
if he tries to run away beneath your feet
[his arms] will carry you
even as far as your father Geb did for you.
Osiris, live!
May the great Listless One rise upon his side!
I am Isis!"
        "I am Nephthys.
How fair are you that rise today!
Like Horus of the Underworld
rising today, appearing from the great flood.
You are purified with those four jars
with which the gods have washed themselves.
Geb has spoken to you
telling you that the evil has been put away,
your mother, Nut, who is before you,

has listened to you.
Horus has cleansed you,
Thoth has glorified you,
—your twin souls, the masters of the Great White Crown
have abolished the troubles of your flesh.
Now you can stand upon your legs completely restored.
You will open the ways for the gods,
for them will you act as the Opener of the Ways.
You have confirmed your glory over your enemies
[who lie] overwhelmed in tears. I am Isis." "I am
Nephthys."'

The vigil of Isis and Nephthys begins with the finding of
Osiris' body lying in pieces 'in this place'. The initial emphasis
is on the unconsciousness of the god as contrasted with the
consciousness of the watchers, the same motif which was noted
in the Pyramid Text on p. 111. It is not yet generally recognized that the Egyptians sometimes explained their myths in
psychological terms. This is quite different from interpreting
them in the language of modern psychology. The plight of
Osiris is generally described as 'weariness' or 'sorrow', but he is
also 'asleep'—he has lost the ability to know. Knowing and
activity are aspects of the same thing.

Isis and Nephthys know that the god in his helplessness is
the dead land waiting to be revived. The rescue of the god *is*
the rising of the flood waters. This text provides an example of
the ancient use of 'name' meaning 'nature'; to create 'the names
of the rivers' is to fill them with water so that they assume their
proper nature. Whereas we say that a dry river-bed is a river 'in
name only', this would have been nonsense to the ancients, who
would only have associated the name with the river when it was
fulfilling its significant role. The second stanza takes the theme
into the world of myth. Horus and Thoth—here called, against
orthodoxy, 'the royal sons' of Osiris—will avenge and protect
him so that he will overcome the power of his murderer and all
creatures, on earth and in the sky, and will see the new power

4 HORUS THE CHILD, still protected by Isis, sets out to avenge his father (British Museum). See p. 187

5 NEPHTHYS weeps for Osiris (British Museum). See p. 125 ff.

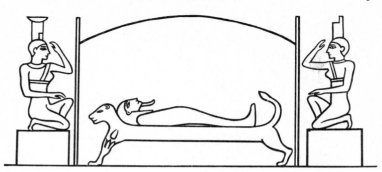

Fig. 17. Isis and Nephthys mourn Osiris

of the god. Horus will take the kingdom from Seth, and the High God of Destiny, Atum, will pronounce the great command 'let the great Listless One arise!'

The Coffin Texts were copied from many sources and remodelled to suit their funerary purpose. Sometimes this was done quite clumsily. Here the scribe has taken a litany based on Osiris rites which was divided up into 'speeches'. One of the headings of the original has been preserved, although it is clear from the length of the composition that there were others in the prototype. This composition is not, in all likelihood, a temple ritual but a poem based on the succession of episodes during the long-drawn-out passion of Osiris. This lasted a long time —at Abydos during the Middle Kingdom it went on for eight days—so what we have is an extremely shortened version of the real thing. It is literature and was intended as such, an exercise in religious sentiment, the product of a refined culture, not a disjointed relic of some old fertility ceremony. It bears a similar relationship to the rituals as the poems of George Herbert do to the Communion Service. One feels that the original was a duet intoned by two voices, sometimes separately, sometimes together.

The request to rise on one side is one of the most important themes in the Osiris cycle. The waters of the annual inundation came from the thigh of the god. This, to us highly artificial, idea is the reason why the thigh of Osiris was kept as a relic in several temples and why modern scholars have been so mystified by references to being 'born upon the thigh'. The new flood will overcome the demons who have been holding the country in thrall during the time of heat and drought. The Egyptians used 'the gods' ambiguously to denote both good and evil spirits—twice in the present poem gods are evilly disposed. One must always be on guard against making assumptions which were not made by the ancients. With them 'the gods' are the bearers of power irrespective of whether that power was used beneficently or not.

The 'call' of Osiris for help is the great turning-point in the drama. Apparently it was 'Come down to me!', '*Ha-k ir-i*', which gave the name Haker to the great festival at Abydos.[1] The old texts hint at the tension of this moment 'when, during the night of the Great Sleep', the call of the god was heard out-side by the worshippers. During this night no sound of music or singing was to be heard, for all were waiting for the moment when the god should cry for help. Also, in the ritual for 'Opening the Mouth' the chief officiating priest pretended to sleep and dream that his father had called out to him. He then rose to answer the call, and this was the beginning of the operative part of the ceremony. In the myth—and it is also implied in the ritual—Horus descends to the Underworld and there embraces his father and 'recognizes' him. That means, as we have seen, that Horus receives the *Ka* of Osiris. On earth the flood flows down the Nile, even as far as Buto in the Delta, says the hymn, thus fulfilling the command of the High God. But water is not the only form of Osiris; he is also seen in the sexual potency of males and the fertility of females.

There follows a stanza declaring that Horus has put things aright. Especially he has constrained Seth to act as, or to be-come, the boat in which the revived Osiris will travel all over the world:

'his arms will carry you
even as far as your father Geb arranged for you'.

Geb, Osiris' father, is the earth who gave the world to his son
as an inheritance. Hence Seth will have to convey his victorious
opponent everywhere. Osiris is the universal spirit of growth.

Finally comes a longer section, which begins by comparing
the reappearance of Osiris with the rising of Horus from the
waters below the earth. Here Horus is the leader of the constellations which determined the Egyptian night sky. After they
had crossed the sky the stars were thought to descend in the
west into the waters of the Underworld which extended everywhere beneath the earth and, passing through them, ascend
with renewed vigour in the east. Hence a descent into the
waters was not only a purification but the prelude to a rebirth.
Osiris' soul was transformed into a star (or, is it the sun?)
typified by a jackal held aloft on a carrying frame—the 'Opener
of the Ways'. With his appearance the passion is ended;
happiness and prosperity have returned, while the enemies are
all overthrown.

The universalizing of Osiris was closely bound up with the
popularity of Abydos as the centre of his cult. Situated midway
between north and south, it was well placed to become a place
of pilgrimage. It had been sacred from time immemorial; the
kings of the First Dynasty had erected cenotaphs there so that
their souls might lie under the protection of the local god of
the dead—a dog or jackal deity called 'The Lord of the
Westerners', i.e. those who lay buried in the western hills.
Sometime before the end of the Herakleopolitan Period (*i.e.*
before 2050 B.C.) the rites of Osiris, as they had been conducted
at his home city of Busiris, were introduced into Abydos and
the local Lord of the Westerners was absorbed into Osiris. If
Kees is right in claiming that the later temple of Sethos I was
modelled on an earlier building, we must imagine the main
shrine as situated in a grove. The most significant part was a
platform surrounded by water and approached by steps. The

mound symbolized the first land which rose out of the original flood and was the prototype of the land emerging from the receding waters of the annual inundation. This was 'the most ancient land', Tai‑wer, which gave its name to the whole district. On this island the body of Osiris was reassembled and the night vigils kept by priestesses playing the parts of Isis and Nephthys. This island, sometimes known as the 'hill', was approached by a descending passage which, to judge by the decorations on the later buildings, was the way down to the Underworld. It was down this passage that Horus went when he came to seek his father. There were other rooms—one, as we know, must have been the place where Seth had to appear before the august Court of the gods. The original shrine of Osiris was probably a mound situated in the middle of a grove, as at Medamud. The mound would have had a room in the centre, reached from outside by a winding passage.

The great annual festival took place during the last month of the inundation when the waters were falling. In the New Kingdom it lasted eight days. It began with the ritual of the 'Opener of the Ways'. There followed three days and nights of lamentation—the period of the passion, when Osiris lay help‑less and was bewailed by Isis and Nephthys. Next came the trial of Seth before the divine Tribunal. The meaning of the next day is not clear; apparently Osiris sailed on the temple lake in his boat, the Neshmet Barque, and a ritual combat took place which symbolized the defeat of Seth and his confederates. There were also days of 'setting up bouquets' and a triumphal return of Osiris to his temple. The final and most sacred act, at least in the later time, was the erection of the '*Djed* Column'—a fetish which was supposed to symbolize the backbone of the god. Its upright position was the final sign that Osiris had 'risen'.

The ceremonies at Abydos were not directly connected with the royal ritual. Apart from being an occasion of popular resort, they were, in fact, a series of mysteries that represented in outward form the fundamental drama of deliverance. A faint echo of the enthusiasm of the pilgrims can be caught from the inscriptions on the stelae which were set up in the outer precincts of the temple—'at the staircase of the God'.

'I would be among the crowd following Osiris when he appears in his final form, praising the god and singing in adoration of the beauty of the Neshmet Barque, fetching the rudder for the boat and honouring the Great God.'

A well-known stela in the Louvre (C15) describes how even the mightiest in the land bowed down and kissed the earth as the Opener of the Ways passed them. The prayer is to share for ever in the zeal of the spectators at the major rites:

'Would that I could see the Opener of the Ways in his first procession when he gleams as a god . . . and Horus the vigorous, who gladdens the people as he passes along the canals leading to the Great Hall.'

Here we can imagine the procession when a priestly actor personifies Horus, or when the god's statue is carried into the 'Great Hall' where Osiris' body awaits him. Horus has heard the call for help during the night 'of the great sleep' and as he hastens to take the message of hope to his father he bears with him the hopes and imaginative trust of the hordes of pilgrims. The conclusion of the festival was marked by the dedication of a new statue of Osiris and the presentation of enormous quantities of offerings—'everything that the land produces, the Nile makes or the sky brings forth'. The pilgrims hoped that by erecting little stelae in the outer temple their souls would share for ever in the wonderful things and thus be assured of all comforts. Similar rites—on a less grandiose scale no doubt— were celebrated all over the country. Osiris was in fact the main god for the great majority of the people. All could share in the excitement of the festivals with their panoply and dramatic tension. The votive tablets at Abydos are generally badly cut or almost illiterate, a unique and moving witness to the genuine piety of Osiris' humble worshippers.

Osiris was not only the fertility demon turned universal god; he was also the prototype of every soul who hoped to conquer death. Just as the kings of aforetime had claimed an Osiris fate, so now the significance of the drama is felt to apply to every soul:

> 'Now are you a king's son, a prince,
> as long as your soul exists, so long will your heart be with you.
> Anubis is mindful of you in Busiris,
> your soul rejoices in Abydos where your body is happy on the High Hill.
> Your embalmer rejoices in every place.
> Ah, truly, you are the chosen one!
> you are made whole in this your dignity which is before me,
> Anubis' heart is happy over the work of his hands
> and the heart of the Lord of the Divine Hall is thrilled when he beholds this good god,
> Master of those that have been and Ruler over those that are to come.'[2]

Anubis is the essential Embalmer of the mummy. Osiris is both the mummy and the hope of transcending the bonds of death. The passion time of Osiris corresponds to the period of embalmment. Seth is the power of death. The combination of Osiris' saga and the fate of the body—and soul—of the deceased is used to give dramatic intensity to a funeral text of this time:

(Isis and Nephthys cry):

> 'How sad is it to see him in the Funeral Hall, struck down by him who would do him harm, by changing himself into a flea and creeping under the soles of his feet.
> Look up, O you who are in the Embalmment Chamber!
> Come hither, O Gods in the Funeral Hall!
> Behold the god's limbs, they belong to him whom the demons fear,

see the stages they have undergone.
Light the lamp, O Gods who guard the Chamber, O
Gods who dwell in this darkness!
and look upon the limbs of this god.
Protect your Master as the hours pass by,
do this for the Lord of the White Crown until Horus
returns from Heliopolis
as the reigning one to whom the great crowns have been
given.'[3]

At this point the interest changes to the preparations for the
coming of Horus the Redeemer. Anubis, the Embalmer,
becomes the Master of Ceremonies while the attendant gods,
'the Ancient Ones', put on the panther-skins to perform their
sacramental task.

'Now is the power of the Embalmer clear
and those in the Chamber rejoice when the Ancient Ones
assume their panther-skins.
"Let the sacred emblems be put up in the Funeral Hall,"
says Anubis,
as he comes, satisfied, as Majordomo. He says
"Watch over him with averted faces!
Purify this place of the confederates of the malefactor (*i.e.*
Seth),
who have come from the slaughter-houses and whose
smell is still fresh,
who have made the offerings for this Great God and
Master of Gods,
and who guard the serpent doors for their Master."
The strong one runs inside the Palace of the Great Weary
One (Osiris) who is lying on the embalming board.
There is great commotion in the Palace when this god
(Horus) comes before him.

"Ah!" says Anubis, "among those that were aforetime,
there was no good thing!

It was said among them that a crime had been perpetrated
in the Palace by him who did him harm.
Seize the miscreant in the darkness! Destroy his band!"

Then the Lord of the Divine Hall (Anubis) rejoices, for
he sees the acclamations in the Funeral Hall [as he
stands] beside Isis, the Mistress of the Mountains.
And Anubis says to Osiris:

"Arise and live! Behold [the manner of your new]
appearance!
Avert the crime of him who did you harm!" '

This is in partially dramatic form. The speeches are interspersed by descriptive passages. The text is based on the funeral
ritual, but the gods take their fictive roles in the Osirian legend.
It is a deliberate attempt to create a new kind of mixed
symbolism, where ritual and legend are woven together to
express the need for a more cogent literature of redemption.

Some versions of Chapter 175 of the Book of the Dead have
preserved a strange myth which must have been composed
when the cult of Osiris was being introduced into Herakleopolis to support the claims of the kings of the Ninth Dynasty:[4]

'There was a cry of acclamation in Henen-nesu, [a cry] of
joy in Naref, when Osiris appeared [as king] in the
place of Rê; he had inherited his throne and was ruling
the Two Lands and all the people—

The company of the gods was well content thereat but
Seth was in great despair:

"[I] would that you give me the panoply of the Universal
Lord," said Osiris to Rê, "for then Seth would respect
me when he saw my appearance as yours and there
would come to me all people, commoners, citizens,
noblemen—all—who would see how you have established my respect and created my authority."
Now it seemed good to Rê to do all that he had said,

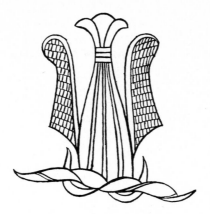

Fig. 18. The Atef Crown

whereupon Seth came and he cast his face upon the
 ground
when he saw what Rê had done for Osiris,
and the blood flowed from his nose
—and that is how agriculture began (variant adds "in
 Henen‑nesu").[5]
But, on the very first day that he wore it
 Osiris had much suffering in his head from the heat of
 the Atef Crown
 which [he wore] that men and gods should respect him.
And when Rê returned in the evening to see Osiris in
 Henen‑nesu
 he found him sitting in his house with his head angry
 and swollen from the heat of the Atef Crown.
Then Rê proceeded to let out the pus and the blood
and Rê said to Osiris "Behold you are freed from the blood
 and the pus which were hurting your head."
—and that is how the majestic pool came into existence in
 the temple at Henen‑nesu.'

This is the earliest myth in narrative form that has come
down to us. Herakleopolis is now the stage for the great

universal drama and the happenings in the legends are told in such words that they provide puns on the names of local ceremonies and religious establishments. The main interest is not in the story as such but in the verbal allusions to which it gives rise. Seth, for example, is made to staunch the blood of Osiris because the word for staunch in Egyptian—*khebi*—sounded very like *khebes*—dig up—thus giving a correlation between a mythical happening and the existence of agriculture or, as in some versions, the ceremony of 'Digging up the ground' which, as Chapter 18 of the Book of the Dead tells us, was the name of a major festival at Herakleopolis. Osiris is not here the dying and reviving spirit of nature but a king—who is not of himself able to bear the full weight of his own authority. Rê, the High God, has departed from the earth and left his throne to Osiris. The significance of the Atef Crown is not known, although the myth assumes that it was the essential mark of dominion over all the world.

The discomfiture of Seth is puzzling. Usually he is the opponent of Horus, but in this text he seems to have had some pretensions to the kingship when Osiris ascended the throne. He must wear the Atef Crown because he must be able to show—visibly—that authority over the world has been granted him by the High God and thus to silence his rival and to be acknowledged by humanity. Osiris is not sufficient of himself; he must have the authorization of the High God if he is to be recognized as world king by Seth and all the classes of mankind.

The episode concerning the Atef Crown emphasizes the subordinate position of Osiris. Rê's crown is so holy that its divine numinous power can harm anyone else. The High God is the source of all authority; it is useless to rule except in his name. This theory, which removes God from direct concern with earthly life, but makes him essential as the ultimate source of power, is typical of the theology of this time.

Another section of Chapter 175 provides a lively dialogue between Osiris and the High God, here called Atum. All the

decisions of the High God previously noticed were accepted
without question. The sceptical spirit of the Herakleopolitan
Age, however, did not stop at minor figures; it queried the
ultimate rightness of the fates determined by God himself.
After his death Osiris finds himself in a cheerless underworld
and remonstrates about his lot:

'*Osiris* O Atum! What is this desert place into which I
        have come?
    It has no water, it has no air,
    it is depth unfathomable, it is black as the blackest
        night.
    I wander helplessly herein.
    One cannot live here in peace of heart, nor may the
        longings of love be satisfied herein.
Atum You may live in peace of heart. I have provided
    illumination in place of water and air, and satis-
    faction and quiet in the place of bread and beer.
    Thus spoke Atum.
Osiris But shall I behold your face?
Atum I will not allow you to suffer sorrow.
Osiris But every other god has his place in the Boat of
    Millions of Years.
Atum Your place now belongs to your son Horus.
    Thus spoke Atum.
Osiris But will he be allowed to dispatch the Great Ones?
Atum I have allowed him to dispatch the Great Ones,
    for he will inherit your throne on the Isle of Fire.
Osiris How good would it be if one god could see
    another!
Atum My face will look upon your face.
Osiris But how long shall I live? says Osiris.
Atum You will live more than millions of years, an era of
    millions,
    but in the end I will destroy everything that I have
    created,

the earth will become again part of the Primeval
   Ocean,
like the Abyss of waters in their original state.
Then I will be what will remain, just I and Osiris,
when I will have changed myself back into the Old
   Serpent
who knew no man and saw no god.

How fair is that which I have done for Osiris, a fate
   different from that of all the other gods!
I have given him the region of the dead while I have
   put his son Horus as heir upon his throne in the
   Isle of Fire;
I have thus made his place for him in the Boat of
   Millions of Years, in that Horus remains on his
   throne to carry on his work.

Osiris   But will not also the soul of Seth be sent to the
   West—a fate different from that of all the other
   gods?

Atum   I shall hold his soul captive in the Boat of the Sun
   —such is my will—
      so that he will no longer terrorize the Divine
   Company.'

This is a direct criticism of the Osirian belief in the survival
of the soul in the life of universal nature. Otto has shown
recently that the scepticism of the age was expressed in terms of
debates;[6] objections were raised with the High God about the
seeming injustices of his ordering of the universe. In the present
case, Osiris complains that the Underworld to which he has
descended has none of the wordly amenities which he had
expected. The High God replies that this may be so, but instead
there is peace and contentment of mind. The lesson is that the
future state is not to be thought of in material terms.

Although the text speaks of Osiris, the god is here the
mouthpiece of the soul expressing its deepest anxieties. This is
abundantly clear in the succeeding section, where Osiris, not

completely satisfied with a metaphorical hereafter, breaks with the traditional mythology and wants to behold the light of day, the face of the Sun God. The Egyptians believed that the soul assumed the form of a bird in order to ascend from the darkness of the tomb to see the daylight and then returned to comfort its body. The supreme beatification in the Pyramid Texts was to join the Sun God's boat or to become 'one of those dwellers in the light'. The Osirian fate did not satisfy this longing for light. Atum's answer is ambiguous and so brings forth the reproach that all the other gods have their places in the divine barque— 'The Boat of Millions of Years'. Atum replies that Osiris must be content that his place has been taken by his son Horus; the older generation must give way to the younger. The royal power has been transmitted to Horus who has ascended the throne in the mythical centre of the world, the Isle of Fire. Humanly enough, Osiris longs to be able to see his son, but even this is denied him. Nevertheless the High God will behold him, for as the all-powerful one he can see down into the depths of the nether world, as the later Amun hymns remind us. Perhaps there is a reference here to the night sun and its visits to the lower regions. Osiris is still dissatisfied; how long will he have to endure his hapless lot? Darkly, Atum replies that he is not to be forgotten; for, one day, millions of years hence, he will bring the present dispensation to an end. Then creation will be reversed and all things return to the Primeval Waters. When all differences have disappeared he and Osiris, the transcendent and the emergent forms of deity, will be reunited in the universal primordial form of life, the original Serpent, the form in which divinity existed before the coming of gods or men. The final fate, then, is to return to the primordial unity. Here we see Egyptian thought reaching out to a concept very like that of the Upanishads.

Atum has not disposed of the enemy. Osiris wonders whether Seth, whose crimes have justified his death, will not be sent down to the Underworld. If Seth is to join him there will be no peace for Osiris. Seth, says Atum, will not be consigned

to the 'West' but will be forced to live in the boat of the Sun
God. There was a legend that Seth stood in the prow of the
sun barque to ward off the attacks of the demon of darkness.
This is quite different from the orthodox doctrine of the
Pyramid Texts, wherein he had become Osiris' boat. By
changing the fate of Seth the whole tone of the legend is altered:
the principle of violent force remains in the world above, but it
will be harnessed to protect the sun from annihilation.

The gods were personifications of natural forces or the em-
bodiments of human desires and aspirations. Originally these
elements existed all together in the various gods. During the era
of the Coffin Texts the different elements began to disentangle
themselves. Seth becomes the storm itself rather than its patron;
Osiris is the growth of the corn rather than the god who
impersonates its force. At the same time this tendency to get at
the natural phenomena behind the personality of a god leads
to a deeper understanding of the principles of existence. Coffin
Text 330 contains the clearest identification of the soul with
nature that the ancients have left us:

'Whether I live or die I am Osiris,
I enter in and reappear through you,
I decay in you, I grow in you,
I fall down in you, I fall upon my side.
The gods are living in me for I live and grow in the corn
that sustains the Honoured Ones.
I cover the earth,
whether I live or die I am Barley,
I am not destroyed.
I have entered the Order,
I rely upon the Order,
I become Master of the Order,
I emerge in the Order,
I make my form distinct,
I am the Lord of the Chennet (Granary of Memphis?),
I have entered into the Order,
I have reached its limits. . . .'

Osiris is now the barley in all its vicissitudes. It is cast upon the ground and enters the soil, the seed decays and growth starts anew. The gods come alive—i.e. are resuscitated in the growth of the new year, and the land is covered with greenery. All this is to be the lot of the soul because it has entered the 'Order'—Mayet—the natural order of the world. As lord of the temple granary of Osiris at Memphis, the soul of Osiris will experience the complete cycle of natural fertility. The theology is different from that in the spell quoted on p. 118; there Osiris was the corn-filled doll, while in this text he is the natural growth in the 'Order'. This repeated word 'Order'— Mayet—is probably the earliest approach to the concept of 'Nature' as understood in Western thought. It marks a break with the old mythical cosmology where the processes of nature were understood in terms of legend and ritual symbols.

There were several beliefs about the survival of the person after death current among the Egyptians at this time. The Osirian fate was one of immanence. To be identified with the spirit of universal nature might satisfy the desire for sheer survival, but it implied the loss of the self, for which the identi-fication of the soul with that of Osiris did little to compensate. In the Pyramid Texts the identity of the deceased with the liberated soul of the god was associated with the rebirth of that soul as a star. During the succeeding period the earthly side of Osiris was emphasized so much that the god could not quite sustain this theology, for the stellar fate was too active for the passive role of Osiris. We have noted that this had contained difficulties for the authors of the Pyramid Texts (cf. p. 116).

One of the Coffin Texts[7] tries to deal with the personality of Osiris in a novel way. The composition is probably a number of selections from a dramatic text. It is certainly highly unorthodox and full of vigour. It begins with Osiris lying in the Underworld, calling out to his son Horus, but instead of the hieratic 'Come to me!' the call is expanded into:

'O Horus, come to Busiris!
Take charge,

make the circuit of my house—for you see my condition.
Raise my soul, instil respect for me, spread my authority,
that the gods of the Underworld may respect me
and defend the gates thereof on my behalf,
so that he who would do me harm may not draw near,
nor see me in the House of Darkness,
nor discover my helplessness which is hidden from him.'

'"This may it be!" say the gods who hear the voice,
and a companion of Osiris who is passing says:
"Be silent, O Gods! A god is speaking with a god!"'

(Horus says):

"May he hear the truth of what I shall tell him!" (aside)
"I am addressing you, Osiris!
Reverse the purport of your speech!
Look yourself to your condition,
set your soul in motion,
make it come forth in control of its motion
so that your seed will proceed thereby among mankind.
Then will you be complete master [down] there,
the gods of the Underworld will respect you
and will guard the gates for you.
Move with the other movers!
Must I remain on your [funeral] mound like a lord of
    [eternal] life?
Must I cohabit with the divine Isis
and entertain him who would do you harm,
so that he does not see your helplessness?
I will journey this way along the roads
and go that way to the limits of the sky,
I will ask advice from Geb, I will seek the opinion of the
    Universal Lord."'

There is obviously a gap here—Geb and the Universal
Lord give Horus advice—when the text takes up again Horus
is once more addressing Osiris:

'"The gods of the Underworld will respect you
when they see that I have sent you one of those glorious
   beings who dwell in beams of light;
I have made his form and his manner like my own,
so that he can visit Busiris, invested with my soul.
He will tell you my news
causing you to be respected, spread your authority among
   the gods of the Underworld
so that they will defend the gates for you."

(The messenger now speaks) :

"Behold, I am one of those dwellers in the beams of light
whom Atum Rê made from his flesh,
who came into being from the roots of his eye,
whom Atum created and glorified,
whose appearances he made distinct
that they might be with him,
who [up to then] had been alone in the Primeval Waters,
who [now] herald him when he appears on the horizon
and spread his respect among gods, spirits, forms and
   powers.
I am one of those reptiles of Atum
which he created in his eye before Isis was born,
she that was to bear Horus.
I grew strong and waxed mighty
so that I became different from the other dwellers in the
   light beams
who had come into being along with me,
and appeared as a Divine Falcon,
and Horus has invested me with his soul,
in order to take his news to Osiris in the Underworld."

(On his journey the Divine Falcon has to pass by the castle
of the Leonine One, a guardian who keeps a magical wig,
the Nemes Crown.)

Then spoke the Leonine One, the dweller in his cavern,
the keeper of the Nemes Crown.

"How can you reach the confines of the sky, seeing that, although you are equipped with the form of Horus, you have not the Nemes Crown in your possession?
That is what will be said to you on the frontiers of the sky."

(Divine Falcon):

"I am taking the news of Horus to Osiris in the Underworld. Horus has repeated to me what his father Osiris told him, as his [last?] wish, on the day of his burial."

(The Leonine One speaks):

"Tell me, then, what Horus told you his father's words were
through the wall on the day of his burial
and I will give you the Nemes Crown,"
says the Leonine One, "and you may proceed upon the ways of the sky.
They who are on the horizon will see you
and the gods of the Underworld will respect you."
"Let him appear at the time of Horus after the [healing of] the damage to his eye!
Beware!
Let there be song and dancing! He has been initiated into the language of the universal gods; he is a uniquely learned one!"
says He who is in his sublimity.[7]
"Take out the Nemes Crown for him," says the Leonine One.

(The Divine Falcon now has to pass through the upper sky, *i.e.* the goddess Nut):

"Ah, Gracious Lady! Allow me to pass
for I have risen thus high in the form of Horus,
The Leonine One has taken out the Nemes Crown for me.
(variant: I have put on the Nemes Crown)
He has given me wings
and posed me firmly on his two great supports.

I shall not fall through the air
for I am one who is sufficient in his beauty,
master of an exalted uraeus.
I am one who knows the way through the sky (?)
The winds will protect me, the bull of the storm cannot
    stop me,
I am bound for the place where the Deserted One lies
in the middle of the Land of Eternity,
whither he was brought through the thick darkness of the
    Westerners—Osiris.
I have come today from the house of the Leonine One,
I left there for the house of Isis,
I saw her hidden mysteries
    in that she let me see the birth of the Great God.
Horus invested me with his soul
—but if I told what was there the columns of the air would
    chase me away
as a punishment for my audacity.
I am the Falcon who dwells amid the light,
who has control over his own light,
who is invested with his own diadem,
who can go to and fro to the limits of the sky."

The Universal Lord [intervenes to say]:

"Do not oppose him—
this form, this agent, this follower of Horus
who is at the frontier of the sky!
Horus has assumed his seats and his thrones
and this one who is in his form
is himself a mighty one as the Divine Falcon;
he is one whom his master has equipped—
Horus has invested him with his soul
that he should set out for Busiris to see Osiris,
and land at the palace of the 'Great Lander' (Osiris).
I will make him spread his authority and respect among
    the gods;

for he belongs to the great Sacred Building
and can make the guard bustle to and fro before him."

So Nut bustles around when she sees him and the other
　　gods see how she inflames "Him of the two eyes" against
　　those who [threaten him with] upraised arms. The
　　"Supreme Power" (Atum) then turns and faces Aker
　　the (gate of the Underworld):

"Let the Sacred Way be open for him
when they (the demons of the Underworld) see his form
and hear what he has to say.
Down upon your faces, O Gods of the Underworld!
O you with repellent (or twisted?) faces and outstretched
　　necks
who hide your faces from what belongs to the Great
　　Palace![8]
Reserve the way, keep guard for the majestic soul!"

(The Messenger speaks):

"Horus has ordained that you should lift up your faces and
　　look upon me,
I have appeared as the Divine Falcon,
the Leonine One has taken out the *Nemes* Crown for me,
I have come with the message of Horus for Osiris,
I have taken (?) the Hoary Heads and assembled the
　　'Powers'.
Be off with you, O Gatekeepers!
Here I am, make way for me!
Let me pass through, O Cavern Dwellers who guard the
　　House of Osiris!
I would tell of the prowess of Horus
and make known how great is the respect for him,
how his horn has been sharpened against Seth,
telling how Horus has taken command
and is now equipped with the power of Atum.

I am the liegeman of Horus, who is now Universal
Master."
"Fair voyage!" say the gods of the Underworld.

The Dwellers in the Caverns and the Keepers of the House
of Osiris show themselves.

(The Messenger says):
"Here I am before you, glorified and fully equipped!
Let the Gatekeepers of the Underworld hurry to me,
let the Powerful Ones clear the way!
I brought the Hoary Heads [to submission], they who
defied Nut,
respect has been shown to me by the Mighty Ones on the
horizon,
the guardians of the sky, the wardens of the [celestial]
roads,
I have established the doorways for the Universal Master,
the roads unto him have been cleared for me.
I have performed what has been ordained.
Horus invested me with his soul and gave me his
instructions,
for he wishes (Osiris) to triumph over his enemies.
Reveal the mysteries to me! Open the secret caverns to me!
That I may enter before the Lord, the great and majestic
soul.
I have come to Busiris to make the circuit of his house
and tell him the news of his son—
how he wished to crush the heart of Seth,
in that I should see the Lord of Infinite Weariness
that he should learn the dispositions of the gods which
Horus has made without his knowing."

(The gods of the Underworld turn to Osiris and say):

"O Lord, great and majestic soul,
Behold, one has come, the Underworld has been opened
for him,

the ways on earth and in the sky have been revealed to him,
and none has been able to oppose him."

(At last the Messenger faces Osiris and gives his message):

"Rise up upon your throne, Osiris!
May life be before you and prosperity behind you!
Rally your heart, defy Seth!
Your son has been placed upon your throne,
The multitudes have been assigned to him,
Geb, eldest of the gods rejoices,
the sky is heartened and Nut exults—
when they see what Atum has done
as he sat presiding over the Divine Council;
he has given his own supreme command to Horus, the son
    of Isis,
that he should govern Egypt, that the gods should serve
    him
and that he should rear and nourish the multitudes
through that Unique Eye, Mistress of the Divine Company
and Lady of the Universe." '

The text begins with Osiris calling on Horus for help. He
lies helpless in the depth of the Underworld, here called
Busiris. His fear is that Seth will discover where he is and
penetrate the dark regions to destroy him. Horus, contrary to
the usual theme, has other ideas. He refuses to come, and tells
his father that he should exert himself without assistance. If he
does so his seed will rise up, men will again become potent
thereby and Osiris will find that he is master of the situation.
He should move along with all the other creatures who 'move'.
This may be a reference to the heavenly bodies, but it is also an
uncompromising exhortation to self-reliance. Ironically Horus
asks whether Osiris expects him to neglect his earthly duties.
He will consult the two great oracles, the God of the Earth and
the High God in the sky. Their advice was probably given in
a section which has been lost, for the text proceeds to assume

that Horus has been advised; he tells Osiris that, although he will not come in person, he will dispatch an envoy to his father to tell 'his news'. The envoy is a 'dweller in beams of light'— one of the primeval beings who were made before the creation of the great gods of the present dispensation. In view of the importance of the commission the envoy is a specially important being; he is the Divine Falcon—presumably the leader of the morning stars who herald the coming of the sun. Horus invests him with his own form—that of a falcon. On his way the envoy has to pass an obstacle, the lair of a demon called 'the Leonine One'—*Ruty*—who, as another text informs us, dwells on the far north of the Underworld. The Leonine One will not allow the Falcon to pass because he does not possess the 'Nemes Crown', a white wig which was one of the royal insignia. At this moment the High God calls down from on high, insisting that the Falcon be given the head-dress because he has learnt the secrets of the two highest beings in the universe after the High God—he knows about the relations between Osiris and Horus. The Leonine One had wanted to know this, or, in his own words, to learn what Osiris had said to Horus through the walls of the tomb after he (Osiris) was buried. The Falcon, however, can now pass on; he is given wings and allowed to perch on the 'great support'—perhaps the stellar pole. From there the Falcon reaches the House of Isis in the Delta marshes, where he learns how Horus was born in secret because Isis was afraid of the machinations of her enemy Seth. Thence the Falcon proceeds to the heights of the sky where he requests a passage from Nut, the patroness of the starry sky. Perhaps Nut demurred in a passage now lost, for the High God has to intervene once more, declaring that the Falcon has the highest credentials and must be permitted to pass. Nut 'bustles around' and instructs the genius of the heavenly vault to keep the Falcon safe from hostile forces. The Supreme Lord then turns round and speaks to Aker, the fear-some sphinx who guards the entrance into the depths below the earth. The monstrous denizens of the dark ways are warned to grant the Falcon free passage. At last he reaches Busiris, the heart of the Underworld, where Osiris lies. He says that he has overcome the 'Hoary Heads' (the clouds?) and all the wards of the celestial roads. He declares to the palace guards that he will inform Osiris how the troubles of the universe have been righted while he has been 'asleep' and the designs of Seth thwarted. He is at last brought into the presence of Osiris and relates to the suffering god how the Divine Council has met under the presidency of the High God and has assigned the ruling power to Horus, who is now king of Egypt and leader of mankind. The message ends with a cryptic reference to 'the Unique Eye'—the secret of executive power personified in the crown.

The tone of the whole composition is rather irreverent, almost flippant. Nevertheless, it is quite clear in its theology. The High God retreated into the upper fastnesses of the sky and entrusted the rule of the universe to his descendants. Osiris was in the line of direct succession but he was 'cast down'. For a while, Seth threatened to bring chaos and destruction on all things, until the gods met in conclave and awarded the rule to Horus. Atum may be a retreated god, but he intervenes twice in this myth to ensure that things go right with the messenger. In general, however, sovereignty in the world belongs to one god at a time; first it was Atum, then Shu and, after him, Geb. Osiris succeeded his father and, following the violent intervention of Seth, Horus is now master of the world. Horus and Osiris are, then,

'the supreme masters after the First Lord'.

The Divine Falcon carefully gives his justification as an envoy on his mission by describing his primeval origin. The legends about the beginnings were much more consistent than has been supposed and the author has carefully fitted the Falcon into the recognized scheme. There was an old tradition about the visit of a divine messenger to Osiris; in Pyramid Spell 606 Horus visits his father and says:

'I have come to you as the messenger of the God Above;
he has confirmed you upon the throne of Atum, the sun,
O my father!'

But here the theme is developed as a way of conveying
Horus' news to the Underworld. Horus is not himself the
messenger as in the Pyramid Text. Nut is treated rather
cavalierly; she 'bustles about' and the Falcon refuses to reveal
the secret manner in which Isis bore her son Horus. Moreover,
the High God interrupts to tell her to let the messenger pass
across the sky. The majestic Great Mother of the funerary cult
is here no more than a minor hindrance. At the end we learn
that Atum presides over a heavenly court which grants Horus
the control over 'Egypt' and grants him 'that Unique Eye'—
the crown, the outward sign of authority.

The chief character is the Divine Falcon; all others are
relegated to minor positions, and the emphasis is not on the
salvation of Osiris but the Falcon's journey. This is a significant
shift of attitude. Although all the obstacles on the way are overcome by the intervention of Atum, the High God, the journey
is nevertheless felt as a great achievement. Egyptian cosmology
is still imperfectly understood, so the exact stages of the Falcon's
progress are difficult to determine. Somewhere in a lost part of
the text the Falcon surmounted the opposition of mysterious
beings called the 'Hoary Heads' and 'assembled the powers'; at
another, there must have been an episode where he was
initiated into the mysteries of the birth of Horus from Isis,
which he cannot reveal to Nut. This is usually located amid
the swamps of the Delta, the far north. After obtaining the
Nemes Crown and wings at the castle of the Leonine One, the
Falcon is given a perch from which he can ascend to the heights
of the sky free from interference from wind or storm. He flies
across the sky and comes down again on the frontiers of the
earth, at the gates of the Underworld. There were two gates of
the Underworld, in the east and west, each guarded by the
foreparts and head of a monstrous sphinx known as Aker.

The demon wards are cowed by the information that the Falcon is equipped with the authority of the new Master of the Universe, and allow him to pass through the dark ways without hindrance to the inmost region where Osiris lies helpless. The recitation of the news that Horus has ascended the throne will presumably rouse Osiris from his lethargy and cause him to 'move along'. There are three stages—through the Earth, the Sky and the Underworld. A comparison with other mythologies would show that the concept of the soul's journey is one of the universal motifs. It is, as always, the voyage from the land of the living to the abode of the dead. The traveller is not, however, a pilgrim in search of some elixir or secret of life like Gilgamesh in the Mesopotamian legend, but a messenger with good news, the essential good news that chaos has been put down and life and order revived. The theme of the 'messenger of the year', which we have already seen on p. 102, has been expanded by someone who realized its dramatic possibilities. Drioton has noted that the original document, from which the compiler of the Coffin Text took his text, contained stage directions which have inadvertently slipped into the extant adulterated version. This is clear from such phrases as:

'a companion of Osiris who is passing says—'

or

'The Supreme Power then turns and faces Aker'

or

'The Dwellers in the Caverns and the Wardens of the House of Osiris show themselves'.

The Lamentation of Isis and Nephthys is a choric song; the Journey of the Divine Falcon constitutes the remains of a

Fig. 19. Forms of the Aker in the Pyramid Texts

drama presented to an audience. Whatever its origin, the latter must have been an independent literary creation which had severed its connection from ritual, although, like Greek Drama, it may have been composed for performance at some festival. The prominent role of the messenger forces the gods into the background and in ceasing to be hieratic

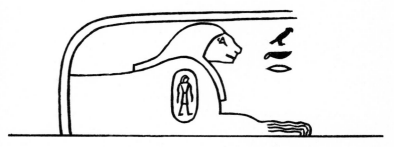

Fig. 20. One end of the Aker at the edge of the world

figures they lose their dignity. If gods are humanized and then subordinated to semi-human characters they inevitably look ridiculous.

Impatience with Osiris as the essentially passive principle was noted in the Pyramid Texts. Here it is put much more forcibly. Horus refuses to undertake the journey to the Under-world or even to carry out his proper filial duties at the tomb. He is much too busy to pay court to Isis or to keep Seth enter-tained—life is for the living. This is a break with the old ideas and one which, if it had been consistently upheld, would have completely upset the Egyptian view of the world. Instead of the old dignity and awe there is a new feeling for the individual. Emphasis had shifted from the passive god to the active angel of annunciation, and this new accent on individuality also appears when Horus tells his father to 'help himself', referring reproachfully to the way the other 'moving bodies' in the universe exert themselves. This is contrary to the orthodox theology of Osiris, who is dependent on others for his regeneration.

Apparently Horus was corrected by the oracles which he consulted. Osiris, so necessary to the life of things, cannot recover by his own efforts; a messenger must be sent to assure him that the disorders of the Upper World have been sup-pressed and universal harmony restored.

CHAPTER V

Esoteric Osiris

ALTHOUGH there were public processions at all the major festivals, the essential rites were performed in the inner rooms of the temples, to which the common people were not admitted. The sacramental acts are described allusively—'on that night of the great sleep' or 'on that day of thrusting into the earth'. Even the major gods are often given epithets rather than mentioned by name; thus Seth is 'he that would do him harm' and Osiris himself is known as *Wennofer*—'Beneficent Being' or *Kai Imentet*—'Bull of the West'. But the priests not only hid their god in awe and mystery; they also taught that the legends and ritual were symbols for metaphysical ideas. Relics of their exegesis exist in the glosses to Chapter 17 of the Book of the Dead. When the Creator declares:

'Mine is yesterday, I know tomorrow',

some glosses say:

'As for yesterday, that is Osiris; as for tomorrow, that is Atum',

thus making Osiris the past and the Sun God the future. Other versions equate Osiris with both aspects—*i.e.* Osiris is past and future—cause and potentiality. The gloss on a coffin from Beni Hassan is more explicit still:

'What is the time in which we are now? It is that Osiris has been buried while his son Horus is ruling. Others comment that yesterday is Osiris and tomorrow is Rê.'[1]

These remarks show that there were disagreements in interpretation and subtle theological distinctions. Elsewhere in the same chapter the Phoenix at Heliopolis is described in the main text as:

Fig. 21.   The souls of Rê and Osiris meet at
Mendes

'He who is concerned with deciding all that shall be.'

'Who is he?' asks an ancient editor, and replies, 'He is Osiris; and as for all that is, that is eternity and everlasting, and as for eternity, that is day, and as for everlasting, that is night.'[2]

In this spirit the High God's twin souls are said to be Osiris and Rê:

'It is Osiris when he visits Mendes, where he finds the soul of Rê, and when they meet they embrace each other and so God exists in two forms.'

This is a basic dogma of the Egyptian religion during the Middle and New Kingdoms. The Sun God as transcendent and Osiris as emergent are the complementary forms of deity. In the tomb of Ramses II the two are represented as one god—a ram-headed mummy; the inscriptions say that each is completed (*hetep*) in the other. The morning of the world, the daily recovery of the sun and the revival of the soul all depend on the combination of both into one concept. The papyrus of Ani has preserved a prayer which indentifies Rê and Osiris:

'Adoration of Osiris, Lord of Eternity, Beneficent Being, Horus of the horizons (*i.e.* Rê), multiple of forms, great of

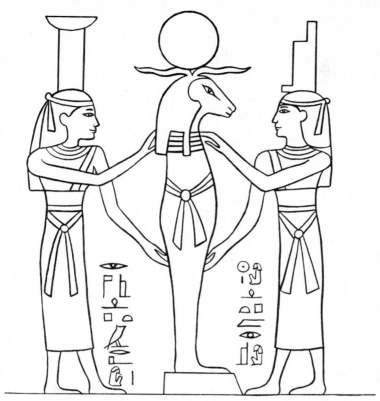

Fig. 22. Rê and Osiris as one god, sustained by Isis and Nephthys.
(Tomb of Ramses II)

manifestations, Ptah-Sokar-Atum in Heliopolis, lord of
the *shetit* shrine, creator of Memphis and its gods, who is
the guide through the Underworld. They (the gods) protect you when you set into the lower sky, Isis embraces you
in peace. . . . You are eternity and everlastingness.'

Prosperity in the hereafter had originally been conceived in a
materialist spirit as sharing in the immense offerings which
were presented in the temples and tomb chapels. During the
Middle Kingdom there is a new interpretation of the offerings.

The earlier versions of Coffin Text 228—an Osiris text—are headed: 'Spell for becoming the first to enter and the last to leave among the banqueters at the feasts of Osiris.' But the scribes of the Twelfth Dynasty added the strange rubric:

> 'If anyone learns this spell he will complete one hundred and ten years of life, of which the last ten will be without weakness and impurity, without transgression or lies, and he will finally consume meals beside that helpful god, every day.'[3]

Sharing the meals of the god has become a general term of felicity. To know the details of Osiris' rites will not only guarantee salvation in the next world but will help to overcome bodily ills and moral shortcomings.

The text itself begins with the soul—or initiate—playing the role of Horus when he claims admission to Osiris' house, here imagined as an aristocratic mansion:

> 'Ah! Old One! Go in and tell the letter
> collector (*sic*), the janitor of Osiris,
> that I have come in all my might, glory, strength, power
>   and divinity!
> Tell him that I have come hither to save
> myself and enliven my two cobras (eyes)
> to sit in the room of Father Osiris
>   and to dispel the sickness of the suffering god, so that I
>   can appear an Osiris in strength,
> that I may be reborn with him in his renewed vigour,
> that I may reveal to you the matter of Osiris' thigh
> and read to you from that sealed roll which lies beneath his
>   side,
> whereby the mouths of the gods are opened.'

The affliction of the god is interpreted as a sickness which Horus will cure. The thigh is, as has already been noted, an oblique reference to fertility; if the wound in the thigh can be cured, the water and the male fluid will gush forth and life

6 HORUS, as the 'Helper of his father' raises the *Djed* Column (Birmingham Museum).
See pp. 132 and 235 ff.

7 THE IBIS OF THOTH (British Museum). See p. 18

8 THE DIVINE FALCON (Papyrus of Ani, British Museum). See p. 145 ff.

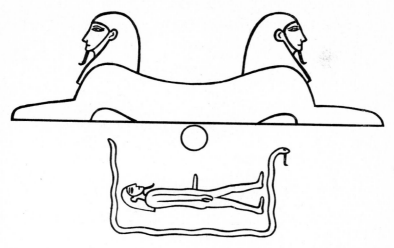

Fig. 23. The serpent enfolds Osiris in the earth (Book of Caverns)

begin again. The heart of the mystery lies in the change of the speaker's soul identity. The Horus role ceases when Osiris begins to revive, the interest shifting to the emergence of the god as a soul in the revival of nature and 'the gods' of the world. The pilgrim has now become *an Osiris*. This is the doctrine of the Osirian resurrection in the Pyramid Texts, as we have seen, but it is now generalized. The situation is comparable with that of the Fisher King in the Grail Legend. He, too, has a wound in his 'thigh'—the same euphemism for sexual organ— and the salvation of the land depends upon the healing of it. He, too, is the monarch of a palace of the lifeless until the hero comes to restore him. In the Grail Legend, also, the active participant takes the place of the suffering king after the cure.

It is easy to see why this text could be regarded esoterically by the author of the later rubric. The beginning assumes the soul's visit to Osiris at the end of a journey or a series of initiations during which the Horus soul-figure has acquired the superlative qualities of a hero—might, glory, strength, power and divinity. In order to cure Osiris, Horus has to inform him what is ailing him, and this is something which the attendants do not seem to know. Here again there is a curious parallel with the Grail motifs, where the courtiers of the Fisher King are ignorant of what is amiss with their master. The roll beneath Osiris is not mentioned elsewhere, but it must contain some all-powerful spell which, when read out in the proper way, will 'open the mouths of the gods', *i.e.* make them live and move again in the life of the new year. This is another way of saying that the suffering Osiris keeps hidden the secret of the renewal of the seasons and human redemption. The roll is like the 'Heavenly Book' with the gospel of the New Year and Age, which the royal son obtains from his father in Mesopotamian religion.[4] Without going into the difficult theme of Egypt's relations with other cultures, it is clear that this text, and the Osirian rituals on which it is based, contains one of the themes which are liable to recur in a religion as it develops from a fertility cult into a mystery of salvation.

Another expression of the Horus, the healer, theme occurs in two early coffins from Sakkarah:

'Ah, Shu, make way for me!
I am the physician for Osiris,
I have come to carry out my treatment,
that there should be no swelling in his body.'

(The physician turns to Osiris):

'Hail to you, O Bandaged One in the midst of the House of Thick Darkness!'
'Do you come to help and cleanse me?'
'Put your arms around you to protect your head.'
'Give me back my mouth that I may speak therewith,
lead me along the fair ways to the sky.'[5]

Herodotus alludes darkly to mysteries of Osiris at Sais in the temple enclosure of Neith:

'Here, too, in Athene's precinct at Sais, is the tomb of one
whom . . .

name I prefer not to mention in such a connection; it stands behind the shrine and occupies the whole length of the wall. Great stone obelisks stand in the enclosure, and there is a stone-bordered lake near by, circular in shape and about the size, I should say, of the lake called the Wheel in the island of Delos. It is on this lake that the Egyptians act by night in what they call their mysteries, the Passion of that being whose name I will not speak. All the details of the performance are known to me, but —I will say no more.'

The reticence of the Greek historian was shared by the Egyptians themselves. Clearly, there were secret rites whose details and significance could not be disclosed to the profane. A passage from an Osiris mystery has become incorporated in Chapter 125 of the Book of the Dead. A dialogue between the aspiring soul and the Guardian of the Hall of Judgment:

A 'Who are you?' they ask me. 'What is your name?'
B Gleaming Sceptre of Papyrus is my name.
A 'Which way did you come?' they ask me.
B I passed by that city to the north of the Cosmic Bush.
A 'What did you see there?'
B The constellations around the Pole.
A 'What did you tell them?'
B I said I had seen the sorrow in the land of the Syrians.
A 'What did they give you?'
B A burning brazier and an amulet of fayence.
A 'What have you done with them?'
B I put them in the coffer beside the river bank during the sacred night.
A 'What did you find beside the river bank?'
B A mace of flint, whose name is 'He who gives the breezes.'
A 'What did you do with the brazier and the amulet after you had put them in the coffer?'

B I wept over them, then I took them out, I extinguished
the fire, I broke the amulet and threw them both into
the lake.

A 'Come then, enter this way into the Hall of Double
Justice!'[6]

In these occult disclosures Drioton sees symbols for the death
of Osiris. The initiate went on a journey to the stars by way,
apparently, of a cosmic tree, and through Syria, the northern
land where the lamentation rites of some Osiris figure were
being celebrated. He was given the key of the winds (primarily
the North Wind, which was essentially the property of Osiris),
a brazier and an amulet (the *Djed* Column?) which must in
some way have signified the god, for he put them in a coffer
beside a river bank, just as Osiris had been struck down beside
a bank. Finally, like Seth, the initiate cast them into the sacred
lake, as Seth had done with the body of Osiris.

The mysteries of Osiris tried to universalize the legends about
the god. In the above dark sayings one can trace the attempt to
transform the passion of the god from a local to a cosmic level.
This tendency was already at work during the Middle Kingdom.
The al Barsha sources transform the Tribunal which judged
between Horus and Seth from the earlier:

'before the Divine Court which sat down to judge in the
presence of Geb'

into

'before the Divine Court which sat down to judge before
Geb (earth) and Rê (sun) . . . on earth and in the sky.'[7]

During the Old Kingdom the theologians of Osiris had tried,
as we have seen, to equate Osiris with the whole earth and had
even tried to put him into the sky world. The god of the
mysteries, however, had developed from the State and fertility
figure of earlier times into something like a personal redeemer.
The fate of the helpless one must be played out with the

universe as stage and, at the same time, must apply not only to collective but also to individual man.

The ancients thought of death as the essential prelude to life. The two form a polarity; one is meaningless without the other, and they alternate in all spheres of nature—among men, animals, vegetation and stars. Death is a passing from one kind of time to another—from life yesterday to life tomorrow. What is in the Underworld belongs to death, but it is in a state of becoming, where the 'form' or shape of things is given in which they will later 'appear'. Life can be seen, becoming is hidden. The chief instance of this great process is the sun, which must somehow be refitted or remoulded beneath the earth or beyond the visible sky. The place where these things happened was called by the Egyptians the *Dat*, which for convenience is called the Underworld. The Egyptians, however, do not seem to have given a fixed location to the Dat; it is usually under the earth but sometimes beyond the visible sky vault ('the belly of Nut')[8] or in the waters which they imagined to extend every-where beneath the land. The Dat is without light and beyond the reach of man. It is the place of the formation of the living out of the dead and the past, the true meeting-place of time before and after. Being mysterious, the anxieties of the living were easily transposed. If it was the source of new life it was also the lair of demons who symbolized the forces of annihilation which threatened re-creation in the early and crucial stages. The demons must be kept at bay, so the gates of the Underworld are protected by still more grisly creatures, the tamed forces of chaos, represented by the authors of the Underworld literature as poisonous fire-spitting serpents, lions, lakes of fire and dragons of mixed form.

Osiris is the spirit of becoming, but in the Dat he has largely lost his accidental characteristics. He is no longer the Dead King, Fertility Daimon or Inundation Spirit but the personi-fication of the coming into being of all things. He is generalized as the secret of what lies beneath the surface and is represented as a mummy figure without any distinguishing marks, the symbol which the Egyptians called '*irw*'—'form'. He is the embodiment of the positive aspect of the Dat. A journey to the Underworld is a descent either to the recumbent Osiris or to view the various stages through which he has to go to be reconstituted.

During the Middle Kingdom the Underworld became a much more frightening place than had been imagined by the authors of the Pyramid Texts. It was divided into sections, each of which was guarded by fearful monsters. The earliest of the special works which deal with these horrors must date from before the Twelfth Dynasty. One of them, the so-called Book of the Two Ways, is a guide through the subterranean paths to the places where the sun and moon are reconstituted, apparently in the far north beneath the world axis. The second is Spell 336 of the Coffin Texts, which divides up the Underworld journey into a series of obstacles or gates which must be passed through by means of magical formulae.[9] In these early Underworld texts the journey is made by the soul, but in the developed works which appear on the tombs of the New Kingdom, the theme is the night journey of the sun. As the latter goes through the subterranean ways it lights up the denizens of the dark. It has been the custom of recent commentators to dismiss these sombre productions as trivial expressions of fear and deficient imagination. This is to misunderstand their intention and overlooks the fact that they remained popular until almost the end of the civilization. When the sun passes along it illumines all the forms which must be in the Underworld and belong to the past or future. As an imaginative exercise it is also a journey into the inner reaches of the mind and an attempt to penetrate to the reality which underlies phenomena. The temptation to people the darkness with the unredeemed dead has appealed to nearly every culture—witness the Underworlds of Homer and Virgil. The Egyptians, too, thought it a place destitute of light and hope, the domain of unregulated power, phantoms and terror. Nevertheless, the Underworld is one of the abiding symbols of mankind. Life

Fig. 24. Seven forms of Osiris within the serpent (cf. A. Piankoff, *The Tomb of Ramses VI*, 2, figs. 19 and 20)

must come from elsewhere and revival of the heavenly bodies must take place beyond human knowledge. The Underworld may be a limbo or a hell, but it is also the source of new life.

Exposed to all the dangers of the Underworld, the hapless Osiris must be guarded, otherwise he would be annihilated by his enemies or disintegrate. He is therefore represented in the Dat as encircled in the folds of a gigantic serpent known as Nehaher—'Fearful Face'—or Mehen—'Encircler'—or, with reference to the old cosmogony, Wer—'Most Ancient One'. In order to be an efficient guardian the serpent must have a frightening aspect. During the early stages of Osiris' Under-world development Nehaher keeps the god closely enfolded; but when Osiris begins to revive, the serpent is an opponent to his recovery as a positive, active force. If Osiris is to 'rise up' the serpent must be straightened out or overcome and chained down. The serpent is both protective and retarding. When he is to be defeated Fearful Face becomes Apopis, the dragon serpent of the darkness who has to be overcome by the atten-dants of the sun before he rises in the morning. At times the serpent may be 'Most Ancient One', or Neheb-kau, 'Provider of Attributes'—the Primordial Snake who held all subsequent creation within his folds at the beginning of the world. To the authors of these Underworld guides all the serpents were one—both the protecting spirit of potential life who saves it from the blind forces of destruction, and the retarding genius of the Abyss which has to be defeated before the 'Divine Soul' can rise into the light of day. Details of the creation drama are taken over to form the mythology of salvation of the prisoner in the Underworld.

Some of the most interesting expansions of Osiris symbolism occur in the Book of Caverns—a work describing the journey of the sun through a succession of caves between sunset and sun- rise. It has been preserved on the walls of the Osiris temple at Abydos as well as in the tombs of Ramses VI and IX and, according to Piankoff, the authority on these matters, probably derives from a cycle of mysteries at Abydos. As the sun proceeds through the dark caverns it lights up a group of mysterious figures in the folds of Neheb-kau. The seven genii wear the divine corslet of gods who took part in primeval events. Their faces are unformed—instead of features they have ovals with horn-like protuberances. Piankoff calls them 'cat- fish', but without referring to the fact that such formless heads occur fairly frequently as early as the Coffin Texts and seem to represent primordial beings before the emergence of properly distinguishable shapes. The serpent is here named Neheb-kau, the Primeval Snake. The genii are, then, half-beings of the time before the emergence of the High God, like the negative or formless creatures of the Hermopolitan cosmogony (see p. 54) who are the characteristics of the Abyss of waters. Their names, however, are not those of the procreation spirits but epithets of Osiris which refer to the various stages of the god's passion and deliverance. They are Osiris, 'he who is preserved', 'he who is mourned' (or, literally 'wept'), 'he who is drowned', 'he whose flesh is made', and two others with names which cannot be readily understood, but seem from their grammatical form to be epithets of the same kind. It is clear that they are seven aspects or elements of Osiris which are individually in- complete but together make up the complete god. There are seven of them because that is a mystic number which conveys the divisions of a higher unity. The creation legends have lent a motif to the Osiris mysteries, but this is more than the trans- ference of a minor trait. The emergence of the High God at the beginning is a symbol which can apply equally well to Osiris, for both he and the Primordial Spirit go through stages of hidden development before their emergence, the High God in the watery Abyss, and Osiris in the initial stages of every living thing. Both are symbols of the liberation of the soul.

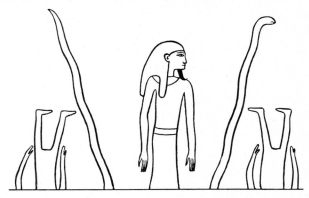

Fig. 25. Osiris breaks out of the serpent's coils, and the enemies disappear
(A. Piankoff, *op. cit.*, 1, fig. 27)

In the Book of Caverns the centre of the Underworld is occupied by an enormous twin-headed sphinx called Aker. In a cavern within this monster's body Osiris lies helpless on his back, feebly moving his legs to and fro. As the disk of the sun passes through the dark cavern, the sexual organ of Osiris becomes erect, a sign of the reviving potency of the god. He is enfolded in the coils of the serpent Nehaher, of whom the accompanying text declares:

> 'This is the manner of the serpent that [hides in the body of Osiris]. In passing through this cavern the sun says "O body of him whose soul is hidden, Osiris of the West, whose decay is invisible and whose rotting is covered up! Whom the dead dare not approach. . . . I will protect your soul and your shadow. I will dispel the darkness from around you and Nehaher in this cavern will hold your body together."'

Towards the end of the Book of Caverns the revival of Osiris is pictured still more dramatically. The god has already half emerged from the earth and is breaking free from the serpent. At the same time the ancillary enemies disappear head-downwards into the limbo. The text has:

'As the sun goes through this cavern it says: "Ah! Osiris! whom the great serpent envelops, and you, O bloody ones [falling] headlong. . . . Behold me as I pass. . . . O you who were in the coils of the serpent, I deliver him to you by the order which comes from my mouth. I will cause you to breathe with what comes from my mouth . . . and may my light . . . give illumination to your caverns without the serpent seeing. . . ."'

The destruction or conquest of the serpent is associated with the rising of Osiris out of the cosmic mound. This idea seems to have been originated at Abydos, where the mound rising from the waters probably gave its name to the whole district—To-wer—'most ancient land'. This, too, is always guarded by an entangling serpent.

In Fig. 26 Osiris rises from the earth which is symbolized by Geb, the earth god, and by Tatenen, the deity of the Primeval Mound. The serpent is held by two ram-headed figures who,

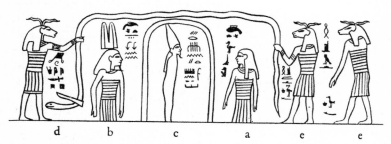

Fig. 26. Straightening out Apopis: the inscriptions read: (a) Geb (the earth), (b) Tatenen (the Primeval Mound), (c) Osiris, (d) 'straightening out' Apopis, (e) 'destroying his (i.e. the serpent's) soul'. The three gods rise from the Under-world (Piankoff, *op. cit.*, fig. 117)

Fig. 27. Osiris enthroned on the Mound

the text says, 'straighten out Apopis'. At the monster's head is a
knife, a reminder that in some versions of the story the serpent
was cut into pieces.

During the late New Kingdom another variant on this theme
became popular on coffins and tombs. In this version the
central object is a mound which is approached by steps. Inside
is either the recumbent figure of Osiris or a symbol which
represented him illumined by the night sun during its Underworld journey. The stepped hill is, of course, the Primeval
Mound but this time it is given directions. The goddesses of
North and South, and sometimes signs for East and West,
decorate the outside of the steps. The Underworld is here the
interior of the whole earth. This idea was not foreign to the
earlier literature but was not depicted so explicitly. Around
the mound the serpent Nehaher winds itself. The Egyptian
artists found it difficult to show a mound surrounded by the
coils of a serpent and still keep the essentials of the interior.
Hence the coils are reduced to two great loops.

Above the mound Osiris sits enthroned, protected sometimes by a goddess, and approached by Horus or Thoth and a
peculiar being carrying two stiff serpents arranged as an X. The
first god to approach Osiris presents him with the Horus eye—
the old motif of the recovery of Osiris which is as old as the

Pyramid Texts. The scene must depict the triumph of the god. The figure with the crossed serpents is probably the Divine Word, the message from the High God which authorizes the enthronement and recovery. Thus the whole picture combines the two main themes of the Osirian fate—the sojourn in the Underworld as a passive body and the triumph when the god receives the Eye as the talisman of active life and the sanction of the ultimate word.

Another version of the theme is given in the Book of the Making of the Sun's Disk which was painted on the walls of the sarcophagus chambers of the tombs of the Ramesside pharaohs. This time Horus is born directly from the inert Osiris at the orders of Atum.

Osiris is usually a personification of the immanent powers in nature; he is not clearly connected with the universe of cause and effect. The Underworld literature, however, tends to interpret his fate by introducing a positive—almost an active—element. Osiris undergoes his transformations because they are ordered by the High God or, as in the Book of Caverns, because the sun passes through the Underworld where he lies. In Fig. 28 Atum bends over the recumbent figure of Osiris with one hand outstretched in the attitude of divine command, like God in the medieval creation pictures. Horus emerges from the loins of Osiris in answer to the command. The dark mystic symbolism of the earlier text has been superseded by a transcendent concept; Osiris is subordinated to Atum as the sole possessor of divine authority. Isis is now unnecessary in her role as Divine Mother. Perhaps this version of the Osiris fate is an importation from the Semitic peoples of Asia, some of whom held more firmly than the Egyptians to a transcendent and obstinately masculine idea of deity.

Atum presides over the whole Osiris drama. Although far away in the sky, he dominates events, using Thoth as an intermediary. In the mysteries the latter, although only carrying out the High God's instructions, occupies the centre of the stage. He is 'the reed pen of the Universal Master', the Lord of Law,

Fig. 28. Horus arises directly from Osiris at the command of Atum
(Piankoff, *op. cit.*, fig. 114)

who announces words of wisdom and understanding. In Coffin Text 338 he is addressed as 'Thoth, who made Osiris triumph over his enemies.' As god of writing and the power of reason his triumph is a legal one, which is why the text continues:

> 'before the tribunal in Heliopolis, on that night when the adversary was fought and overthrown,
> before the tribunal in Busiris, on that night when the twin pillars were erected . . .'

and so on through a list of the main centres of Osiris worship to be found at the time of writing of the text, thus asserting that Thoth was the chief actor in all the temple dramas where the passion of Osiris was enacted. To share in the mysteries was to be 'a follower of Thoth'. Chapter 183 of the Book of the Dead, a composition of the early New Kingdom, preserves a moving hymn based upon this theme. The singer is a deceased person who has come before Osiris to be judged. On earth he had been a spectator of the mysteries and so a follower of Thoth. Osiris is addressed:

'I have come before you, O Son of Nut, O Prince of
 Eternity!
I am a follower of Thoth, rejoicing in all that he has done:
 he bought the sweet air for your nose,
 life and vigour to gladden your face
 and the North Wind that comes from Atum for your
  nostrils.
O Lord of the Sacred Land!
 He made the light shine on your inert body,
 for you he illumined the dark ways,
 for you he dispelled the weakness in your limbs through
  his potent spell,
 for you he reconciled the Two Lands,
 for you he put an end to the storm and confusion,
 for you he pacified the Two Lands
 so that they are at peace together,
 putting away the anger in their hearts
 so that they fraternise together.'

Osiris was revived by the North Wind, which was sent by the
High God, and heralds the inundation, the annual sign of the
god's new life. As the Moon, Thoth can illumine the dark
ways through the Underworld; as the patron of learning, he is
the master of powerful spells to charm away the sickness and
recall the helpless deity from his lassitude. In the political sphere
Thoth put an end to the 'storm and confusion'. The Two
Lands mean more than Egypt in this context. When they
began their contention, Horus was the leader of the north, while
Seth commanded the south, so in bringing the gods together
Thoth brought peace to the two kingdoms, which henceforth
lived in peace with one another.

In the next section there is a description of the triumph of
Horus and its universal significance:

'Your son Horus has been upheld by the unanimous court,
 kingship of the earth has been granted him
 and sovereignty over the whole world;

the throne of Geb has been assigned to him
while his office, the special task of Atum, has been
    confirmed
  by the writings in the Archive House,
  inscribed upon a tablet of copper
  according to the ordinance of your father Ptah⁄tenen
  —he is upon the "Primeval Place"—
  so that the waters might be brought up to the mountains
  to enliven what should grow upon the highlands, the
  mountain and the plain.
Your son Horus has enlivened the gods of earth and sky,
they come in homage to his audience chamber
and whatever he orders them to do, they perform straight⁄
  way.
May your heart be happy, O Lord of the Gods!
for all joy is his: Egypt and the Desert are at peace.
  They serve under your leadership,
  the temples are established in their proper places,
the towns and districts are confirmed in their names.'

Thoth belongs to myth but Horus is the living king. The
throne of Geb—mastery of the earth—and the sovereignty
—the special task of Atum—are now his. Monarchy was
founded by the Creator upon the first land to emerge from the
Abyss and its rules drawn up on a metal (*i.e.* eternal) tablet by
Ptah⁄tenen, the High God as personification of the Primeval
Mound at Memphis. Using a Memphite creation myth, the
hymn goes on to credit Ptah⁄tenen with the separation of
the waters below from the waters above the earth. By lifting the
upper waters upon the supports of Shu—the air—the god pro⁄
vided the rain for the high land. The positive creator is here
called 'the brother' of the Primeval Waters. After this digression
the Horus theme is resumed; the powers of the world become
his courtiers, obeying him implicitly. Osiris should now be
completely reassured—law and order have been reasserted and
all the world is at peace.

In the new dispensation Osiris can receive the attention. The speaker hopes to share in the god's good fortune:

'May we join with you in the offerings
    and the gifts which will be made for ever in your name.
Paeans will be sung in your honour,
    libations poured out to your *Ka*,
sepulchral meals will be presented to the spirits in your
    train
and water poured on both sides on the . . .
    for the souls of the dead in this land.
Now have all your dispositions been perfected
    according to the instructions at the beginning
so that you are crowned, O Son of Nut! as Universal
    Lord in full glory.
Verily you live [once more]—established, vigorous and
    justified,
while your father Rê invigorates your flesh
    and the Divine Company praises you.
Isis is with you, she will not leave you
    before your enemies have been overthrown.
The chiefs of every country extol your beauty,
    which is like that of the sun in its rising at dawn,
    when you (seem to?) rise up on his standard
    and your beauty heightens the face and quickens the
        step [as his does].
The sovereignty of your father Geb—who created your
        beauty—
    has been granted you,
while your mother Nut, who gave birth to the gods,
    gave birth to you as the firstborn of the "five gods",
    forming your beauties and fashioning your limbs,
    with the Great White Crown upon your head, grasping
        the crook and flail;
    for when still in the womb, before ever you had appeared
        on earth,

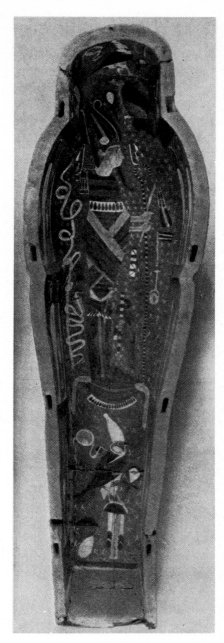

9 OSIRIS in the starry underworld,
protected by the Cosmic Serpent
(British Museum). See p. 167 ff.

10 THE SOUL rising from the Primeval Lotus (Papyrus of Ani, British Museum).
See p. 239
See p. 239

you were fully panoplied as Lord of the Two Lands
with the Atef Crown of Rê upon your brow.
The gods come bowing before you, respect for you
    envelops them
    when they behold you in the majesty of Rê,
    respect for your majesty fills their hearts,
Life is yours, Command is all around you,
    Mayet is offered to your face.'

Osiris is extolled as Lord of the Universe and essential king.
The original master, Atum, has retreated beyond creation. He
transmitted his power to Shu and then to Geb, the earth. In
turn, Osiris, as Geb's son, received the kingship. There must
have been a myth, now lost, which told how Osiris was born
directly into the royal state, Geb having retreated to become the
earth. From Geb and Nut came five children, Osiris, Haroeris,
Seth, Isis and Nephthys, of whom Osiris was the eldest and
heir because he emerged fully crowned from his mother's womb.
Kingship is the supreme manifestation of earthly power whose
glory can only be compared with that of the sun (Rê). As
king, Osiris has the majesty which formerly belonged to the
creator, Rê, before he departed from the world; he is master of
all living things, of government and of the Cosmic Order
(Mayet).

Osiris dwells in the Primeval Place; his throne is placed
upon the creation mound, which the deceased now reaches in
what he calls 'this city':[10]

'I have come to this city, the region of the "First Time",
    to be a soul, a *Ka*, a spirit, a dweller in "this land";
    its (the city's) god is the Lord of Righteousness, master
        of provisions in full sufficiency;
    [the people] of every country are brought hither,
    the South comes sailing downstream,
    the North with the wind in its sails for its festal occasions
        in the glorious palace
    as its god commands, who is master of peace therein.

He will not repulse anyone who rejoices in doing right,
[rather] he gives a long and happy old age to him who
   does right,
so that he (the latter) reaches beatitude, attaining it after
   a fair burial in the necropolis.
I have come before you, my hand holding righteousness;

as for my heart, there is no lie therein;
I offer Righteousness before your face
   for I know that it is that wherein you live
   and I have done no wickedness in this land
   nor have I defrauded any man of what was rightfully
   his.'

Osiris sits in judgment in a palace on the Primeval Mound,
which is in the middle of the world. He has become the
Master of Righteousness. These are particular symbols for
the High God in most of the religions of mankind. According
to the older theology, Rê or Atum was the Lord of the Universe
and Mayet—the World Order of righteousness—was his
especial prerogative. We have seen how Osiris gained
possession of the 'order' of nature in his capacity of spirit of
growth in vegetation. The transcendent god was removed from
the world in order to make room for the immanent deity who
assumed all his attributes except that of Creator—for when
he is being worshipped Osiris is the only god that matters. The
reconciliation of the two ideas of deity is therefore incomplete.
Step by step Osiris takes over from Rê the judgment of the
dead. The process was not complete before the end of the New
Kingdom. In the hymn given above, Osiris is the incorporation
of right rather than the judge of it. On the well-known papyrus
of Ani in the British Museum the deceased is judged in a hall
before forty-two judges, and then, when he has been found
guiltless, he is brought by Horus into the presence of Osiris.
The god sits in a garden pavilion erected on a platform
approached by a short flight of steps which is situated in front
of a shrine. The cornice of the pavilion is hung with bunches

of grapes. The pavilion is exactly the same as that in which the earthly kings of the time sat to receive the gifts of their subjects on New Year's Day (Davies, *Tomb of Ken Amun*, 1, pl. XI). The details of the pavilion, however, are cosmological. Osiris' throne seems to be in front of a pool of water, from which rises a lily, and out of the opening flower come four little mummy-like figures—the four so-called 'Sons of Horus' who are the gods of the cardinal points. This seems to emphasize what Chapter 183 of the Book of the Dead has already taught us, namely that Osiris sits enthroned on the Primeval Mound in the midst of the waters. The goal of the soul's journey is the 'first place'—the essential abode of divinity.

Osiris can sit alone in his shrine, but generally he is guarded by one or two goddesses—Isis and Nephthys, Mayet or Imentet, the Spirit of the Western Mountain where the dead are buried. Even in his glory, then, he is not self-sufficient, for he is neither alive nor completely dead. He is the helpless ruler who is at the same time the vital source of all life. The symbol of his revival is depicted above the shrine, whence the hawk-form Sokar emerges, guarded by twelve cobras.

There was always an anomaly in the position of Osiris. He is the fountain of all living things on earth and even in the sky, for even the phases of the moon can be symbolized in terms of his passion and recovery. He is subordinate to the High God, but the latter is not directly concerned any longer with his creation. Osiris is God as refuge, sympathy and invisible power, who 'saves you when you are ill-treated'. He is what the Egyptians called a '*neb tem*'—'universal master'—human yet mysterious, suffering and commanding.

Throughout Egyptian religion, from the hymns of the Pyramid Age to the speculations of the New Kingdom, there is an underlying theme. The passion and triumph of the god may symbolize the cyclic events of external nature or the theory of the kingship, but they also externalize a drama of the soul. The presentation of the Eye signifies the achievement of full consciousness but at a different level from what had existed before

—Osiris is not revived in his original form as an earthly king. The triumph, as has been shown, enables the god to send out his soul; that is, to assume another and higher form of life and to escape from the trammels of material things as well as to be associated with the power which sets them moving. He is the prototype of the liberation of the human soul from the helplessness of death as well as the symbol for the liberation of the soul from its psychic hindrances in this life. On some of the tombs which contain funerary texts we are told: 'This will be useful for a man here on earth as well as when he has died.' In its comprehensiveness and lasting vitality the symbol of the dying and triumphing Egyptian god was perhaps the greatest imaginative concept of Oriental antiquity.

CHAPTER VI

Some Myths about the Great Gods

I

HOW RÊ LEFT THE LOWER WORLD

AT THE BEGINNING of time the High God rose out of the Primeval Waters, but now he is the sun in the sky. The Egyptians sought to explain how this has come about. In the Pyramid Texts there is a statement that the 'gods'—the former kings—have, in dying, left the sad and restricting conditions of earthly life for a carefree existence among the stars:

'Your purity is the purity of the gods who have gone to their
   Ka's,
   your purity is the purity of the gods who went away to
   avoid earthly sorrow.'[1]

This was, of course, just wishful thinking about the souls of deceased pharaohs, but it stimulated the development of a myth on the basic theme of disgust with the world of men and the wish to escape from it. During the Herakleopolitan Period this was expanded into a considerable myth:

'Rê, the god who created himself,[2] was originally king over gods and men together, but mankind schemed against his sovereignty, for he began to grow old, his bones became silver, his flesh gold and his hair [as] real lapis lazuli. When he realized that mankind was plotting against him he said to his suite:
"Go, summon me hither my Eye, together with Shu, Tefnut, Geb, Nut and all the fathers and mothers who were with me in the Primeval Waters, as well as the god

Nun himself[3] and let him bring his court with him. You must gather them together secretly, do not let mankind see. . . . You shall bring them to the Great Palace that they may give their advice [as they have been accustomed to do] from the time I emerged from the waters, up to the place where I now appear."[4]

So the gods were brought together. They entered in before him and cast their heads to the ground in his presence, waiting for him to speak—first to the father of the most ancient ones, he who created mankind, the king of men.[5] And they said, "Speak to us that we may hear."

So Rê addressed Nun: "O Eldest God, in whom I myself came into being! And You, O Ancient Gods! Behold mankind, who came from my Eye, have been scheming against me. Tell me what you would do about it, for I seek [a solution]. I would not kill them until I had heard what you have to say."

Then Nun said: "O Rê, my son! O God greater than he who made him and mightier than they[6] who created him! O You that now sit upon your throne! If your Eye were turned against those who are plotting against you, how greatly would they fear you?"

But Rê said: "See, they have fled into the desert, for they were afraid in their hearts that I might speak [reproachfully] to them."

Then the others who were about him said: "Let your Eye be sent out to seize those who are plotting evil against you. Of itself the Eye is not strong enough to destroy them. Let it descend upon them as Hathor."

So that goddess came and slew mankind in the desert. This god (*i.e.* Rê) said: "Welcome, Hathor, for having done the deed which I came (to see ?). She said: "As truly as you live for me[7] I have prevailed over mankind and it is pleasant to my heart."

Then Rê said: "Now that I am in control of them, do not reduce them any more."

And that is how Sakhmet came into being.[8] Then Rê said:

"Go, summon swift messengers, that run as fast as a body's shadow."

The messengers were brought straightway. Then this god said:

"Go to Elephantine[9] and bring me red ochre." And red ochre was brought him. Whereupon this great God . . . and "He with the side lock" in Heliopolis[10] ground up the red ochre. Then a group of servant girls crushed barley for beer and the Majesty, King of Upper and Lower Egypt, Rê, came with his [attendant] gods to inspect this beer.

The day dawned for the final slaughter of mankind by the goddess, and as they went southwards Rê said:

"How fair it is! I will save mankind with it," and Rê also said, "Come! Carry it to the place where she expects to slaughter [the last remnant of] mankind." Then Rê set to work in good time, even in the middle of the night,[11] to get this soporific poured out. The fields were flooded to a depth of three palms with the liquid, through the power of this great God.

At dawn the goddess set out and found everywhere flooded. Her face seemed beautiful in it (the reflection?). Then she drank and it seemed good to her heart and she returned drunken, without noticing mankind at all.

Then Rê said to this goddess: "Welcome, O Beautiful One!" And that is how beautiful women came into being in the city of Yamit.[12]

Then Rê said of this goddess: "Let [intoxicating] drink be made for her at all the yearly festivals and let it be entrusted to servant girls." And ever since that first time people have entrusted to servant girls the making of drink at the festivals of Hathor.

Then Rê said to this goddess: "There is a scorching pain and sickness in me." And so the state of sickness came into being.

Then Rê said: "As I live, my heart is weary of staying with them (*i.e.* mankind). I have gone on killing them [almost] to the very last one, so the [insignificant] remnant is not my affair."

The gods who were in his suite declared: "Do not be disᐟappointed or weary, you [still] have all the power you may wish for."

Then this god said to Nun: "My limbs have become feeble, as they were in the Primeval time, but I will not return [into the waters of the Abyss] until another cycle overtakes me."[13]

So Nun said: "O Shu, my son![14] May your eye [behold] your father and protect him!"

"And do you, O Nut my daughter, sustain him!"

Then Nut said: "How shall I do that, O Father Nun?"

When Nut has spoken (thus?) she disappeared into the Primeval Waters and she was transformed into a [cow] and he (Rê) was on her back. And all mankind were astonished when they saw him on the cow's back.

They said to him: "We will overthrow your enemies . . . plots. . . ."

So he proceeded to his palace on the back of the cow and he joined them (the gods?).

The world was in darkness. When it was light, in the morning, mankind came out with their bows and shot arrows against their enemies.

Then this god said: "Beware of this massacre, for killing has been put far away . . . and so killing among mankind."

Then this god spoke to Nut: "I have put myself on your back to be high up."

Thus he spoke, and Nut became the sky. Then this god requested:

"Keep far away from them (mankind on earth) so that I can see them."

Thus the upper sky came into being. Then, as this god looked at her, she said: "Make me a multitude."'

(The text is faulty. It must refer to the creation of the stars, the spots on the belly of the cow.)

'Then this god said: "How peaceful it is in this field!" and that is how the Field of Abundance came into existence. Then the majesty of God said: "I will plant green plants therein."

And that is how the Field of Reeds came into being. Then Nut became dizzy. . . .

(And this god said): "I will provide it with all good things," and that is how the Akhakh stars came into being.[15]

Then Nut began to shake because of the great height, and Rê said:

"Let my son Shu be put beneath my daughter Nut to keep guard for me over the Heavenly Supports—which exist in the twilight. Put her above your head and keep her there." '

The legend falls into two parts. The first deals with the disaffection of mankind and their punishment, as well as the escape of a remnant to form the ancestors of the present human race. This, of course, is the theme of the Biblical Flood story—as of its Mesopotamian precursors. The Egyptian myth differs completely from the Asiatic one in detail and in spirit. Rê may be the master of the universe but he is unsure of himself. He summons a council and acts on its advice—up to a point! His 'Eye' is somehow distinct from himself. Mankind came from the tears of Rê—as we have learnt on p. 72—so it is possible that the Eye might not wish to annihilate its own offspring. First, the Eye assumes the form of Hathor, and then of Sakhmet, the goddess of slaughter and plague. The Eye, then, is the Great Goddess and in her terrible aspect.

The second part of the story is a string of puns explaining the origin of various details of the world. The legend of the separation of earth and sky has here degenerated into a trivial episode. There are signs of satire as though the intention was to burlesque the great creative scheme of Heliopolis.

2

THE DELTA CYCLE

After the death of Osiris, Isis went in peril of her life. According to a late source, Seth put her in a spinning-mill with the bondwomen—in plain terms enslaved her. Above all things, she had to hide from her vicious brother the fact that she had conceived a child, and that this child might be a boy who would grow up and seek to avenge his murdered father. But with Thoth's help Isis escaped and fled into the marshes of the Delta. There, hidden in the swamps, she gave birth to her son Horus. As early as the Fifth Dynasty various legends had grown up around the little child. Isis had to leave him alone while she wandered about begging food to keep them both. The swamps were full of dangerous snakes and insects and Horus went in great danger from them. In one version, he was bitten in his mother's absence and cured by a magical spell. In another, he stamped on the snake that came to assail him. Judging from some statues, there was an episode with a scorpion. The snake was really Seth in disguise, for, as we learn from the myth given on p. 190, Seth could not come near the marshes of the Delta in his true form:

> 'for I was the Pure One who overthrew his serpent (enemy).
> I was a little unweaned child.
> Although I was still a weakling I overthrew Seth and ensnared him on the bank at the New Moon.'[16]

Echoes of this legend are to be found in snake spells in the Pyramid Texts:

> 'Horus lifted himself up to escape a hostile snake . . . quickly . . .
> there was no one to warn him, all help had been taken away.'

And:

> 'O Snake! O Vile Miscreant!'[17]

O You on whose mouth Horus trod with his foot!'[18]

While another allusion to the young Horus stamping on a snake occurs in:

'The sandal of Horus it is that trod on a dangerous snake,
dangerous for Horus, when he was but an infant
with his finger in his mouth.'[19]

In another spell the deceased tries to share Horus' secret:

'The serpent to the sky, the millipede to the earth!
Horus is careful as he walks; I walk the rounds of Horus.
I am ignorant of what he does not know,
but I am watching you, O Bush-dweller!
Creep away, O Cave-dweller!
O Stew-meat of Horus![20] glide back into the earth!
Hey! Come, Desert Monster, roll into a ball!'[21]

But the myths and the place-names of the Delta make it clear that, presumably as a result of Horus' misadventure with the snake, Isis asked various local nymphs to watch over her son while she was away. The hiding-place in the marshes was known as Chemmis—'Swamp of the Bee King'—a stretch lying near Buto, an ancient city in the north-east of the Delta.[22] In it was the sacred 'Bush', the thicket in which Isis hid away to give birth to her son and which, as we have seen, was part of the mystic pilgrimage in the Osiris rites (see p. 163). It was from Chemmis that Horus set out, when he reached his manhood, to see his father and to begin his struggle with Seth. The Pyramid Texts say:

'. . . the great Isis, who knotted the girdle (on Horus) at Chemmis, when she brought his clothes and burned incense before Horus, her son, when as a growing lad he set out to traverse the land in his white sandals, when he went to see his father Osiris. N. (the deceased) has set out with him as a bird hunter . . .'[23]

Looked at in one way, the adventures of Isis and Horus in the Delta form a group of tales about earthly events of long ago. But Horus is the Saviour of the World, the essential hero who is destined to bring back order to the whole universe. As he rests, a baby in the marshes, he is watched over, sometimes by the marsh-nymphs but also by the Great Goddesses of the Delta, Nephthys, Sekhat-Hor, Neith and Selkis, who are really forms of the supreme Goddess and sky beings.[24] One text says Horus was guarded by the seven cows of Hathor, who are all the reaches of the sky.[25] Isis can be identified with Sirius, the Dog Star, whose appearance on the eastern horizon just before sunrise heralds the New Year, so in giving birth to Horus she has brought forth the New Year itself.

'It is Horus the intrepid that will come forth from you (Osiris), in his name of Horus who is within Sothis.'[26]

The motif of the World Saviour lying helpless in a wild place and yet watched over by the most august powers in the universe occurs in Indian religion and is not without echo in Christmas Carols.

Fortunately two large fragments from the Delta Cycle have been saved through being incorporated into magical spells against snake-bite. These texts are written all over the supports of figures of the baby Horus stamping on snakes and mastering scorpions. They date from the last millennium B.C. but obviously derive from much earlier works. The stories are told in a down-to-earth style, like a European folk-tale. Nevertheless, the first of them is highly dramatic; indeed it has been thought that it comes from some ancient play.[27]

(1)

'I am Isis, who conceived a male child, who was pregnant with the divine Horus and gave birth to Horus, the son of Osiris, within the "Nest" at Chemmis. I was exceedingly happy about it, for I foresaw that he would become the avenger of his father. I concealed the child, hiding him for fear of what that "Cursed One" (*i.e.* Seth) would do. I left him there [alone] and wandered about as a beggar woman, [disguising myself] out of fear of the evil doer. All day, while I was caring for his needs, I was longing for my little boy. When I returned, expecting to embrace him, I found my beautiful golden Horus, my innocent, fatherless child, lying on the ground with water streaming from his eyes and saliva dropping from his lips. His body was limp, his heart was weak, the pulses of his body did not beat. I cried out, saying, "Here I am, here I am!" but the child was too weak to reply. My breasts were full but his mouth wanted food, it (*i.e.* my breasts) was as an overflowing well, but the child was still thirsty. My heart yearned to save him. It was a dreadful deed to perpetrate on an innocent child, one who was still un-weaned. He had been left alone too long. I was afraid, for I knew that no one would come if I called for help. My father was in the underworld, my mother was in the land of the dead, my elder brother lay in his coffin while my younger brother was my constant enemy and my younger sister lived in his house. Then to whom, of all mankind, should I appeal for help, hoping for immediate sympathy? I thought I would call on the dwellers in the Marshes; they, I knew, would come straightway to my help. And indeed the fishermen left their huts and came hurrying when I called. They all cried out, exclaiming at the greatness of my sorrow, but none of them could cure him with a magical spell. They all wept copiously but there was not one of them who knew how to cure him.

Then there came to me a woman who had a reputation for learning in her city and was a great lady in her province. She approached me bearing a Life sign and was confident in all that pertained to her knowledge: "Nay, do not fear, little Horus! Nay, do not despair, O Mother of the God! The child is protected against his uncle's malice, for he is hidden in a bush. Death cannot penetrate it, for it is the power of Atum, the Father of the Gods, he who is in the sky, which created this Life sign. Seth cannot enter this province, he does not prowl around Chemmis. So Horus is protected against his uncle's malice, nor can his followers harm him. Seek [another] reason why this has happened. Then Horus will revive—to his mother's delight. It must have been a scorpion or a poisonous snake that bit him."

Then Isis laid her nose to his mouth to find out whether there was any smell in his skull. She examined the disease of the divine heir and found that he had been poisoned. She seized him in her embrace, leaping about with him like fishes that have been put on a fire.'28

Up to now the story has been laid in human surroundings. The intervention of the learned woman introduces the rational note which one finds in the medical papyri. The power of the High God can protect Horus against Seth and his friends but does not seem to extend to natural hazards. Isis gives her son a medical examination, smelling his breath and confirming from his symptoms that the child has a toxic infection. In wild despair she seizes the little boy and darts about with him.

The atmosphere changes at once. The sickness of Horus is a cosmic event. Isis gives vent to a passionate litany of woe which is an appeal to the High God that her child's fate is a divine concern:

'Horus has been bitten,
    O Rê! a scion of yours has been bitten!
Horus has been bitten!
    the heir of your heir, a direct link with the kingship of Shu,
Horus has been bitten!
    the babe of Chemmis, the infant of the House of the Prince,
Horus has been bitten!
    the beautiful golden child, the innocent orphan child,
Horus has been bitten!
    the son of the "Beneficent Being", born of
        the "Tearful One",

Horus has been bitten!
him I watched over so anxiously, for I foresaw that he
would avenge his father. . . .

The blameless little child wept in pain, those who were
by him were sore distressed. Nephthys came running to
him in tears; her cries rang out across the marshes. Selqet
cried: "What, what is the matter with the child? Ah, Isis,
my sister! Beseech heaven and the divine crew will bring
Rê's boat to a standstill and the cosmic wind will cease
to blow for the boat of Rê while Horus lies on his
side."

So Isis uttered her cry to the sky and her request reached
the "Boat of Millions of Years". When it drew level with
her the sun stopped and remained stationary. Then Thoth
came down to her—he who was equipped with power and
the supreme authority to set things right.

"What is the matter, O Isis, you who are so divine and
skilful and know your spell? Surely nothing has gone
amiss with Horus? An assurance of his safety is in the
boat of Rê. I have just come from the barque. The sun is
in its place of yesterday[29] so that all has become dark and
the light has been driven away until Horus recovers his
health—to the delight of his mother Isis."

Then the divine Isis said: "O Thoth! How confident
you are, but how slow are your dispositions! Can it really
be that you have come down here equipped with power
and the supreme authority to put things right? Disaster
is heaped upon disaster—innumerably. Look at Horus
suffering from poison. This evil thing must be the deed of
his uncle. His (*i.e.* Horus') death will mean complete
annihilation.[30] Would that I were with his mother's
eldest son,[31] for then I would not have seen what has
befallen after his departure. I was reconciled with that
because I was waiting for revenge. Ah, Horus! from the
day I conceived him I have been longing to beseech the
Ka of his father whenever the child suffered."

[Then Thoth answered]: "Do not fear, Divine Isis! and you, Nephthys, lament not! I have come down from the sky with the breath of life to cure the child—to his mother's delight. Horus! may your heart be firm, let it not weaken because of the fever. The magical protection of Horus will be the same as that of the sun[32] when it lights up the world with the splendour of its two eyes."'

Here follows a series of instances of the divine security of the High God, Osiris, Isis and, finally, Horus himself. Thoth ends:

' "Back, O Poison! You are exorcised by the spell of Rê himself. It is the speech of the Greatest God which turns you away. The boat of Rê will stand still and the sun remain in its place of yesterday until Horus recovers—to his mother's delight.

Down! to earth! Then will the boat begin to move and the sky crew begin to sail once more. There will be no food and the temples will be closed until Horus recovers —to his mother's delight.

All the present misery of [the world] will keep coming back (?) until Horus recovers—to his mother's delight.

Darkness will cover everything and there will be no distinction of times, nor will any shapes of shadows be seen until Horus recovers—to his mother's delight.

Wells are dry, crops wither, vegetation is withheld from mankind, until Horus recovers—to his mother's delight.

Down, to earth, O Poison! so that all hearts rejoice and the light of the sun go round once more. . . .

The Poison is dead! its fever has stopped hurting the Lady's son. Go hence to your homes [O Gods!] Horus is now living again—to his mother's delight."

Then the divine Isis said: "Give orders concerning him (*i.e.* Horus) to the dwellers in Chemmis, the 'nurses' who are in Buto. Give them careful instructions to guard the child—for his mother's sake. And do not let them know

11 THE PHOENIX (Papyrus of Ani, British Museum). See pp. 37 and 245 ff.

12 SITO, the Primeval Serpent (Papyrus of Ani, British Museum). See p. 239 ff.

my condition in Chemmis—that of a beggar woman, a fugitive from her own town."

Then Thoth spoke to the gods and to the dwellers in Chemmis: "O Nurses who are in Buto, who tear your-selves with your hands and beat your arms for that Great One (Osiris) who has departed from among you! Watch over this little child, seek to bring him up among men, turn aside the ways of those who would rebel against him until he has taken the throne of the Two Lands. Rê in the sky will answer for him, his father will watch over him, the magical power of his mother will be his protection in that she will spread the love of him and make him respected among mankind.

But they are waiting for me to push off in the Evening Boat and, thereafter, to set sail in the Morning Boat. Horus is now your [responsibility.] I will tell his 'Father' that he is alive and well, thus giving happiness to the passengers and joy to the crew, and the boat will set sail once more. Horus is alive and well—to his mother's delight. The poison is powerless." '

(Then, in what seems a stage direction, we read):

'the official is praised for carrying out his task when he makes his report to the one who sent him out.'
(And Thoth delivers his succinct report to Rê):
'Rejoice, O Rê of the horizon. The life of your "son" Horus has been saved!'

(II)

'I am Isis, who escaped from the spinning-mill in which my brother Seth had put me. It was Thoth, that great god who is master of justice in heaven and earth, who spoke to me.

"Come away! Goddess Isis!" he said. "It is good to listen; a man lives by letting another guide him. Go into hiding with your little boy so that, one day when he is

fully grown and his strength developed, he may come back
to us. Then he will be granted to sit peacefully on his
(rightful) throne and assume the office of Ruler of the Two
Lands."

When evening came I left, and seven scorpions accompanied me.[33] I gave them strict orders, my words entered
their ears:

"Ignore the Black One (*i.e.* Osiris), do not acknow-
ledge the Red One (*i.e.* Seth), make no distinction
between the well-born and the commoner, but keep your
faces to the road. Beware of pointing the way to him who
may be looking for me until we reach Crocodile Town,
that lies at the edge of the Marshes, the tarns of Buto."

On the way I came on a settlement of people. There
was a certain rich lady there who, as soon as she saw me
coming along the road, shut her door in my face. This was
very grievous to the hearts of my companions. After dis-
cussing the matter they put all their poison into the sting
of Tefen.[34] But there was a poor little girl belonging to the
fisher folk, who opened her door, inviting [us] into her
humble dwelling. Meanwhile Tefen had crept in under
the double doors of the rich lady's gateway and stung her
son. It was as if a fire had broken out and there was no
water to put it out, or as if the sky was pouring its torrents
of rain into the rich lady's house at the wrong season. She
bitterly regretted that she had not opened her door to me,
now that she did not know whether her son would live.
She rushed around the town lamenting, but none would
answer her call.

At this point my heart misgave me about the little child.
I wanted to cure him—for he, after all, was quite innocent.
So I cried out to her saying: "Come to me! Come to
me who have the secret of [restoring to] life. I am a
'daughter',[35] one well known in her town, who can expel
poison with her spell. This knowledge my father taught
me and I am his beloved and rightful daughter."

So Isis laid her hands on the child to soothe him as he lay panting for breath. "O Poison of Tefen, come, flow to the ground! . . . May the child live and the poison die. . . ."[36]

It was as if the fire had been extinguished and the sky calmed down through the spell of the divine Isis. Then the rich lady went and brought her possessions out of her own house. She filled the fisher maiden's hut with them, for she knew full well that it was the fisher maiden who had opened her hut door to me. But all that night the lady grieved, tasting the results of her hard speech. She would be ready to give away all her possessions if she could undo the results of her not opening her door to me.'[37]

Reduced to bare essentials this myth tells how Isis had to leave her child alone in the bushes in the marshes while she went begging. On her return she found that the child had been bitten and sought for a magical remedy. But the facts are less important than the feelings which the tale called forth—the love and anxiety of the mother, the desperate situation of the lonely and unprotected child. Many medical prescriptions to abate fever are prefaced by moving allusions to this story:

(a) 'Ah, baby boy! Ah, my son! Are you burning, O my nestling? Are you over-hot, there in the bush? Your mother cannot be by you, nor is a sister there to fan you, nor a nurse to give you succour.[38]

(b) 'Ah, Horus, my son! Lying in fever in a lonely place! There is no water there, nor am I there. May there be brought me water between the banks of a stream to quench the fire.'[39]

3

THE GREAT QUARREL

Horus and Seth are the essential contestants, the Egyptian version of the Lion and the Unicorn. Their long battle for supremacy is only an episode in the Osiris myth, but the opportunity it gave for the interplay of opposed characters led to the growth of independent legends. One is reminded how the quarrel of Agamemnon and Achilles—a minor theme in the whole history of the Trojan War—was magnified into the chief motif of the *Iliad*. Similarly an unknown Egyptian took the contest of Horus and Seth and worked it up into a long and rather rambling narrative. As in the *Iliad*, the gods receive scant respect. Rê and his company seem a most changeable group, their opinions veer this way and that with every telling remark. The purpose of the narrative is entertainment, not religious instruction. The Egyptians loved conversation with its various highlights, the smart repartee, the apt proverb, the humorous or obscene allusion, the pun and the occasional touch of pathos or characterization.

Hence the general form is dialogue with a minimum of description. As mythology in the hierarchic sense this work is deliberately shallow, for it is a satirical *jeu d'esprit*. For this very reason the allusions are often obscure to us, as is always the case with humorous literature. An Egyptian would have understood in a moment the point of some dark saying which modern scholars find completely intractable. The text is written in New Egyptian and the manuscript dates from about 1150 B.C., but this is probably a revision of an earlier recension. Spiegel thinks that the theology is characteristic of the early Middle Kingdom. He may well be right.[40]

When the story begins Horus has left the Delta where he grew up and is appealing for his rights before the Council of the gods, which has assembled at Heliopolis under the leadership of Atum.

> 'A youth sat down before the Lord of All, claiming his father's office. . . . Thoth brought out the "Holy Eye" and laid it before the Great Prince in Heliopolis.'

(The 'Eye' is the crown and symbol of sovereignty.)

> 'Then Shu, the son of Rê, said: "Justice should prevail

over sheer strength. Deliver judgment saying 'give the office to Horus'." '

(This is the clue to the characterization. Seth is the figure of brute strength while Horus is a David figure, young and intrepid.)

'And Thoth said to the Company: "That is right, a million-fold."

Then Isis gave out a cry of sheer joy, as she stood before the Lord of All, calling: "Hence, North Wind! to the west and tell the good news to the 'still vigorous one'." '[41]

(Isis, however, is over-hasty; the issue is not so readily decided.)

'Then Shu, the son of Rê, said: "Let the 'Eye' be presented [to Horus] for that is the justice of the Company."

But the Lord of All exclaimed: "Stop! What do you mean by acting by yourselves? . . ."[42] And he was silent for a while, for he was angry with the Company.

Then Seth, the son of Nut, spoke: "Let him (Horus) be sent out from here, together with me, so that I may show how to prevail against him, for no one seems to know how to strip him [of his pretensions]!" '

(Seth proposes trial by combat.)

'But Thoth interposed: "Should we not rather seek to find who is in the wrong?[43] Is the office of Osiris to be given to Seth, while his (*i.e.* Osiris') son is standing by him?" '

(Thoth, as the Spirit of Ordered Justice, opposes the trial by combat.)

'Then Rê of the Horizon[44] became exceedingly angry, for he wanted to give the office to Seth—as the stronger one and as the son of Nut.

Then Onuris said to the Company: "What are we to do?" '

(Recourse is then had to the Ram of Mendes, a god of generation, and to Ptah of the Primeval Mound, but these ancients
say the gods are acting on insufficient information. They are
advised to consult Neith, the oldest of the goddesses.)

'So the gods told Thoth: "Write a letter to Neith, the
Oldest One, the Mother of the Gods, in the name of the
Lord of All."

"I will do that, very willingly," said Thoth, and he sat
down and wrote: "The King of Upper and Lower
Egypt, Rê-Atum, beloved of Thoth, the god in Heliopolis, the Disk of the Sun . . . to Neith, the eldest, the
Mother of the gods, who shone in the primeval time. . . .
Your servant[45] passes the night worrying about Osiris, and
the day concerned with the business of the Two Lands,
while Sobek endures eternally. What are we to do about
the Two Fellows who have now been before the Court for
eighty years without being able to decide finally between
them? Please, write and tell us what to do." '

(This is ironical. It is a formal letter couched in diplomatic
language. Atum has to worry about the fate of Osiris during
the night and about the government of the world during the
day. But Neith has no cares, for her son Sobek, the Crocodile,
is immortal.)

'Then Neith . . . sent a letter to the Company as follows:
"Give the office of Osiris to his son Horus! Do not go on
committing these great wrongs, which are not in place, or
I will get angry and the sky will topple to the ground. But
also tell the Lord of All, the Bull who lives in Heliopolis,
to double Seth's property. Give him Anath and Astarte,
your two daughters, and put Horus in the place of his
father." '

(This is a compromise. Seth is to be given two Syrian
goddesses as wives—he already has Nephthys—presumably
together with lordship over Asia.)[46]

'When Neith's letter reached the Company they were sitting in the great hall known as "Horus, whose horns are in front of him" and the letter was put in Thoth's hands. He read it out before the Lord of All and the entire Company. Whereupon they cried out with one voice: "This goddess is right!"

But the Lord of All was still angry with Horus and said to him: "You are still weak in your limbs so this office is too much for you, O Stripling whose mouth is yet bad!"[47]

At this Onuris became very angry indeed, and so did the whole Company—the whole thirty of them. Baba[48] arose and shouted at Rê of the Horizon: "Your shrine is empty!"

Rê was so hurt by this retort that he lay down on his back and was very miserable.

Then the Company went outside and turned on Baba, saying: "Away! You have committed a serious offence!" And they all went back to their tents.

The Great God spent the day lying on his back in his house, alone, with very unhappy heart.'

(Rê is sulking. He cannot solve the problem, his sympathies are with the unpopular party and now he has been publicly insulted by an inferior deity. Hathor cheers him up.)

'After a while Hathor—lady of the Southern Sycamore[49] —came and entered in before her father, the Lord of All. She bared her private parts before him, so that he was forced to laugh thereat. He arose and went and sat down once more with the Company, saying to Horus: "Have your say!"' '

(Rê throws the debate open.)

'Then Seth, the strong one, the son of Nut, said: "As for me, I am Seth, the strongest of the Divine Company. Every day I slay the enemy of Rê when I stand at the helm of the Barque of Millions of Years, which no other god dare do. I am therefore worthy to receive the office of Osiris."

Then they said: "Seth, the son of Nut, is right."

But Onuris and Thoth raised their voices, calling: "Should one give the office to the mother's brother, while the direct son of Osiris' body is at hand?" '

(This is the crux of the matter. The Great Quarrel is a clash between two systems of inheritance.)

'Then the Ram of Mendes cried out: "On the contrary, should the office be given to a mere lad while Seth, his elder relative, is at hand?" '

(This reveals the weakness of the patrilineal system. In an uncertainly ruled society the ruler must be of age to exercise his authority, no matter how acceptable his title may be.)

'Then the Company turned loudly against Horus, saying: "Those words which you have to say are not worth listening to!"

But Horus, son of Isis, declared: "It is not fair that I should be put down before the Company and cheated of my father's office!"

Then Isis grew angry with the Company. She swore an oath before them, saying: "As true as my mother Neith lives, as true as Ptah-tanen lives . . . these words shall be laid before Atum, the prince in Heliopolis, and Khopri in his barque."[50]

But the Company said to her: "Be calm! He who is in the right shall have his due and all shall be done as you say."

Whereupon Seth's wrath broke out against the Company when he heard what they said to Isis . . . and he said: "I will take my spear, four thousand five hundred cubits long, and kill one of you with it every day!"

And Seth swore an oath to the Lord of All, saying: "I will have nothing to do with the Court as long as Isis is a member of it!"

Then Rê of the Horizon spoke to them: "Go hence to Middle Island[51] and there decide between them. [And on the way] tell Anty, the ferryman: 'Do not transport anyone who looks like Isis.' "

And the Company crossed over to the Middle Island and there sat down to eat. Then Isis came and accosted Anty as he sat by his boat. She had transformed herself into an old woman walking with bent back. There was a little gold ring on her hand. She addressed him: "I have come to you to ferry me over to Middle Island. I am taking a jar of barley to the little boy who is tending the cattle on Middle Island. He has been there five days and will be getting hungry."

He answered her: "I have been told to ferry no woman across."

She replied: "But was it not about Isis that you were warned?"

He (*i.e.* Anty) said: "What will you give me if I ferry you over to Middle Island?"

Isis replied to him: "I will give you this barley bread."

He said: "What have I to do with your bread! Should I take you across to Middle Island when I have been told to ferry no woman across—just for your bread?"

She said to him: "I will give you the golden ring in my hand."

Then he said: "Give me the golden ring."

She gave it to him and he took her across to Middle Island. Then, as she was walking about underneath the trees, she looked out and saw the Company as they were sitting dining with the Lord of All in his pavilion. Seth looked up and saw her afar off. Now she had cast a spell with her powerful magic and had transformed herself into a maiden of lovely form, one whose like was not to be found in the whole land—and he fell wildly in love with her.

Then Seth arose from where he was sitting eating with the rest of the Company and went across to meet her—for no one else had noticed her. He hid behind a bush[52] and called out to her: "I would like to tarry here with you, Fair Child!"

She said to him: "Ah, my great lord! I am one who was married to a shepherd and I bore him a son, but my husband died and the boy had to look after his father's cattle. Then a stranger came and hid in my byre. He spoke in this manner to my son: 'I will beat you, I will take away your father's cattle and I will chase you away.' That is how he spoke to him. It is now my wish to persuade you to help my son."

And Seth said: "Indeed, should one give cattle to strangers while a man's son (heir) is at hand?"

[Immediately] Isis transformed herself into a kite. She flew up and perched on the top of a tree and called down to Seth: "Bewail yourself! Your own mouth has said it! Your own judgment has judged you. Do you wish for anything more?"[53]

So he arose and wept. He returned to Rê of the Horizon, weeping all the while. Rê said: "What is wrong with you this time?"

Seth replied: "That wretched woman (Isis) met me again and played me a scurvy trick. She had transformed herself into a beautiful maiden. . . .'"

(And Seth recounts the whole tale word for word.)

'Rê asked him: "What did you reply to her?"

Seth said: "I told her—should one give cattle to strangers while a man's son is at hand? Rather one should throw him out and put the son in his father's place. That is what I told her."

Then Rê of the Horizon declared: "But see! You

have judged yourself. Do you wish for anything more?"

Then Anty the ferryman was brought before the Company and they cut off the lower part of his legs. And so Anty has forsworn the use of gold until the present day. . . .[54]

The Company then crossed over to the western bank of the river and sat down upon the mountain. When evening came Rê . . . sent them a message: "What are you doing sitting there? You will make the Two Fellows spend their whole lives before the Court. When my letter reaches you, you are to put the White Crown on the head of Horus, the son of Isis, and install him on the throne of his father Osiris."

At this Seth became enraged, so that the Company said to him: "Why are you so angry? Should it not be done according to what Rê of the Horizon has said?"

Then, when the White Crown was put on the head of Horus, the son of Isis, Seth gave out a great shout of fury before the Company, saying: "Should one give the office to my younger brother[55] while I, the elder brother, am at hand?"

He swore an oath and said: "One should tear the White Crown from Horus the son of Isis and throw him into the water, so that I can fight him there for the princely office."

And Rê agreed with him, so Seth spoke to Horus: "Come! Let us assume the forms of hippopotamuses and dive into the water in the middle of the lake (or sea). Whichever of us emerges before three months are up, he shall lose the office."

So they both submerged. But Isis sat down and wept, saying: "Surely Seth will kill my son Horus!" And she fetched a length of rope which she made into a cable. Then she took an ingot of metal and beat it into a harpoon-head. She tied the cable to it and threw it into the water where Seth and Horus had submerged. Then the bronze[56] pierced the sacred body of her son Horus. Then Horus cried out loud: "Help, Mother Isis, my mother! Order your weapon to free itself from me!"

Then she called loudly: "Free him! See, that is my son Horus!" and the weapon freed itself straightway. She cast it again into the water and it pierced the body (?) of Seth, who called out: "What have I done to you, O Isis my sister? Order your harpoon to release me. I am your brother, I come from the same mother as you, Isis! Do you love a stranger more than your own brother?"

Her heart was deeply touched . . . and she said: "Release him. See! It is my brother . . . whom you have bitten."

And the harpoon-head released him.

Then Horus became very angry against his mother Isis. He emerged [from the water] and his face was fierce as that of a leopard. His knife of sixteen bars weight was in his hand. He cut off the head of his mother Isis, took it up in his arms and climbed up into the mountains. . . .

Then Rê of the Horizon called out loud to the Company: "Let us hurry to give him severe punishment!"

The Company then climbed the mountains, looking for Horus, son of Isis. But he spent the night under a *shen-usha* tree out in the oasis country. There Seth found him. He threw him on his back on the ground and tore his two eyes from their sockets and buried them on the mountain-side. And there the two eyeballs became two flower buds which grew into lotus flowers which light up the earth.[57]

Meanwhile Seth went and spoke deceitfully to Rê of the Horizon: "I cannot find Horus," he said, although he had indeed found him.

Then Hathor, the Lady of the Southern Sycamore, went and found Horus lying weeping on the mountain-side. She took a gazelle, milked it, and addressed Horus. "Open your eyes that I may rub in these drops of milk." She did

this in the right and in the left eye. "Open your eyes," she
said to him. He did so. She looked upon him and found
that all was well again.

Then she went to speak to Rê of the Horizon, saying:
"Horus is found! Seth had brought him to a sorry state in
[the loss of] his eye, but I have restored him. Behold! there
he comes!" '

(There follows a series of events which violate every canon of
modern man. They are obscene, brutal and inconsequential.
Nothing in the tale is so alien to us; it shows that the Egyptians
lived much closer to the dark Powers of the unconscious than
we realize. A truce seems to be called and the two contestants
go off and rest together. In the night Seth violates Horus.
Apparently the latter is an innocent still, for he runs to his
mother with Seth's seed in his hand. Isis cuts off her son's con-
taminated hand and throws it into the water. In revenge, Isis
obtains some of her son's semen and sprinkles it on a lettuce in
Seth's garden. We are told that Seth eats nothing but lettuces.
Seth eats the plant and becomes pregnant with the seed of
Horus. Then the two go before the Court and Seth claims that
Horus is unworthy of the royal office because he allowed Seth
to treat him homosexually.)

'The Company called out loud and spat in the face of
Horus, but Horus laughed at them. He swore an oath and
said: "It is all false what Seth says. Let the seed of Seth be
called and we shall see from where it answers. And then
let my seed be called and we shall see from where it
answers."

Then Thoth, the Master of Divine Words, the Scribe
of the Truth of the Company, put his hand on Horus' arm
and called: "Come forth, Seed of Seth!" and it answered
from the water in the ditch. Then Thoth laid his hand on
Seth's arm and said: "Come forth, Seed of Horus!" and
the seed said: "Where shall I come forth?"

Then Thoth said to it: "Come out of his ear!"

But it answered: "How should I come out of his ear, seeing that I am a divine liquid?"

Thoth then said: "Come out of his shoulder, then!"

And there emerged a golden disk on Seth's head. He became very angry at this and extended his arm to take it away. But Thoth snatched it from him and put it on his own head as a decoration.

Then the Company called out: "Horus is right, Seth is wrong."

But Seth swore a great oath and said: "Let not the office be given him until he has been sent away with me that we may build a pair of boats of 'stone',[58] and let us have a race, the two of us. Whichever beats his opponent, let him be given the kingly title."

Then Horus built himself a boat of cedar and caulked it with gypsum and launched it into the water at evening, without anyone at all seeing him. Then, when Seth saw Horus' boat, he thought it was made of stone, so he went off to the mountains, cut off a peak and built himself a stone ship, one hundred and thirty-eight cubits long.[59]

They got into their boats before the Company, but Seth's boat [immediately] sank, so he changed himself into a hippopotamus and assailed the boat of Horus. At this he seized his harpoon and was about to cast it into the sacred body of Seth when the Company said to him: "Do not transfix him with it!"

Horus took his equipment, put it aboard his boat and sailed north to Sais to say to Neith, the oldest goddess, the Mother of the gods: "Let a final decision be made between Seth and me. We have been eighty years before the Court but no one can pass final judgment on us. He has not been judged in the right against me, but a thousand times, right up to now, have I been right over him—all the time—but he pays no attention to anything the Company says.'"

(Horus enumerates the various 'halls' where the Company has sat when they declared him in the right. Neith's reply has been lost, for the next scene shows Thoth suggesting that a letter be sent to Osiris.)

'Now after some days the letter reached the King, the Son of Rê, Great of Flood, Master of Food. When the letter was read out to him he gave a loud cry and sent an answer back double quick to the place where the Lord of All was sitting with the Company, saying: "Why should my son be thus ill-treated? Was it not I who made you strong, for I was the one who created barley and spelt to nourish the gods, and cattle after the gods. No other god or goddess ever did anything like it."

And the letter of Osiris reached the place where Rê of the Horizon was, sitting with the Company in the "White Field" in Xois. When the letter was read out to him and the Company, Rê of the Horizon said: "Be quick and answer Osiris' letter, writing to him in reply—'If you had never existed, if you had never been born, barley and spelt would have existed nevertheless.'"

The letter of the Lord of All was taken down to Osiris and read out to him. Then he sent again to Rê of the Horizon, saying: "All that you did was very, very fine, O Creator of the Company of Gods! Indeed! when the divine justice was let down into the Underworld. Look again at your own condition. The land in which I reside is full of grim-looking messengers who fear neither god nor goddess. If I let them out they will fetch me the heart of anyone who does wrong, and they are here with me. What does it mean, that I am here in the west (Under-world) while you are all in the upper world.[60] Who among you is stronger than I? You have imagined false-hood as a great deed. When Ptah . . . created the sky, did he not speak to the stars in it, saying: 'You shall go to rest every night in the west where King Osiris is.' And to me he said: 'After the gods shall all men and all mankind[61] go to rest where you are.'"'

(But this does not decide the case. Seth calls for another trial by ordeal or combat. Isis is told to bring Seth, bound in hand⁄ cuffs, before the court . . .)

'. . . as though he were a criminal, and Atum said to him: "Why will you not allow the case to be decided between you [legally] instead of trying to take the office from Horus by force?" '

(Once more we are back at the central theme—the triumph of legality over brute force.)

'Then Seth said unto him: "Not at all! My good Lord! Let Horus, son of Isis, be called and let him be given the office of his father Osiris."

So Horus was fetched and the White Crown was put on his head and he was placed on the seat of his father Osiris. And he was addressed: "You are now the fair King of Egypt. You are the goodly master of every land for all eternity!"

But Ptah asked: "What shall be done with Seth? . . ."

Rê of the Horizon said: "Let Seth the son of Nut be given to me so that he can abide with me as a son. He shall raise his voice in the sky and men will be afraid of him."'

(Seth is recompensed for losing the contest by being made the God of Storm.)

This is, effectively, the end of the story, although there is a stanza acclaiming Horus, which adds nothing to the sense.

4

SETH AND APOPIS

Seth is a storm god. Most of his activities are connected with his implacable hostility towards Osiris and Horus, the spirits of fertility and order. He was, however, an immortal and

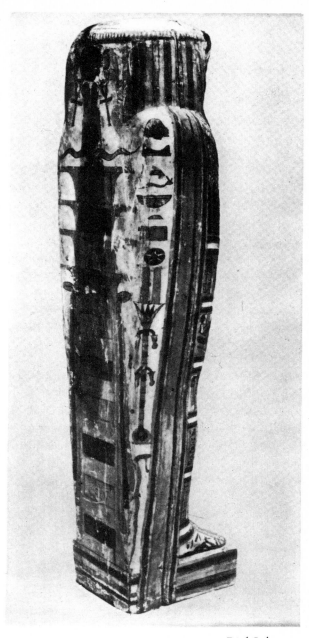

13 SYMBOLS OF UPWARD MOVEMENT: *Djed* Column,
Primeval Lotus and Rearing Serpent
(Birmingham Museum). See p. 238

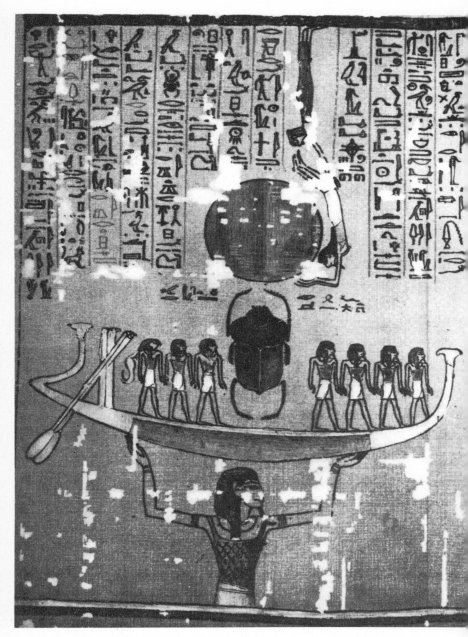

14 SUNRISE—The god of the Primeval Waters lifts up the boat of the sun
(British Museum). See p. 249

so a place had to be found for him in the cosmic scheme. The Pyramid Texts hint that after the final judgment in favour of Horus, Seth's life was saved on condition that he became the breeze upon the water which bore the boat of Osiris. Hence, as the hymns say, 'Seth has escaped his day of death'.[62] In the *Contendings of Horus and Seth*, a composition of the New Kingdom which seems to reflect the theology of the Herakleopo⁄litan Age,[63] the long and bitter contention between the two gods is decided by giving Horus the world of mankind while Seth is put at the bow of the sun's boat. He has to ward off the attacks of Apopis, the serpent dragon of darkness, who threatens to overwhelm the divine barque at sunrise and sunset.

Chapter 39 of the Book of the Dead has preserved part of a scenario about the defeat of Apopis at dawn. Seth plays the chief role, although at the end all the other gods join in, with the exception of Geb, the earth, who is still half asleep and is peevish at being roused. Some acting directions have been retained in the text, showing conclusively that this is a genuine dramatic piece and not a tale told in direct speech.[64] The atmosphere reminds one of Spell 312 in the Coffin Texts which, as was shown on pp. 150 ff., is also dramatic. There is the same light⁄hearted attitude towards the gods, while the humour is even broader. The introduction has been lost, for the text begins with someone, obviously Seth, uttering imprecations against Apopis:

> ' "Back, Villain! Plunge into the depths of the Abyss, into the place where your father ordained you should be destroyed!
>
> Keep far away from this station of Rê, at whom you should tremble!" '

(Rê, the sun, calls from within the horizon):

> ' "I am Rê, at whom all should tremble!" '

(Seth resumes):

> ' "Back, Fiend! from the onslaught of his light!

If you speak, your face will be overturned by the gods. Your heart will be seized by the lynx, your reins will be bound by the scorpion, you will be punished by Mayet, she will bring you to grief." '

(Those who are upon the roads say):[65]

' "Fall back, Apopis! Enemy of Rê! Leave the edge of the sky at this voice of roaring thunder!" '[66]
The gates of the horizon open for Rê to appear.
He (Apopis) is helpless beneath the blows [of the gods].[67]

(Apopis cries out that he will conform to the divine will.)

' "I will perform your will, O Rê (*bis*), I will act properly! (*bis*) I will act peacefully, O Rê!" '

(Seth speaks again):

' "Bring your ropes, O Rê! that Apopis may fall to your snaring or be trapped by the gods of north, south, east and west in their traps. The Earth Dragon[68] has overthrown him, the spirits of the reddening sky have trapped him.
All is now well, O Rê! Proceed in peace!
And you, Apopis! Down! Away, Apopis, O Enemy of Rê!" '

(During the fight with Horus, Seth loses his tecticles—as related on p. 109. Apopis now taunts Seth with this.)

' "But what you felt is worse than the sting of the scorpion. What she (Mayet)[69] did to you was so dire that you will suffer from its effect for ever! You will never go a⁄courting, you will never make love!" '

(Stung by this retort, Seth determines to destroy Apopis rather than just keeping him in bondage. He is not quite brave enough, however, to face up to him and kill him face to face, but craftily orders him to turn his face away.)

' "Apopis, O Enemy of Rê! Turn your face away! Rê hates the very sight of you." The head is then cut off, hacked in pieces and thrown away on either side of the roads.'

(Seth continues.)

' "Your head is crushed, O Groundling![70] Your bones are broken up and your flesh cut in pieces. He (Rê) has consigned you to the Earth Dragon, O Apopis! Enemy of Rê!" '

(Having performed his task, Seth turns derisively to the Sun God):

' "[From now on] your crew are accountable for your welfare. Your safety is assured, so are your chattels. Come on, come on out here! Bring hither your Eye, O Fair Servant![71]

But let no evil appear in your mouth against me. Do not turn against me, for I am Seth who sets up the storms and thunder within the horizon of the sky, like a fury!" '

(This is deliberately insulting. The paraphernalia of the solar barque are the most sacred things in Egyptian religion. Seth calls them 'chattels'—'*henu*'.[72] This includes the 'Eye'—the sun itself—which the god can now bring out like an attendant bringing gifts to a master, now that the enemy has been over-thrown. Finally Seth utters dark threats to use his storms against the Sun God's boat if he is reviled.)

'Atum says: "Attention, O soldiers of Rê! Chase me this villain from the company!" '

(Geb, who, as will presently appear, does not want a rumpus, gives somewhat contrary instructions.)

'Geb says: "Sit down on your seats on the deck of the Boat of the Rising Sun. Start off, but keep [ready] the weapons which have been put in your hands."

Hathor says: "Take up your swords!"

Nut says: "Come, let us chase away this windbag!" '

(Seth is the god of winds and his threats are vain. He is, therefore, a windbag in both senses. One must imagine that Seth is
driven away into the wings at this point.)

 'Then *He* comes in his shrine; that He who set himself
in motion, all alone, the unsurpassable Universal Master.
And some of the gods, gathering in groups around the
turquoise pools, call:

(This piece of exquisite description needs emphasis. The sky
has now changed from rosy dawn to the clear blue of full day.)

 "Come, Mighty One! Let us adore our deliverer, the
Mighty One in his shrine!"
 The Divine Company gathers around him, hailing and
extolling him.
 "Herald him with me!" says Nut to that god who is still
taking his ease.[73]
 Some of the gods say: "He has arisen! He has found the
way! He has brought the [hostile] gods to subjection. He
has aroused the whole sky!"
 Geb rises, bewildered, and says: "The Company of the
Gods is acting as if the mouth of Hathor had drooped.
Damn the triumph of Rê over Apopis!" '

 This little satire explains why Seth, who repulses the attack
of the monster of darkness from the prow of the solar barque,
is not usually depicted among the crew. He disgraced himself
by overweening pride and was driven away. The Sun God has
two enemies, darkness in the person of Apopis and storms in
the person of Seth. Only when both have been put out of the
way can he set off across the blue sky. The other gods are now
fully awake but the Earth Spirit is only roused with difficulty.
He would rather remain asleep, and in his dazed state is bewildered by the dawn chorus of the exultant celestials. He
hints that night is the time for love-making and that he would
rather stay under the smiling face of the love goddess.

5

THE BIRTH AND FLIGHT OF HORUS[74]

Here and there one comes upon traces of an old myth that the sun had burst out as a bird from the great egg which the Primeval Being, a goose, had laid in the waters of the Abyss. One of the Coffin Texts has combined this motif with the tale of the birth of Horus. The text, as it has been preserved, was compiled from fragments of a dramatic sketch which must have been a singularly powerful work. It begins with the dark days immediately after the death of Osiris, when Seth and his henchmen are tyrannizing over the world. Atum, the Master of Destiny, has retired to his boat in the sky and seems to want to hand over control of the lower world to someone else. Isis dreams that she will give birth to a saviour who will redeem his patrimony. She has to justify her claims and then asks Atum to allow her son, when born, to have a place in the sun boat. But, as soon as he is born, Horus assumes control of his own destiny. He appears as a falcon and soars up into the sky, beyond the flight of the original bird-soul,[75] beyond the stars (the 'gods of Nut') and all the divinities of olden time whose souls inhabit the constellations. He seems to fly out into the vast regions beyond the limits of the divinely created universe and alights upon the ramparts of the eastern horizon, the boundary of the world. In so doing he brings back light and the assurance of a new day, thus subduing Seth, who personifies the terrors of darkness and death. The atmosphere is almost messianic. One feels a transition from the anxiety of the opening, through the uncertain deliberations of Isis' pleading, to the tremendous call of triumph at the close. The opening section moves within the Osiris myth, but this disappears when Isis suddenly realizes that she will give birth, not to a child, but to a falcon. The Osirian world is transcended as the bird flies up.

'A storm is raging, the gods are in terror,
  as Isis awakes, [realizing that she is] pregnant with the seed of her brother Osiris,

She rises, a woman in a hurry, her heart rejoicing
in the [effect of] the seed of her brother Osiris.'

(She dreams prophetically that the child quickening in her
womb will grow up to restore the rightful order of the world.)

'She says: "Attention, O Gods! I am Isis, sister of Osiris,
who wept for the Father of the gods, for Osiris,
whose [fate] began the time of carnage in the Two Lands.
The seed of that god is in my body.
I have formed the body of a god as an egg,[76] who is the
son of him who formerly presided over the Companies
of the gods,
[and it shall be that when born] he shall rule over this
land,[77]
inherit the patrimony of Geb, speak up for his father and
slay Seth, his father's enemy.
Come, O Gods! Protect him while he is in my womb,
realize in your hearts that he will be your master, this god
who is as yet but an embryo, so still and unformed.
[He will one day be] Lord of the gods, although they
themselves are so mighty, so fair and bedecked with
blue feathers." '

(At this point Atum, the High God and Master of Destiny,
intervenes):

' "Amen!" says Atum. "Consider, O Woman! How
do you know that he whom you have formed in embryo
will be the god who will inherit the presidency of the Twin
Companies?"
(Isis replies): "Am I not Isis, fairer and nobler than any
of those lesser gods? Furthermore, the god who is in my
womb is the seed of Osiris."
Atum says: "Since you have conceived in secret, O
Damsel, you must surely be one who has conceived and
will give birth through the intervention of the gods! Truly
it must be the seed of Osiris!

Let not that god who slew his father draw near to break
the egg inside which the young one is growing, and may
the Great Magician respect him!"[78]

"Obey this command, O Gods!" says Isis. "Atum,
master of the Castle of Primeval Forms, has spoken. For
me he has decreed that my son shall be protected while he
is within my body. He has stationed a guard all around
him while he is in my womb.

Keep him safe, for he (Atum) knows he is heir to
Osiris." '

(Here begins a new scene. The birth is about to take place. Isis
comes forward to Atum, who must be imagined surrounded
by his divine courtiers.)

' "Make way!" (She turns to Atum.) "It is a falcon that
is within my body!"

Atum speaks (addressing the Horus falcon still unborn):
"Come! Appear upon the world!" '

(Horus is born at this point, for Atum says):

' "I salute you! May the followers of your father Osiris
serve and worship you. I will create your real name when
you have reached the horizon, when you have passed over
the ramparts of 'Him whose name is hidden.' " '

(Isis says):

' "That strength which was within my flesh has now left
me,[79] the vigour which was within my flesh will reach
(the horizon?), that vigour which is so keen will be
transporting the sunlight.

May he now take his proper place and sit among the
gods, among the crew of Prince Rê. (Turning to Horus)
Ah! O my son Horus, sit in this land of your father
Osiris in this your name of 'Falcon upon the ramparts of
Him whose name is hidden.'

I request that another seat be made amid the followers of

Rê as he sits in his boat, at the prow of that Primeval Boat that is for all time."

Isis approaches the "Retreated One".[80] Horus is brought forward. Isis asks that he be admitted as a "distant one",[81] among the guides of eternity.'

(Meanwhile Horus has flown up of his own accord. Someone calls out):

' "Look at Horus, O Gods!" '

(Horus calls):

' "I am Horus, the great Falcon upon the ramparts of the house of him of the hidden name. My flight has reached the horizon. I have passed by the gods of Nut. I have gone further than the gods of old. Even the most ancient bird could not equal my very first flight. I have removed my place beyond the powers of Seth, the foe of my father Osiris. No other god could do what I have done. I have brought the ways of eternity to the twilight of the morning. I am unique in my flight. My wrath will be turned against the enemy of my father Osiris and I will put him beneath my feet in my name of 'Red Cloak'." '

(The gods must have protested at this point, for Horus brushes their objections aside with):

' "The flaming breath of your mouth will not harm me. What you can say against me will not damage me at all, for I am Horus whose domain stretches far beyond gods or men and also I am Horus son of Isis." '

There were two gods called Horus; the first was the original falcon who flew up at the beginning of time—the most ancient bird—and the other was the son of Isis and heir to Osiris. They are compounded in this piece. Instead of being born in the Delta swamps and growing up in secret, Horus is offered a place in the sun's boat, but he transcends both his earthly fate and that as a subordinate to Rê. He flies up and across the night sky of the Underworld to land on the edge of the world, bringing with him the twilight that comes just before full day. This links up with the old belief that Horus was the leader of the decanal stars which circled around the sky in the path of the sun. The appearance of Horus in the sky just before dawn is the mark of the new year. Out of the fear and confusion of Seth's reign, the time of troubles, has come the herald of the new dispensation. The world's great age begins anew.

CHAPTER VII

Mythological Symbols

THE NUMBER of basic symbols in Ancient Egypt was fairly small. Some of them can be paralleled in other cultures—the Tree of Life, for instance, or the Phoenix Bird of annunciation. This is to be expected on psychological grounds. There are others, however, which were peculiar to the Egyptians alone, such as the Divine Eye or the *Djed* Column. But this is to look at the matter from the outside. It is not the symbol itself, but the thoughts that gather around it, which make it significant. Symbols are, by their very nature, things which act as focal points for emotions or imaginative speculations. They belong to the world of myth, even if they have mundane origins. They are not distinct entities, for they readily merge into one another, making patterns of bewildering complexity. Nevertheless, the combinations of symbols are not haphazard; it is just that the rules governing their use are not understood.

I

THE EYE

The Eye is the commonest symbol in Egyptian thought and the strangest to us. Crawford has recently shown that the fertility goddess of the Neolithic world, both in Asia and Europe, was represented by an eye—or eyes.[1] Egypt almost certainly came within the orbit of this primitive eye cult, but the Egyptian sacred 'Eye' was so complex and individual that it is as yet impossible to relate it with ideas in other parts of the world.[2] One fact does stand out—the Egyptian Eye was always a symbol for the Great Goddess, whatever name she may have in any particular instance.

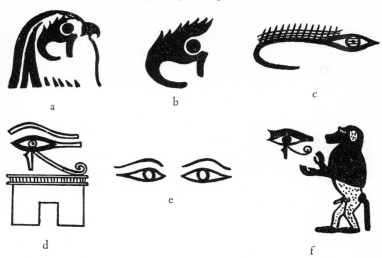

Fig. 29. Falcon and human forms of the Eye: (a) Falcon Head; (b) Falcon Eye; (c) The hairs around the Eye; (d) Wedjat on the gate; (e) The 'Two Eyes'; (f) Baboon (=Thoth) remakes the Moon Eye

At the beginning of history the High God of the Egyptians was a falcon which was shown either as perching on a building or emerging from the Primeval Waters.[3] Its right eye was the sun and its left one the moon, so this bird cannot be taken in an absolutely literal sense. Certainly, whenever the Egyptians pictured the eye of their god they depicted a falcon's eye, not a human one;[4] but at the back of their minds there was another and almost forgotten deity, a man or just a face known as 'He who commands both eyes' or, in his alternative form, 'the Sightless One'. In either case the eyes were regarded as separate things. The phases of the moon and the cycle of the sun's power were symbolized in rites and myths connected with healing or uncovering an eye. The general word for eye in Egyptian is '*iret*'—a feminine noun. When its parts were put together in the calendrical rites the name was '*Wedjat*'—'the Hale One'— again feminine.

The widespread popularity of the eye symbol must be based
on common experience. Most peoples have been sensitive to the
power and vitality which seem to reside in the eye. The
Egyptians felt this so much that they exalted their feelings to
cosmic dimensions. When Shakespeare conjured up the image
of the dawning sun in the words:

> 'Full many a glorious morning have I seen
> Flatter the mountain tops with sovereign eye'[5]

he was using an Egyptian symbol. But in a semi-tropical
country the searing heat of the sun makes the 'sovereign' aspect
of the eye seem terrible rather than majestic. So the eye became
the sign of destructive force, blinding light, fire and the
emotions which can be described in such terms, namely, anger
and incontrollable fury. Because one symbol for the terrible can
flow into another if the words for them belong to the same
gender, the eye merged with the image of an enraged, rearing
cobra with its poisonous bite. The cobra was the protector of
the crown and is shown attached to the front, just above the
king's forehead. Hence we get the fundamental symbol
equation of Egyptian religion:

$$\text{Eye} \equiv \text{Flame} \equiv \text{Destructive Goddess} \equiv \text{Cobra} \equiv \text{Crown.}$$

This holds true from the Pyramid Texts to the end of the
civilization.

The Eye of the High God is the Great Goddess of the
universe in her terrible aspect. Originally it had been sent out
into the Primeval Waters by God on an errand to bring back
Shu and Tefnut to their father. Thus the Eye is the daughter
of the High God. When it returned, it found that it had been

$$= \triangleleft + O + \frown + \triangleright + \searrow + \P$$

$$= \tfrac{1}{2} + \tfrac{1}{4} + \tfrac{1}{8} + \tfrac{1}{16} + \tfrac{1}{32} + \tfrac{1}{64}$$

Fig. 30. The parts of the Eye

Fig. 31. Vicissitudes of the Eye; (*left*) Completely restored and rising in the sky (*right*) Flying through the Underworld

supplanted in the Great One's face by another—a surrogate eye—which we can interpret as the sun or moon. This was the primary cause for the wrath of the Eye and the great turning-point in the development of the universe, for the Eye can never be fully or permanently appeased. The High God, using the formula given above, turned it into a rearing cobra, which he bound around his forehead to ward off his enemies. This is why, on the terrestrial plane, the eye denotes the kingship of the pharaohs in terms of sheer power, while cosmically it is the 'sovereign eye' and burning heat of the sun. Spell 316 of the Coffin Texts assumes that the Eye has just been put in its present place by the High God at the time when he emerged from the waters.

'I am the all-seeing Eye of Horus,
    whose appearance strikes terror,
    Lady of Slaughter, Mighty One of Frightfulness.'

This is a reference to the activity of the Eye in the chastisement of mankind as told on pp. 181 to 185:

'who takes the form of blazing light,
    whose appearance Rê ordained, whose birth Atum
        established when Rê said to her:
    "Great will be your power and mighty your majesty
    over the bodies of your enemies.

> They will fall howling on their faces,
> all mankind will cringe beneath you and your might,
> they will respect you when they behold you in that
>   vigorous form
> which the Master of the Primeval Gods gave you."
> Thus did he speak to me. Yes, the Master of the Primeval
>   Gods, even to me.
> . . . I am—yes—I am a burning flame, but also
> the boon companion, the darling of Rê. . . .
> I have seized the gods, there is no opposition to me—
> as the Master of the Primeval Place[6] declared.
> "And when did this god come?"
> "It was before the shadows were separated
> or the outlines of the gods were visible." '

This means that the Eye, like all the essential characters of the universe, was given its role by God while he was still in the dark and in his primordial condition. Having equipped him-self with the Eye—now a rearing cobra—God can assume his solar form. He rises with her from the Isle of Fire, the mystic land of origin beyond the horizon, and all the denizens of the ocean and the night sky—the gods of former ages—are blinded by the light.[7]

> 'Look with your faces, O God of eld! O Primeval
>   Ancestors!
> upon this spirit who comes today, taking the form of a
>   beam of light, coming from the Isle of Fire.
> "I have to raise my hand to shade myself, for fear of the fire
>   of her mouth," says one of the elder gods.
> "Behold it (the Eye) will be stronger than all the gods,
> It has mastered the dwellers at the ends of the Earth,[8]
> it is sovereign over every god." '

The Eye itself then speaks again:

> ' "Behold me, O Men and Gods! that is how I became the
>   burning Eye of Horus . . .

the Flood, the parent of the gods, it was that clothed me, creating therefrom the eye for his body." '

This is an allusion to the origin of the Eye in the Primordial Ocean which is now called 'the Father of the gods'. The 'clothing' is a picturesque expression for giving characteristics, but for an Egyptian it would also have had an allusion to the 'Clothing'—one of the ceremonies in the temples.

> 'No one will come who can withstand me, except Atum, for it was he who originally moved and put me before him so that I could wield power and throw out my heat.
> It was as Atum said:
> "May the one Eye be more powerful than all the [other] gods."
> And I said to my father Atum:
> "By your utterance has strength come into me."
> And that is how I became the mightiest of the gods.
> It was [really] I who overthrew Seth and forced his confederates to submit. . . .
> It was I who stood upon his coils.'

The theme is generalized. The Eye is the striking-power of the High God in all his manifestations. Strictly it was Horus the son of Isis who overthrew Seth, but Horus is only a symbol of the divine spirit as victor, so his aggressiveness really comes from the High God, whose aggressiveness is in the Eye. Seth is the eternal enemy, so he, too, is not only a figure in the Osiris myth but a form of the essential hostile power, whose first form was the serpent dragon of the waters who was overthrown by the High God in primeval times. The authors of the Coffin Texts had realized that their myths were not always about different things but conformed to patterns and were symbols of certain underlying themes. They had come to see that the gods were the expression of psychic needs. The hero and the enemy remain essentially the same whatever their names.

Towards the end of the utterance the Eye is called:

'Most ancient female of the world
and conductress of the One Lord'

—a typical piece of Egyptian stylistic parallelism where the first
line alludes to a myth about something that happened at the
beginning of things and the other refers to the organization of
the present world.

But there were two sacred eyes. So far we have been considering that of the High God—the '*iret*'. There was also the
eye of Horus, son of Isis, which Seth tore out during the great
quarrel. If the Eye of the High God was the sun, the other was
the moon. A well-known text explains:[9]

A 'I filled the eye when it was deficient
    on the day when the Two Fellows fought.
       (Explanatory gloss.) That was Horus and Seth, when
       Seth laid hold of it and tore it out of Horus' head
       and when Horus seized Seth's testicles. But it was
       Thoth who did that thing (*i.e.* filled the eye).
B I raised the hair from the *Wedjat* Eye at the time of storm.
       (Explanatory gloss.) What is that? It is the right eye of
       Rê when it became enraged against him after he had
       sent it forth. But it was Thoth who raised the hair
       from it.
C I have seen the sun born from yesterday on the shanks of
    Methuer.[10]
       (Explanatory gloss.) What is that? It is an image of the
       morning sun as it is born every day. As for Methuer,
       that is the *Wedjat* Eye.

Section *A* deals with the left eye, which is both the Eye of
Horus and the moon. Seth flung it away beyond the edge of
the world, and Thoth, the moon's genius and guardian, went
and found it lying in the outer darkness. Apparently he discovered it lying in pieces. He brought them back and
assembled them again to form the full moon. This is the
strangest part of all. The *Wedjat* sign can be taken to pieces as
shown in Fig. 30 (p. 220).

15 SUNRISE—alternative version—with adoring baboons and sky cow
(British Museum). See p. 251

16 NIGHT AND MORNING SUN (British Museum). See p. 252

It will be seen that if each part of the *Wedjat* represents a fraction of the descending geometric series $\frac{1}{2}$, $\frac{1}{4}$, $\frac{1}{8}$, etc., put together, they make $\frac{63}{64}$, *i.e.* they approximate to 1. So Thoth can say:[11]

> 'I came seeking the Eye of Horus,
> that I might bring it back and count it.
> I found it [and now it is] complete, counted and sound,
> so that it can flame up to the sky
> and blow above and below. . . .'

When Seth flung the Eye away the night sky was plunged into darkness. This was the symbol of lunar invisibility—the new moon. Thoth's return with the parts means the time of waxing moon. Full moon is a sign that all is well, so Thoth is, in a way, the saviour of the world's order—Mayet.

> 'I am Thoth, who brings back Mayet,
> who makes the *Wedjat* Eye begin moving in the House of
> the Leonine One,'[12]

or

> 'I am he who returns the *Wedjat* Eye,
> I am he who abolished its dimness, when its brightness
> was damaged . . .
> I am the returner of the *Wedjat* Eye
> when it is saved from its misfortune . . .
> [so that all is now well] in the House of the Moon.'

Section *B* deals with the right eye, the original Eye of the Creator, a sort of original sun, which he sent out into the Primeval Abyss to find Shu and Tefnut. The comment is based on a pun between 'rage'—'*neshen*,' and 'hair'—'*shen*'. The rage of the Eye when it returned to the creator and found that it had been supplanted by another, the *neshen*, is identified with the hair which hides the eye. The latter is a symbol for the strands of cloud which float across the sun, hiding its light. Thus the storm that the Eye raised at the beginning of the world is the same as the dark clouds covering the sun. In both cases it is Thoth, the genius of cosmic order, who puts things right. This is esoteric theology with a vengeance! The Egyptians were quite aware that their creation myths were not to be believed in as historical events but as symbols of the way in which the universe was run.

Just how far even the priests of the Old Kingdom could go in wrapping a symbol around itself can be shown from a Pyramid Text, an apostrophe to the crown of Lower Egypt:

'Ah, Crown of Lower Egypt!
You have appeared from him (*i.e.* you have appeared on his head)
just as he appeared from you.'

(Addressing the king):

'The "Great Matter" has born you,
the great Cobra has born you . . .
for you are Horus who fought in defence of his Eye.'[13]

Crown and Cobra and Mother Goddess (the 'Great Matter') are one. We remember that the enraged Eye became the cobra which Rê wound around his head and that this is the first coronation. In the waters the Eye had come from the High God, so *he* was its progenitor. The Eye is also the Mother Goddess because all mankind have come from the tears of the Eye when it became enraged. So the king's mother—or primeval mother—is the Eye. But as the Eye is the cobra which decorates the crown and is part of it, we can see why the same goddess can adorn the king's brow and be his mother at the same time. This ought to be complication enough, but even then the prayer has one further symbolic equation. There may be two eyes, one in the Primeval Waters and the other in the Horus and Seth story; but they, too, are one. The king is Horus who fought for the crown—*i.e.* the Eye—and who first lost and then regained his actual eye during the contest with Seth.

Section *C* returns to the naturalistic idea—the eye of the blazing sun as it shines over the horizon at dawn. But the symbolists are again at work. The sun emerges from the sky beyond the world, the sky is a cow-form of the Mother Goddess who, as we have learnt, is also the Eye. So Methuer has to be explained as the Eye itself. One is tempted to think that priestly subtlety has overreached itself here. But what passed as profound spirituality for two millennia must somehow have been reasonable. The complex meshes of eye symbolism are woven all round the Egyptian Mother Goddess and she cannot be understood or compared with other goddesses of the same type until they are unravelled. The Eye is the key to the religion.

Egyptian literature of all periods abounds in allusions to the 'bringing back of it'—meaning the Eye. The meaning of this motif was elucidated by Junker.[14] It is founded on one of the most widespread of all saga motifs—the return of the conquering hero. In Egypt it took the form of a hunter who comes back to his people, bringing with him a wild but now subdued animal—lioness or hippopotamus. Onuris, 'he who brought back the Distant One', is the name of the essential hunting hero. His cult figure was a man wearing a long skirt, his feet poised well apart to enable him to aim a spear downwards at some monstrous foe. His worship was centralized in Thinis, a district which also included Abydos. There he had a mate called *Mehit*—a lioness whose name means 'she who has been filled'. In other contexts 'filling' always refers to the filling of the parts of the Eye as representing the moon. So it is likely that here, too, Eye, moon and hunting motif have been put together.

Junker pieced together a myth from scattered references in late inscriptions from Edfu and Dendera, but stray allusions make it certain that it was in fact very ancient. Rê, the High God, is still on earth, playing the part of an Egyptian king. For reasons unknown Rê's daughter Tefnut becomes estranged from her father and departs for Nubia. There, in the form of a savage lioness, she prowls around, a terror to men and animals. We get graphic descriptions of her ferocity—how she feeds on flesh, drinks blood and puffs fire from her eyes and nostrils. But exact details are unimportant; they are impressionist traits to build up the image of the savage goddess as the opposite of the gentleness and humanity of the civilized state. Rê regrets his daughter's departure, for she is his kin and he longs for her company. Perhaps he also wants to make use of her ferocity to defend him against his enemies. Shu and Thoth are therefore sent to the Nubian Desert to persuade Tefnut to return to Egypt. They disguise themselves as monkeys—an intrusive detail from another myth cycle. It is Thoth who first finds the wild lioness. He extols the amenities of Egypt, the land of civilization, as against the uncertainties of the desert. He tells Tefnut that all the game which she now has to hunt down in the desert wadis will be offered up to her upon the altars of Egypt, and that in the Nile valley there is security, jubilation, singing and dancing without end. Thoth's persuasions imply two of the basic assumptions of Egyptian theology: first, that the fauna that are presented dead upon the altars of the gods are supposedly trophies of the chase, even if they are, in fact, domestic animals;[15] second, that the absence of the goddess (the Eye) has plunged the country into gloom and sterility. The first of these points harks back to the hunter chieftain offering up his kill to some primitive deity; the second echoes the theme of the Mesopotamian cult of Tammuz and Ishtar, wherein the life of the land dies away when the god—and sometimes the goddess—departs from the city, the civilized area, and resides in the 'Edin', the Underworld or desert. Shu joins Thoth and, ultimately, Tefnut is persuaded to accompany the two gods back to her homeland. This introduces the most widely illustrated episode in the myth, when Tefnut returns accompanied by a Bacchic rout of Nubian musicians, baboons and comic figures.[16] She progresses in triumph from city to city; her advent is a signal for universal rejoicing, the 'festival of drunkenness'. Tefnut loses her ferocity as she proceeds

Fig. 32. Onuris, who rescued the Eye

northwards; she may even change into a comely maiden. This may, of course, be a way of describing the gradual softening of the sun's heat as one gets into higher latitudes, but it is really a victory for the powers of civilization over the untamed ferocity of the desert.

Tefnut has taken the place of the Eye in the other versions, but Thoth has kept his old place as the bringer-back of the Eye. The tale has been changed from moon into sun symbolism. The old hero who presumably fought a lioness and brought her back captive has been supplanted by Thoth and Shu who overcome their opponent with words, not heroic deeds. What does become clear is that the time of absence of the Goddess—whether the Eye or another—is the season of fear and lifelessness. A New Kingdom hymn speaks of the full moon as the time of dancing. Through all this one catches the fear of ancient man at the dark and his relief when the moon once more shines out in the night sky, or the calendrical rhythm of the dead season followed by the beginning of a new year, ushered in with carnival and holiday. Over all this presides the Eye.

2

THE WATERS OF ETERNITY

This symbol denotes the 'God of Millions of Years'. He is nude except for a girdle with three strips hanging down in front. This was the standard uniform of watermen during the Old Kingdom and so may refer to the god's watery nature, but as such a brief garment was no longer worn when the picture was painted, it is probably a sign of ages long ago—before the introduction of the loin-cloth. The body is green and covered with extended water signs, which can also be seen in the pool on the right of the picture. The god has distended pectoral muscles and a pot belly; he is old and fat. The long, curved beard denotes divinity—men wear short tufts under the chin. He holds a notched stick and wears another fixed in his head-band. A stick with one notch means 'year', but one with many notches means 'millions of years' or 'eternity'. The figure can therefore be read off as the god of the waters of eternity which last for ever and are older than any created thing.

The god is making passes with his left hand over an oval which contains the right eye of a falcon. There is a twofold meaning here. It is a reference to the legend of the Eye of the High God which was sent out into the waters before the beginning of the world. But this is the prototype of the nightly journey of the sun through the waters of the Underworld—which are part of the eternal Abyss.[17] The Eye is that of a falcon because the High God in his primeval form can be thought of as a monstrous falcon, whose eyes are the sun and moon. The spirit of the eternal waters is protecting the Eye on its dark and dangerous journey.

Plate 1 shows one of the standard illustrations to Chapter 17 of the Book of the Dead. The ancient commentators have provided several explanations. One calls the god 'The Seed of Millions'. As the Primeval Waters, this god contains the germ of the countless beings that are to come. The Egyptian idea of Primordial Ocean as the basic stuff of the universe could not be expressed more clearly.[18]

3

THE *KA*

Fig. 33. Forms of the *Ka* sign: (*left*) standard form; (*centre*) *Ka* on a standard; (*right*) the *Ka* encircles a royal name

What is an embrace? For us it is a gesture of love or protection but for the Egyptians it meant much more than that, both in religion and everyday life. They called it the act of *Ka* and represented it as two arms extended upwards from a schematic base which was supposed to show the breast muscles. The hands are extended as if the palms were raised in adoration, but this is in conformity with Egyptian rules of dealing with three-dimensional space, as can be seen from *Ka* figures in the round, where it is obvious that an embrace is meant.[19] To put one's arms around another meant, to the ancients, to impart one's vital essence. So the *Ka* is a symbol of the transmission of life power from gods to men. But it is not only the act, it is also the source of this power. Everyone is a receiver of divine power and everyone is an individual, so each has his own *Ka*.

'If a great man is presiding over the meal
  his humour will be according to his *Ka*. . . .

> But it may happen that, as evening draws on
> his *Ka* will stretch forth its arms
> and the great man will give [titbits] to anyone he can
> reach.'[20]

Here the *Ka* sign comes alive as a figure describing the giving of favours. The great man in this extract is really God dispensing good fortune to whom he will. So God has his *Ka*, too, the source of all the good fortune in the world. In fact, with the High God, self and *Ka* are one. This is why the *Ka* is often depicted on a carrying-frame, showing that it is above the weaknesses of the world and truly divine (see Fig. 33, centre).

The individual *Ka* is a kind of spiritual double which determines the good or fortunate aspects of one's fate. Hence the Egyptians said 'To your *Ka*!' where we would wish good health and prosperity. The *Ka*—or *Ka's*—are the dispositions which the good fairies bestowed on the new-born child, at least when these are favourable.

An embrace is protective. The pharaohs had several names, one of which was inscribed above the palace façade and surmounted by a massive falcon, the symbol of Horus, the patron of the kingship. The royal *Ka* puts its arms around the Horus name to protect it from harm. The Horus name is an epithet concerned with the king's vigour, such as 'Bull of Truth', 'Appearing as a God', or 'Victorious Bull'. The *Ka* therefore protects the martial or vigorous qualities of the king. On p. 43 the *Ka* idea has got into a creation myth: the High God put his arms around his progeny to shield them from the disintegrating powers of the Primeval Waters.

The *Ka* is also male generative power. Ptah-hotep, in speaking of parental care, exhorts a father to treat his son with every care:

> 'for your son belongs to the generation of your *Ka*'.[21]

The *Ka's* in general are the ancestors, and to beget a child is to forge a link with them. A father, then, is an agent of the *Ka* or, perhaps, the *Ka* acts through the father. Male potency is

Fig. 34. A child dandled by its own *Ka* (good luck)

symbolized by the bull, the name of which in Egyptian was written with the same signs as *Ka*; so the two words must have sounded very like one another. The Egyptians were prone to relate ideas, however dissimilar, if the words for them sounded alike. In other words they were inveterate punsters, so the concepts of *Ka* and masculinity were inevitably linked together.[22]

To 'go to one's *Ka*' means to return home to the land of the ancestors, to die. In early times the ancestors were believed to dwell in the cemetery itself—the 'west'. As the funeral procession wended its way up into the desert hills figures representing the ancestral *Ka's* came forward dancing to welcome the new arrival:

> 'The mountain will hold out its arms to him and the living
> *Ka's* will accompany him. . . .
> His arms will be grasped by his *Ka's*, by his ancestors.'[23]

The *Ka's* run out and lead the procession home 'along the lovely roads of the west'. One feels a quickening of feeling whenever the *Ka's* are mentioned:

'How fine will it be to reside with your *Ka* for ever and ever!'

In the Pyramid Texts the *Ka's* have been removed beyond the world, to the sky by the eastern horizon:

'King N is on his way to that distant palace of the *Ka*-Lords,
where the sun is greeted every morning . . .
to be the god of those who have [already] gone to their *Ka's*.'[24]

In the Osiris drama the *Ka* doctrine became complex. Osiris is the *Ka* of Horus because he is his father and the source of his fortune. In the ritual, however, Horus puts his arms around Osiris' body, thus acting as his father's *Ka*. Each is, or mediates, the *Ka* of the other. This is why, on paintings in Tutankhamun's tomb, Osiris and the late king embrace one another, and, in the pyramids:

'King Pepi has come to you, his father . . . Osiris!
he has brought you this *Ka* of yours',[25]

while elsewhere:

'Horus has not kept away from you, for you are his *Ka*.'[26]

As the source of his people's prosperity the king is their *Ka*. In a general way the *Ka's* are the dispensers of all the goodness and wealth in the world. When they act, all is well, whether this is considered in terms of material happiness or moral worth. A sin is 'an abomination to the *Ka*'. There are statues which depict the *Ka's* of their owners; they are idealized youths at the height of physical vigour and beauty. The *Ka* is therefore both the source and the giver of those values which the Egyptians thought most desirable. Part primitive ancestor spirit, part ideal, part benefactor, the beliefs of many generations were united in this compelling symbol of human affection.

4

THE *DJED* COLUMN

Fig. 35. Forms of the *Djed* Column

Osiris did not rise up as an active man and leave the tomb or Underworld. In the developed theology it was his soul that was set free, to ascend as a star or in the life-forces of the ensuing year. The god was more than his myth, he was the spirit of life itself, manifest in the sprouting of vegetation and in the seed of animals and men. But the greatest religious achievement of the Egyptians was to take this general fertility god and make him into the saviour of the dead; or, more exactly, the saviour from death. It was in the soul of Osiris that the Egyptians believed they would live on. The rising of the Osiris soul was therefore the sentimental core of life, the central fact in the structure of the universe. To signify this tremendous thing they used a fetish from their half-forgotten past, a strange wooden object called the *Djed* or 'Stability' Column.

The rites of Osiris simulated the passion of the god in great detail. On the last day, the ceremonies culminated when the king or chief priest set the *Djed* Column upright. This act probably began as a simple harvest ritual, carried out by the prehistoric peasants of the Delta. All over the ancient world

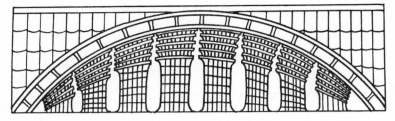

Fig. 36. *Djed* Columns supporting an arch

the reaping of the harvest was imagined as a killing and dis-
memberment of a spirit whose vital essence was kept in the last
sheaf, and the harvest ended with rites which reasserted the life
of the spirit. The *Djed* certainly comes from this world of folk
custom, however complex it may later have become.

The idea of the *Djed* Column is that it stands firmly upright
—for to be upright is to be alive, to have overcome the inert
forces of death and decay. When the *Djed* is upright it implies
that life will go on in the world. The raising of the column was,
however, not the final act in the drama. A loin-cloth was tied
around the middle and feathers were stuck in the top. It was
treated as a living god, so much so that in the later examples a
pair of human eyes were painted in to make the identification
with Osiris more emphatic.

The word *Djed* meant 'stable' or 'durable'. If this is taken
into consideration it is easy to see why the column could be
used as a cosmic pillar or sky support as well as a symbol of
revival. Judging from the wall decoration in the Step Pyramid
the royal palace windows of the early period were lattices with
curved or arched tops and the vertical supports made from *Djed*
columns carefully graded in size to fit the arch. Thus, when one
looked up through the window, the *Djeds* were actually supporting the sky. In more formal settings, such as the elaboration
of the royal protocol, the royal name has to fill the world below
the sky vault. To show this the top of the name enclosure is
always formed by a sky sign and the ends of it rest on cosmic

Fig. 37. *Djed* Columns supporting the World Space occupied by the name King Neterikhet (Zoser)

supports. As early as Khasekhemui of the Second Dynasty a well-known stele has a support made from a composite column formed of a *Djed* and, underneath, a strange object known as a *Tit*, a knot of cloth or leather. This was the emblem of Isis or of the Mother Goddess in general.[27]

There are several stelae in the Zoser buildings at Sakkarah where the *Djed* and the *Tit* are used together as supports. It is to be presumed that the combination of both emblems denotes the union of Osiris and Isis. This union of male and female obviously has some meaning, but it is impossible to see how it links up with the rest of the symbolism. The purpose is clear: as with Khasekhemui the *Djed* Columns are world pillars, holding up the sky and so guaranteeing the space of air and world in which the king's authority holds good. It is basic for all royal symbols of antiquity that kingship is universal; it means rule over the whole earth and all that is beneath the vault of the sky. Hence the frame of a king's name is the delimitation of the world. Taken horizontally, this is shown by a coil of rope with the ends tied together—in early times the coil is circular, but later it is spread lengthwise to accommodate longer names. This is the origin of the royal cartouche, the expanded oval in which royal names are written. In the Zoser name the *Djed* and *Tit* signs delimit the world vertically while the coil of rope does the same thing horizontally. Zoser is master of all that is beneath the sky and to the ends of the earth.[28]

In the later periods of Egyptian history the rich were buried in stone sarcophagi or in wooden or plaster mummy-cases. The sarcophagus was decorated as if it were intended to lie flat, whereas the mummy-case was painted as if to stand upright, although in fact it was placed flat inside the sarcophagus. The reason for this discrepancy is that the sarcophagus was put into the tomb before burial, whereas the mummy-case was brought to the tomb at the funeral and during the final commitment ceremonies stood upright to receive the final consecration, the 'Opening of the Mouth'. In fact, the whole purpose of the mummy-case was to hold the body upright during the rites which preceded the interment. Hence the mummy-case nearly always has a series of interlocked representations of the cosmic pillar which are designed to emphasize the uprightness of the divine world. It is in these complexes of uprightness that the *Djed* comes into its own as a dominant symbol. This can be seen very clearly on the back of a case in the Birmingham Museum. The central figure is the *Djed* in its final state, with the tie-pieces of the loin-cloth showing at the sides and, above it, the horns and double feather crown—the so-called *Atef*—which Osiris wore in his triumphant phase.[29] At the sides of the *Djed* rise male serpents (with beards!) and, above them, lotus flowers crowned with stylized feathers. The serpents are double figures of the great Primeval Serpent, who reared up out of the Abyss at the beginning. Similarly, the lotuses are figures of Nefer-tum, the original cosmic flower, whose petals opened to reveal the sun which then rose up and flew (hence the feathers) across the sky. In both cases the symbol recalls a myth of origins, having as central idea a rising upwards. The two creation symbols have been doubled to provide supports for the central *Djed*, itself a symbol of the same thing but, with its Osirian connotations, immediately connected with the identification with Osiris and the rise and permanence of the soul. The whole design is a triple statement about the victory of the vertical as the manifestation of eternal life.

5

THE LOTUS

Like the Indians, the Egyptians sometimes symbolized the appearance of the great Life Spirit out of the waters as a lotus —a water-lily—rising and opening its flower. The petals bent back to reveal the rising God of Light and Movement. In Plate 10 the soul is emerging, reborn, from the interior of the flower. By the side are buds in various stages of growth. Sometimes the flower discloses a young child, the morning sun. The lotus is itself a form of the High God and is mythical in that there must have been a belief that the origin of life could be expressed in terms of a flower symbol. There is, however, another version, based on the way water-lily flowers blossom in the rays of the morning sun. They open to give up their scent to the Sun God. So the text appended to this vignette begins:

'I am the pure Lotus that rises in the glorious light
to be the peculiar delight of Rê.'[30]

6

THE COSMIC SERPENT

In Egyptian lore all serpents tend to merge into one another, at least if they belong to the same sex. To emphasize the male, the masculine ones have beards. The cobra is the ideal form of the female serpent; in fact, a rearing cobra became the determining sign for goddess in the later stages of the hieroglyphic script. The major symbolic activities of male serpents are:

(1) as creator or most ancient manifestation of the emergent spirit,
(2) as a monster which has to be overcome before the world can be said to be really in order;
(3) as *Sito*, a serpent god who encircles the world, either

with many coils or with its tail in its mouth or walking
—with legs provided!

(4) as the spirit or guardian of the earth or Underworld;

(5) as cosmic enemy, the serpent-dragon Apopis, who
personifies the powers of darkness and has to be overcome at dawn and sunset;

(6) as fertility spirit—chiefly in the form of the Corn God
Neheb-kau;

(7) as Water God, especially living in the caverns out of
which the Nile flood was believed to come;

(8) as a distinguishing mark of the non-human—the serpent
is a primeval creature, living in the dark earth or the
depths of the water (the eel?), uncanny and hostile—and,
possibly, very wise.

The Primeval Serpent has already been discussed. The
monster who has to be destroyed before the world is reduced to
order exists in several forms. He, too, has already appeared in a
Heliopolitan myth, mentioned on p. 54. A casual allusion
in a medical papyrus of the New Kingdom informs us that
Seth must have conquered a serpent monster who represented
the sea[31] while the Instructions to Merikare, a document of the
Herakleopolitans, says that the High God himself restrained
the greed, or greed-monster, of the waters.[32]

The world has to be protected against the disintegrating
forces of the surrounding chaos. All the peoples of antiquity
felt that light and life were constantly threatened by very real
cosmic enemies, everywhere beyond their own immediate
environment. Hence the need to put a guard around the earth
or its symbolic alternative, the Primeval Mound. The world
area, usually called Hermopolis in this connection, is surrounded by a monstrous serpent with its tail in its mouth. This
creature was called Sito—'Son of Earth', *i.e.* 'the essentially
earthy one'—a common expression for snakes. There is a
picture of him in Chapter 87 of the Book of the Dead, which
begins:

17 THE SOUL BIRD flies through the underworld with the sun
(British Museum). See pp. 253–4

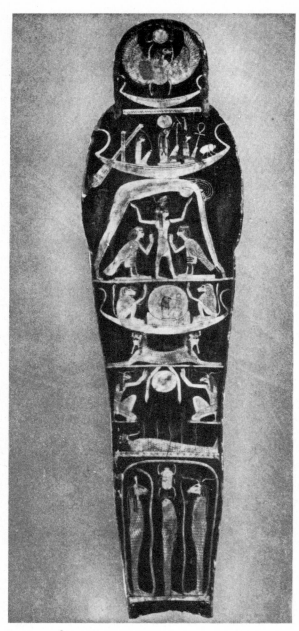

18 TRANSFORMATIONS OF THE SOUL
(Fitzwilliam Museum, Cambridge). See p. 254

'I am Sito, dilated with years, I die and am reborn every
    day,
I am Sito, who dwells in the farthest regions of the world.'

So the serpent is eternal, it will last as long as time. Because it
surrounds the world it is to be found at the ends of the earth.
In a sense, it is the surrounding ocean; but it is also the power
which defends the world from that water.

Most symbols that are used defensively against spirit enemies
come singly or in pairs, when they are placed on either side of a
sacred person or thing like heraldic supporters. This is noticeable in Plate 13 where the two rearing serpents are really
based on the one great Primeval Serpent who raised himself up
at the beginning, but by being doubled they protect the *Djed*
Column. Sometimes there is a compromise, and the serpent
has two heads, so that it can face both ways at once (see
Fig. 7, p. 52).

Generically, the serpent was a left-over from the earliest ages
of the world. There are many spells for driving away poisonous
snakes. In many of them the creature to be expelled is equated
with the Primeval Serpent. There must have been a myth
which told how Neheb-kau, the 'Provider of Attributes', the
Primeval Serpent Spirit at Hermopolis, was overcome by Atum
in the shape of a mongoose. In a Pyramid Text the priest is
made to hold up some instrument, probably an adze, and say:

'This thing is the claw of Atum which grasped the claw of
    the Neheb-kau Serpent, to drive away the confusion in
    Hermopolis.'
(And then, turning to the snake)
'Down! Away!'[33]

Another name for the Primeval Serpent was Amun—'Invisible One' because it came into being before the sun.

'Back! Amun-Serpent! Hide yourself! So that you do not
    let me see you nor come where I am.'[34]

The point of this spell lies in interweaving two ideas—the invisibility of the Primeval Serpent and the desired disappearance of the snake.

The cobra was the ideal female snake. The original rearing Cobra Goddess was Ejo and came from a city in the Delta. In the later periods of Egyptian history the cobra drove out its rivals and became the general sign for goddess. Most cobra symbolism has been absorbed into that of the Eye, but the rearing snake is a sign of the uprightness of the universe. The name—'*Iaret*'—means 'the rearing' or 'the upright one'. It represents the cosmic force which lifts things—a quality derived from its name. One of the commonest symbols is a rearing cobra which holds out a sceptre or mark of prosperity to a king or god.[35] Another is a cobra with the sun on its head. We know from sportive writings of the name of Queen Hatshepsowe of the Eighteenth Dynasty that this form of the cobra stands for Mayet, the World Order.[36] In other words the cobra merges, in one direction, into the terrible concept of the Great Goddess; in another she assimilates the attributes of 'the Gracious One'. In this latter respect it is equated with Tefnut or Mayet, whom the High God lifted up and kissed at the beginning of time, thus starting the scheme of ordered life, as was told on p. 46.

The skies teem with rearing cobras. The sun's boat is towed across the day sky by racing dogs or jackals (the winds) and through the Underworld by cobras.

Dangerous snakes were to be found everywhere. As a Pyramid Text vividly puts it:

'When walls are knocked down and bricks dislodged,
    may that which comes out of your mouth be turned back
        against yourself (O Snake!).'[37]

Another telling remark comes in a curse against Seth, the god of Ombos, who is death itself:

'When the light is extinguished and a lamp cannot be found
    in any house where the Ombite is,

may a biting snake creep into the house to bite him unawares.'[38]

As the spells show, these creatures lurk in the ground under stones, in caves, thickets or long grass. When they bite they cause 'fire', that is, fever and perhaps death. Having neither arms nor legs they do not belong to the animal world but to something primeval. They are the suppressed forces that lie below the outward appearance of the divinely appointed scheme of things. They must be treated carefully, for they are kinsmen of the gods:

'If you become dangerous to me I will step on you,
  but if you recognize me I will not tread upon you,
  for you are that mysterious and shapeless thing, of whom
    the gods foretold
  that you should have neither arms nor legs
  on which to go following your brother gods,'[39]

where we catch a reference to a myth telling how the snake came to have its shape. This is strangely reminiscent of the Serpent in the Garden of Eden which was doomed to go upon its belly. The snake was a form of the Primeval Serpent:

'Whatever you do, wherever you pass by,
  tread carefully, beware of the Oldest of the Old!'[40]

A myth which probably dates from the early Middle Kingdom, describes how the power of the primeval snakes was curtailed.[41]

This God (*i.e.* Atum) called to Thoth, saying:
  'Summon Geb to me, saying, "Come, hurry!"'
So when Geb had come to him, he said:

'Take care of the serpents which are in you. Behold, they showed respect for me while I was down there.[42] But now you have learned their [real] nature. Proceed to the place where Father Nun is, tell him to keep guard over the serpents, whether in the earth or in the water. Also you

Fig. 38. Time and Form emerge from the Cosmic Serpent. (Tombs of Ramses VI and IX)

must write it down that it is your task to go wherever your serpents are and say: "See that you do no damage!" They must know that I am still here (in the world) and that I have put a seal upon them. Now their lot is to be in the world for ever. But beware of the magical spells which their mouths know, for Hikê[43] is himself therein. But knowledge is in you. It will not come about that I, in my greatness, will have to keep guard over them as I once did, but I will hand them over to your son Osiris so that he can watch over their children and the hearts of their fathers be made to forget. Thus advantage can come from them, out of what they perform for love of the whole world, through the magical power that is in them.'

The serpents are the demonic, chaotic powers who dwell in the lower world. As long as the High God dwelt in the Abyss or on earth they were under control, but after the rebellion of mankind he departed to the sky. The serpents thought that God no longer existed and began to show their true colours. He therefore sent Geb down to them with a written message. They were to keep within the earth, where they would live eternally. They have power—*Hikê*—but Geb, with his written instructions, has knowledge. This is the oldest statement of the belief that the forces of nature have to be curbed by 'knowledge'. In the theocentric universe of the Egyptians this knowledge derives from the High God and is transmitted to the Earth God. The theology is dualist. The energy which the

Fig. 39. Serpent containing the Cardinal Points

serpents have in their mouths is the force of nature. Set against this inchoate energy is intelligent direction, stemming from Atum. In the Primeval Age of Oneness this was unnecessary, but with his elevation to the sky, God and creation are distinct. As myth this is a declaration of the divine transcendence, but as theology it contains the germ of the scientific attitude. Geb is only an intermediary. Ultimately the task of curbing the serpents devolves on Osiris. This is a strange statement, because Osiris is usually passive and his theology cannot be reconciled with the concept of nature found in this myth. In the Herakleopolitan Period, however, Osiris became an active god and this gives a hint to the date of composition of the present text. There is an echo of a similar belief in the 'Great Quarrel' where Osiris has to keep in check the denizens of the Underworld. But Osiris is only a name for his rites. The implication for the Egyptians was that they must carry out the prescribed ritual of the Osirian cycle in order that the forces of nature work advantageously—this is the word used in the text—for the benefit 'of the whole world'.

7

THE PHOENIX

The Phoenix, known to the Egyptians as the *Benu* Bird, was one of the primeval forms of the High God. The Shu Texts epitomize the appearance of light and life out of the original darkness and chaos as:

'that breath of life which emerged from the throat of the
Benu Bird, the son of Rê in whom Atum appeared
in the primeval nought, infinity, darkness and nowhere.'

One has to imagine a perch extending out of the waters of the
Abyss. On it rests a grey heron, the herald of all things to come.
It opens its beak and breaks the silence of the primeval night
with the call of life and destiny, which 'determines what is and
what is not to be'. The Phoenix, therefore, embodies the original
Logos, the Word or declaration of destiny which mediates
between the divine mind and created things. It is essentially
an aspect of God, self-created, and not a minor deity. But
the heron form is not to be taken too literally; it is a way of
expressing one of the basic activities of God rather than a
historical or naturalistic figure. It is the first and deepest manifestation of the 'soul' of the High God.

Underlying all Egyptian speculation is the belief that time
is composed of recurrent cycles which are divinely appointed:
the day, the week of ten days, the month, the year—even longer
periods of 30, 400 or 1460 years, determined according to the
conjunctions of sun, moon, stars and inundation. In a sense,
when the Phoenix gave out the primeval call it initiated all
these cycles, so it is the patron of all division of time, and its
temple at Heliopolis became the centre of calendrical regulation. As the herald of each new dispensation, it becomes,
optimistically, the harbinger of good tidings. During the
Middle Kingdom the *Benu* Bird became the 'soul' of Osiris and
the symbol for the planet Venus—the morning star which
precedes the sun out of the Underworld and is the herald of a
new day. In spite of these minor roles, however, the *Benu* Bird
continues to be 'he who created himself'—a form of the High
God. In fact, Atum-Rê, Shu and Osiris meet in the bird as
the symbol of the godhead in time.

The Egyptians had two ideas about the origin of life. The
first was that it emerged in God out of the Primeval Waters;
the other was, that vital essence—*Hikê*—was brought hither

Fig. 40. The Phoenix
(in Coffin Text 335)

from a distant, magical source. The latter was 'the Isle of Fire' —the place of everlasting light beyond the limits of the world, where the gods were born or revived and whence they were sent into the world. The Phoenix is the chief messenger from this inaccessible land of divinity. A Coffin Text makes the victorious soul say:

> 'I come from the Isle of Fire, having filled my body with Hikê, like "that bird" who [came and] filled the world with that which it had not known.'[44]

So the Phoenix came from the far-away world of eternal life, bringing the message of light and life to a world wrapped in the helplessness of the primeval night. Its flight is the width of the world:

> 'over oceans, seas and rivers,'[45]

to land, at last, in Heliopolis, the symbolic centre of the earth where it will announce the new age. We are told that 'the watchers tremble' with joy when they behold it coming, with the assurance that creation is still active and the world is not yet to be reabsorbed into the Abyss. It is for this reason that Atum can say, in Chapter 17 of the Book of the Dead:

'I am that great *Benu* Bird in Heliopolis, who determines
what is and what is not to be.'

This great symbol, the most persuasive in the Egyptian
repertoire, was misunderstood by Herodotus who, as a stranger
to the inner meaning of Egyptian religion, brought it down to
the level of a fairy-tale:

'There is another sacred bird called the Phoenix. I have
never seen it myself except in pictures, for it is extremely
rare, only appearing, according to the people of Heliopolis,
once in five hundred years, when it is seen after the death
of its parent. If the pictures are accurate its size and appearance are as follows: its plumage is partly red and partly
gold, while in shape and size it is very much like an eagle.
They (the Heliopolitans) tell a story about this bird which
I personally find incredible: the Phoenix is said to come
from Arabia, carrying the parent bird encased in myrrh;
it proceeds to the temple of the sun and there buries the
body. In order to do this, they say it first forms a ball as big
as it can carry, then, hollowing out the ball, it inserts its
(dead) parent, subsequently covering over the aperture
with fresh myrrh. The ball is then exactly the same weight
as it was at first. The Phoenix bears this ball to Egypt, all
encased as I have said, and deposits it in the temple of the
sun. Such is their myth about this bird.'[46]

This is very different from the hieratic figure in Chapter 83
of the Book of the Dead—the 'Spell for becoming the *Benu*
Bird.' The soul declares:

'I flew up as the Primeval God and assumed forms—
I grew in the seed and disguised myself as the Tortoise,
I am the seed corn of every god,
I am yesterday . . .
I am Horus, the god who gives light by means of his
    body . . .
I come as day, I appear in the steps of the gods,

I am Khons (the moon) who proceeds through the universe.'

Here the Phoenix is the principle of life, not so much in any particular form but the constant divine power in all its supreme manifestations, whether natural or mythological. For the author of the rubric to this text, the Phoenix was a synthesis of the main forms of life, a general symbol to include all particular ones.

8

THE PRIMEVAL OCEAN (PLATE 14)

One of the chief difficulties in the interpretation of cosmic symbolism is that the symbol is a two-dimensional picture of a three-dimensional reality. In this picture Nun, the ocean, half emerges from the waters, holding the sun in a boat above his head. The sun is being pushed up by a beetle; in other words, this is the rising sun. The arms lifting the boat and the beetle pushing up the disk are parallel symbols of the same event. Above are two figures, upside-down. The large one is 'Osiris as he encircles the Underworld'; he is bent in a circle with his feet touching his head. He is the rim of the land below the earth or, if one likes, the celestial river. This is a rather forced way of expressing that he is lord of the land of the past night, where the sun has been prepared for the task of the ensuing day. On him rests Nut, the sky, who takes up the sun with her arms.

The words above the boat run: 'This god rests in the Morning Boat; the gods about him are'; and underneath are the gods themselves: Geb, the earth, Thoth, *Hikê* (the Divine Word), 'Command' and 'Intelligence' and three 'Look-out men'. Isis and Nephthys support the beetle. In other words, the sun is accompanied by Geb and four primeval spirits concerned with creation in terms of the Logos doctrine (see pp. 54-5). It must be remembered that the solar barque is the centre of the regulation of the universe, so it is suitable that it should be manned by personifications of intellectual qualities. This is allegory more than symbolism.

This is a standard picture of the late New Kingdom. Several copies are known. They come from 'The Book of Gates', a work about the night journey of the sun which reflects the ideas of the time just after the collapse of the heresy of Akhenaton, say about 1320 B.C.[47]

9

SEPARATION OF EARTH AND SKY (PLATE 3)

The separation of Earth and Sky is a common theme on the shoulders of coffins of the Twenty-first and Twenty-second Dynasties. The Sky Goddess Nut is an enormous maiden bending over in an arc to represent the heavenly vault. She is being lifted up by Shu, the Air God, who bears the sign of his name fixed upright on his head. Geb, the Earth, is a green man, falling or lying in an awkward, listless position. The inscription on the right runs: 'Words said by Nut, the Primeval Mistress, who gives birth to the gods (*i.e.* stars), who creates the sun that he may rule the districts of both lands.' Around Shu the signs read: 'Shu, the son of Rê, who raised Nut aloft.' In front of Shu's mouth is the sign for spitting. The emission of air is the coming of the breath of life which is the other aspect of the separation of the two parts of the universe—life begins with the act of Shu. In the picture, two birds with rams' heads and human arms help to sustain Shu's arms.[48] They are 'souls'—the ram alternates with the bird as the symbol of the soul—spirits of life and air who are drawn up into the mighty creative act. By Geb's feet is a composite creature named Shay—a fabulous animal connected with Seth. He appears in several of the mythological scenes but his significance is unknown. Is he 'Fate'?

10

DAWN

An arched sky sign resting on a mat surrounds two symbols of the rising sun. In the upper picture the sun's disk encloses the scarabaeus beetle (see Plate 15) and rests on the twin-peaked mountain of sunrise. Against all verisimilitude this figure, mountain and all, is being conveyed across the waters of the heavenly ocean in a boat whose extremities are shaped like papyrus flowers. Iconographically this is not strictly correct, for a boat of this form belongs to the rites of Osiris at Abydos, not to the sun. However, it has been borrowed for a solar context because its shape fits compactly into the arch. The steering oars and their supports end in the heads of falcons and the guide rope is a rearing cobra. The boat is therefore alive and moves of its own accord. In the bow is a somewhat debased harpoon, also magically propelled because it has been given a leg. This harpoon is always to be found in the solar boat. It probably descends from the harpoon stick and knife which was carried in the boats of prehistoric chieftains as a sign that they had power to inflict the death-penalty—a kind of Fasces. It might come in useful in overcoming the denizens of the waters (see the Apopis Myth, pp. 208–12).

Immediately underneath the heavenly ocean is the head of a brindled cow. This belongs to Nut, the Sky Goddess, who can assume a cow-form. Below that, the head and arms of the Primeval Waters emerge. The arms are lifting up the sky, or maybe the boat. Strings of dots simulate beams of light falling from the sky ocean upon the world beneath. Heraldically placed on either side are two baboons, the creatures who adore the rising sun, and may be the morning stars. In front of each baboon is a loaf and an open-mouthed container for liquid— symbols of the offerings which were made every day to the rising sun. On either side are the names of Amenophis I (1550 B.C.) whose cult enjoyed popularity at Thebes during the New Kingdom. The animals' legs are in profile but the feet are shown in plan, and both are the same way up! The bottom of the picture is a flattened wickerwork basket.

An interesting constructional detail is the ends of the poles which are fixed across the hull of the boat and provide the support for the platform on which the sun symbol rests.

11

THE TRANSFORMATION OF THE SOUL

The combination of day and night sun in one diagram is a common theme because it symbolizes the journey of the soul through the Underworld of the coffin to its rebirth into the light of day. In the upper section of Plate 16 the rising sun is shown as a disk with a beetle in the middle. It rises from a sandy hill—the eastern horizon—the sand being marked by red dots on a yellow ground. This hill is incongruously placed in the solar boat. The sun is being fanned by the wind god/ desses, this time shown as cobras with outstretched wings. One of the cobras is called Ejo,[49] the personification of the Delta. In this case the unnamed cobra stands for the south. Sacred Eyes are being wafted towards the disk by the wings of the cobras.

In the lower section a hawk's head hangs downward from a sky sign. From the top of the reversed head stars and circles of light fall upon the body of a recumbent mummiform figure. Four hieroglyphs say, 'The House of the Underworld'. Immediately to the left of the hawk's head is the usual flying cobra wearing the white crown of southern Egypt. This is significant: in the upper picture the north is on the right but in the lower one the directions are reversed. The directions are emphasized by two standing mummies, one on either side. That on the left is Kebhesennuf, with hawk's head; the one on the right is Duamowetef with a jackal's head. These are two of the four sons of Horus the Elder, the gods of the cardinal points. The scene depicts the passage of the sun through the

Underworld, illuminating the figure of the deceased lying helpless in his tomb—who is, at the same time, Osiris in the Underworld. The eye with suspended wing is probably the moon being brought back to Egypt, but the white crown on the guarding cobra hints that this is the savage Eye (lioness) whose return from the south has been described on pp. 227–9. The cobra wafting the Eye appears in both pictures. It is not yet understood.

An alternative representation of night journey and sunrise— the normal theme for the inside head of a coffin—comprises a sky sign bent round to fit the head of the flat portion and to act as a frame for a diagram (Plate 17). The ends of the sign rest on a mat and, under it, a much flattened wickerwork basket, symbolizing 'festival'. The upper section beneath the vaulted space contains the usual boat of the rising sun, flanked by two semicircular signs for 'bread'. Offerings are scattered all over these pictures; they seem to denote that the various objects and persons shown are very holy and receive daily meals in the temple ritual. The boat is floating in, or on, another sky sign—straight this time —which must be the celestial ocean. It is upheld by a cartouche with a white ground, in which is written 'Amenophis, ruler of Thebes'—Amenophis I (1557–1530 B.C.) whose cult tended to replace aspects of Osiris-worship in the late New Kingdom. The name is crowned by a sun disk and two feathers. The whole thing acts as a support for the sky, as is clear from the attitude of Isis and Nephthys, who are steadying it. The god-desses wear patterned slips, not the white clothes of Egyptian ladies of the time.

Above, in the curved head section of the coffin, is a strange creature with human head and body of a falcon. It is shown full face with outstretched wings. On its head is the sun disk guarded by a twin-headed cobra, wearing the white crowns of southern Egypt. The great bird-man has flown across the Underworld sky, so its disk has had to be guarded from hostile powers by the cobra. The day sun has no need for such defences. Above the bird-man the beetle of sunrise pushes his disk up, adored as it goes by the baboons of dawn. Below the baboons are two soul birds, twin versions of the human soul of the man buried in the coffin. Just as the sun traversed the dark ways of the Underworld every night and alighted on the horizon at dawn, so the soul of the deceased would be able to leave the dark tomb each day to greet the first light. On either side of the dawn sun, behind the baboons, are sacred eyes and winged cobras who are using their wings as fans—they are called Ejo (North) and Nekhabit (South).

Plate 18 represents the interior of a Twenty-first Dynasty coffin in the Fitzwilliam Museum, Cambridge. It is a veritable compendium of symbols.

At the top is a solar disk, guarded by a two-headed cobra, which is being pushed up or supported by a winged beetle with a ram's head. The ram denotes the night sun on its journey through the underworld, whereas the beetle is the sign of the sun at dawn. The beetle rests on a boat which is sailing across a stretch of water—the heavenly ocean—marked by a wavy line and two fish. Beneath the beetle's legs is the ring of totality, flanked by two more cobras. The snakes may be just magical defenders of the sun symbols or they may refer to the two goddesses, Ejo and Nekhabit, who, as we have seen, can signify north and south.

Immediately underneath is a compound scene. Nut bends over to form the sky. A text beside her head calls her 'Nut, the great, who gives birth to the gods (*i.e.* the stars).' Two bird-souls support the Air God, who stands with extended arms, holding up the sky. The Air God should be Shu, but here he is called 'Hikê, Great God, Master of the Sky' and bears on his head a lion's hind-quarters, resting on a standard, which is the sign for 'Creative Word' in the so-called 'Enigmatic Hiero-glyphs' of the New Kingdom. The equation of Shu with Creative Word is the fundamental innovation of the creation texts discussed on pp. 80–7. Over Nut's back sails the sun boat, this time with an anonymous helmsman. In the centre sits Rê, the Sun God, and in front of him is Mayet, the Cosmic

Order, and a grasshopper, a form of the cosmic enemy which is defeated by the forces of Order.[50] On either side of Nut are great eyes, flying on wings through outer space towards the central figures.

The third picture shows the sun resting on the dawn mountain—in a boat and adored by baboons, who may be the morning stars. The boat rests on the Aker monster (see Chapter V, p. 153) on the earth. Below this, two arms, probably belonging to the goddess of the Underworld sky, enfold or hold a sun disk which sheds its beams upon the inert body of Osiris. Out of the latter sprout five plants. This is the earliest known representation of the sprouting Osiris; the others occur in the temples of the Graeco-Roman Period.

At the bottom is a headless mummy, out of which is rising a beetle. This figure, with its attendant genii, is wrapped in the convolutions of the cosmic serpent.

So far this coffin has been described as a series of separate and unrelated mythological pictures. If, however, they are interpreted from the bottom upwards, we are given a scheme of the salvation of the soul. In the tomb the soul lies together with its body in the darkness of the mummy-case. It is immobile and helpless, without the distinction of a head, and has to be protected by the serpent and its attendant demons. Nevertheless it is a potentiality, for out of it rises the beetle, the sign for 'form' and 'coming into being'. In the next, the Osirian stage, the night sun penetrates to the Underworld and its rays fall upon the soul in its new form as the body of Osiris. As in the life of nature, where Osiris is the potential life in the earth and the solar rays call forth the vegetation, so the soul can say:

'I am the plant of life which grows through the ribs of Osiris.'

But in the next scene the Osirian fate is transcended. The symbol of the rising soul has now become the sun as it mounts above the eastern horizon, adored by the morning stars. Then, in the Nut and Hikê diagrams we have the breaking of light into the world and the sailing of the sun in its true day-form as Rê. Finally, in the top picture of all, the sun is Universal God, persisting through all his forms, whether by day or night, cosmic and universal. This, the ram-headed beetle, is the supreme form of the High God in the funerary literature of the New Kingdom. Chapter 42 of the Book of the Dead says, when the soul claims absorption into Him:

> 'I am he who is constantly appearing, whose real nature is unknown,
> I am yesterday, "He who has seen a million years" is one name of mine,
> I pass along the ways of those sky-beings who determine destinies,
> I am the master of eternity, ordering how I am fated,
> like the Great Beetle.'

MAJOR RELIGIOUS SYMBOLS

1 Earth

2 Ground and
underworld
(The 'Aker')

3 Underworld

4 Star
(always five-pointed)

5 Sun
(red circle in white ring)

6 Moon

7 Sunlight

8 Water

9 Mountains: hill

mountain of sunrise

foreign lands

10 Primeval Mound

11 Building

12 Palace
(of High God or King)

13 Shrine   or

14 East

15 West

16 Crown of North
(red)

17 Crown of South
(white)

18 Goddess of North
(Ejo, the cobra)

19 Goddess of South
(Nekhabit, the vulture)

20 Supports: steps

    mat

    bowl

    pylon

27 Eternity   or

(A notched stick or a man with upraised arms having the stick on his head)

28 Mayet (Truth or World Order)

21 Throne   or

    or

22 Horizon

29 Soul   or

(ram)

23 Gateway

30 Rule   and

(crook)   (rattle)

31 Life

24 Doors

32 Stability or resurrection

25 Air   or

33 Prosperity
(stick of desert sheikh)

26 Totality

(a coiled rope)

34 Youth (child,
    New Year or Dawn)

35 Place and seat or

43 Recitation of hymns of praise

36 Eye (the *'uiat'* — can be sun, moon, etc.)

44 Worship of sun

37 Solar boat

45 Submission

38 Osiris boat

46 Sun at dawn

39 Gold

47 Sun at night

40 Divinity signs

48 Phoenix

49 Osiris

41 Ramparts or

50 Goddess

42 Edge of world or

CHAPTER VIII

Conclusion

FOR US the past is over and done with. Time is irreversible and its passing inexorable. However much we may wish to alter past history or to make it present, we know that we cannot do so. In fact, we have become so used to this attitude that it is hard to appreciate that our concepts of time and history are not those of ancient man. The verbs in modern languages possess a definite tense structure so that one is sure whether events are present, past or future, but this was not the case with Ancient Egyptian. There the verbs had complex and subtle forms, but in translating a text it is often difficult to decide whether to render it into past or present time in English. Thus, in Coffin Text 335, the soul hopes that it will not come to grief because, it says:

> 'I was one of the ministrants of the Master of Things, he who kept the "Book of Forms",'

or, it may mean:

> 'I am one of the ministrants of the Master of Things, he who keeps the "Book of Forms".'

In the first case we are to assume that there was a myth about a Master of Destiny—God or his Demiurge—who drew up a book in which was written all that was to happen in future ages. This is mythical in the modern sense; that is, it is a reference to an event in the past which is not historically verifiable; it is not a description of divine activity at the present time. But if the Egyptian *'ink'* is taken to mean 'I am', then the text says that there is a God who directs the affairs of the universe here and now, and that the soul wishes to become one of his agents and so, by implication, free from the restricting circumstances of death or the danger of annihilation. It does not mean, as the other rendering does, that all fates were laid down at the creation of the world. The apparent uncertainty of the translation is due not so much to our ignorance of the Egyptian verb—or Independent Pronoun in this case—as to the uncertainty of the Egyptians themselves.

For them, myths were about the doings of the gods at the beginning of the world, but these events were symbols expressing the present organization of things. The mythical era did not exist in its own right but only to explain or justify the world of historical times. Myths belonged to the past but they were really valid in the present. The 'Book of Forms' was written at the start of everything, but it is still being compiled. Moreover, it contains a quasi-philosophical idea which can be expanded in accord with the great Egyptian concept of 'Forms' to mean stages of development, species and visible signs.

During the Old Kingdom the mythical past and the divinely regulated or conserved present were not distinguished from one another very clearly. It is impossible to disentangle them in the Pyramid Texts. Later on, in the Herakleopolitan Period (Ninth and Tenth Dynasties), there are signs that the mythical epoch is seen as distinct from its influence on the present. The notes which were added to Spell 335 of the Coffin Texts make this quite clear. In its wish to share the essence of the High God in his various manifestations, the soul wants to be part of the mythical creation of the world and to be the sun when it rises at dawn every morning. These are, of course, two quite separate ideas. The older doctrine had been that the High God Atum or Rê had produced a Primeval Twain. The soul says:

'O Primeval Ones, give me your arms!
I am the soul who came into being in you (twain).'

An early editor added:

'Who are these "Primeval Ones"? They are Command and Intelligence.'

But the original goes on:

> 'as one who is with my father Atum throughout the course
> of every day',

thus recognizing that Command and Intelligence are really
one being. A later editor gives, however, a mythical interpretation of the 'soul':[1]

> 'It is the blood that descended from the phallus of Rê
> after he proceeded to circumcise himself,
> and these gods are those who came into being [im
> mediately] after him.'

The underlying myth is the one about how God—Atum or
Rê—had procreated a first couple. In the Herakleopolitan
Period these were generally depersonalized as Command and
Intelligence. They are abstractions and, in a sense, a 'form' of
God as active force. They are one 'soul', hence the prayer,
although they are two individuals. Now the supreme form of
God in the present world is the sun, who governs through his
power of command and his omniscience. The soul desires to be
associated with these two qualities, which are theologically one
but mythically two. Later on, a New Kingdom editor, with
more acute time sense but crass misunderstanding of the earlier
theology, devised a myth that God had circumcised himself
and that the Primeval Twain had issued from his blood.[2] He
was careful to add, however, that Command and Intelligence
arose later in time than Rê, thus making the temporal status of
myth more precise. In the New Kingdom the mythological age
was quite distinct from the present age of humanity. This is an
advance in the concept of time but it marks a decline in theological acumen. The cosmic speculations of the earlier periods
depended on a belief that the myths were eternally valid. As
long as this belief was held myths could be altered, transferred
to other gods or expanded creatively to suit the requirements of
a developing world and psychic consciousness. When the
myths were relegated to the past they could only become

stereotyped fairy-tales. Thus the developing sense of time and history was, on the whole, an intellectual loss.

Myths told as long connected narratives are a comparatively late phenomenon. In the earlier ages of Egyptian history myths can inform rituals or even dramatic and mime performances and choric songs, but there are no long sagas. These make an appearance, in rather primitive form, in the texts of the Ninth Dynasty, *c.* 2150 B.C., while the myth as entertainment first appears in 'The Great Quarrel'. Most early Egyptian myths are quite short episodes and can be told in one or two sentences. They are not long involved relations like those which have been recovered from the contemporary Sumerians of Mesopotamia.[3] For the Egyptians, mythology was not a collection of texts but a language. This is fundamental. It explains why the doings of the gods could be altered, be expanded and even reappear with other protagonists without apparent inconsistency. But myths do not have to be consistent. They belong to a way of thinking in which consistency in the logical sense is irrelevant. The myth was a way, and before the emergence of lay philosophy with the Greeks, the only way, to express ideas about the cosmos or the needs of the human soul. This is why Egyptian mythology is so simple, so absurd and sometimes so profound. It is dream, metaphysics and poetry, all at once.

The creation of myths was founded on certain principles. These are strange and, as yet, only partially understood. The most important elements seem to have been as follows:

(*a*) The basic principles of life, nature and society were determined by the gods long ago, before the establishment of the kingship. This epoch—'*Tep zepi*'—'the First Time'—stretched from the first stirring of the High God in the Primeval Waters to the settling of Horus upon the throne and the redemption of Osiris. All proper myths relate events or manifestations of this epoch.

(*b*) Anything whose existence or authority had to be justified or explained must be referred to the 'First Time'. This was true for natural phenomena, rituals, royal insignia, the plans of temples, magical or medical formulae, the hieroglyphic system of writing, the calendar—the whole paraphernalia of the civilization.

(c) All showings of force, whether natural or human, were re-enactments of some myth. The sun rose at the beginning of the world, but this great drama of creation is repeated every morning and every New Year's day. Whenever the sun drove away the thunder-clouds it was a repetition of the defeat of Apopis by Rê in the mytho-logical past—'for so it was determined of old', as the texts say. But our words re-enactment and repetition give a mechanical and false impression of the immediacy of the myths. When the thunder roared it *was* Seth roaring; when the plants began to grow it *was* the soul of Osiris rising.

(d) All that was good or efficacious was established on the principles laid down in the 'First Time'—which was, therefore, a golden age of absolute perfection—'before rage or clamour or strife or uproar had come about'. No death, disease or disaster occurred in this blissful epoch, known variously as 'the time of Rê', 'the time of Osiris', or 'the time of Horus'.

(e) The Golden Age was disturbed. The entry of evil was generally thought to have happened when the eye of the High God grew angry seeing that it had been supplanted by another in its absence. The partial restoration of this Golden Age—*hetep*—is the chief theme of the ritual. Hence the emphasis on the constraint of evil forces and the defeat of the powers of chaos. After the triumph of the Osiris cult the chief disturber of cosmic harmony was Seth.

(f) Divine power is ambivalent. Peace and prosperity are always precarious and depend on holding in check the powers that threaten them. The warlike defenders of order are but the powers of evil and chaos held in thrall

and turned to righteous purposes. This is the under,
lying theme of the cycle of myths connected with the
'Eye'. Even the Sun God has to be championed by Seth
when he has to overcome the demon of darkness.

(*g*) The hostile forces are divided into major enemies and
their subordinates. No major deity, Osiris excepted, can
be killed, otherwise the myth would have no further
relevance for the organization of the world. Hence the
cosmic enemies, Apopis, Seth and the Eye, are constrained but their followers are annihilated.

(*h*) One of the commonest ideas in Ancient Egyptian
religious thinking was that of the 'soul': the form,
symbol or manifestation of a divinity, which was distinct
from the god himself. The stars were, in general, souls—
in fact, the Goddess Nut, the sky, was named 'she of a
thousand souls'. The soul was not earthbound. It moved
readily from place to place. It reconciled the recognition
that all power belongs to God with the vivid sense the
Egyptians had for the multiplicity of the world. The sun
was the soul of the High God, vegetation the soul of
Osiris, the Dog Star the soul of Isis. By the use of this
concept the gods could develop individually as richer
and more interesting beings.

(*i*) Related to the 'soul' is the 'form'—'*khepru*'. The High
God went through a series of changing forms as he
developed from the first life to come from the waters.
He can be a shepherd herding his flock, a king on a
throne, the idol in its shrine, as well as his past forms as
lotus flower, Divine Child, hawk, serpent, ram, and
so on. It was through this idea that the Egyptians
could readily understand how Khnum, the ram of
Elephantine, when shaping mankind on his potter's
wheel was also the High God in another form. The
'forms' held the mythology together and prevented
Egyptian religion from becoming a mass of independent
cults.

(*j*) All the major goddesses are really forms of the one Great Goddess. This is why the 'Eye' in the tale about the rebellion of mankind against Rê can become Sakhmet, and explains how Isis and Hathor can be easily confounded.

(*k*) The connecting link between the events in the mythical texts is generally a play on words. We can see how elaborate this can be from a drama preserved on the temple of Sethos I at Abydos. Horus had lost his eye during his battle with Seth and the recovery of this eye is both the creation of the moon and the symbol for its waxing every month.

> Geb says to Horus: 'I apprehend (pick up?) that which you fit into your face.'[4]

This only makes sense when it is realized that in Egyptian the words for 'moon', 'apprehend', 'face' and 'fit' form a complex pun. The text is built around the assonance of three words in the speech of Geb and the word for 'moon' which is understood but not mentioned. This strange proceeding is no longer part of our conscious thinking, but the psychologists have shown that similar verbal exercises underly the free association of ideas. It is, of course, the technique of James Joyce in *Finnegan's Wake*. The Egyptians lived closer to the forces of their unconscious minds than we do. If two words had similar sounds, what they expressed must have something in common.

(*l*) The addiction to punning was related to a reverence for the 'Word'. Words meant ideas and the domination of mind over sheer matter. The Egyptian theologians were convinced that the world was governed by ideas, the 'words' of the gods. Most myths lead up, not to a deed, but to the saying of something significant. One of the most eloquent testimonies to this power of the Word appears in a recently published text:[5]

'[God's] powers are exercised in creating reverence for
    him in the gods who came after him,
the millions of attributes are in his mouth.'

(*Gloss*) That is, the Creative Word of the Self-Creator.

'The gods rejoice to see him,
    the gods live on his dew,
the hills are created and the ores inserted therein.'

God as the mythical first being, as the Divine Word and
Creator, and as the object of worship, are united in a cry of joy.
The creation of the hills and the insertion of the ores into their
rocks are artfully mentioned as the most wonderful of God's
works. But the commentators have been busy, inserting the
note to explain that the multitudinous 'attributes' of the world
are in fact the Creative Word at work. The Egyptians held to
the Creative Word as the rationale of their world, the stage on
which God played out his role as regulator and sustainer of all
created things. The notes show how seriously the texts were
taken. However extravagant the punning or the events, the
older texts hint almost always at a deeper, subtler and more
intellectual meaning. Mythology was not the same thing as the
telling of tales. It was the explanation of the universe by a
believer in the Egyptian religion.

It is the present writer's conviction that if Egyptian myths
are understood, not as a collection of tales but as a religious
language, many contemporary controversies will seem to be of
minor importance. For instance, whether or not Egyptian
myths grew out of a pattern of ritual common to the ancient
Oriental world or more directly out of the rites of the temple and
funerary cults, is probably of less significance than what the
myths said in themselves and the truths they were trying to
bring out. The Pyramid Texts, the Coffin Texts, the Book of
the Dead and the Underworld Books are the remains of a
literature, not just a collection of magical spells. Most of the
mythical material was composed within pious but orthodox

circles. However, as has been shown, occasionally the Egyptians tried to free themselves from the trammels of theology. They then began to use their mythological language as humour or natural description, or to enlarge their apprehensions of individual character. But this is only to say that Ancient Egypt was a complete civilization and its myths were as rich and various as the life which they reflected.

NOTES

PREFACE:

1 *cf.* H. Grapow, *Forschungen und Fortschritte*, 26, 1950, 297.

INTRODUCTION:

1 S. Schott, *Mythe und Mythenbildung im alten Ägypten*, Leipzig, 1945, especially Chapter 5.

2 The usual translation—'The Field of Reeds'—misinterprets the word '*Sekhet*', which often refers to a marshy or watery place inhabited by birds and fish. The Egyptians were peculiarly affected by marshes.

3 At Edfu the celebrant was even named 'the King himself'!

CHAPTER 1:

1 K. Sethe, *Urkunden der 18ten Dynastie*, Leipzig, 1934, 248, 16.

2 W. Spiegelberg, *Der Mythos vom Sonnenauge nach dem Leidener demotischen Papyrus*, Strassburg, 1917, 36.

3 H. Kees, *Der Götterglaube im alten Ägypten*, 2nd ed., Berlin, 1956, 316 ff.

'He who presides over his pool' may refer to a lost creation myth.

4 A. de Buck, *The Egyptian Coffin Texts*, II, Chicago, 1939, 33.

5 Apparently '*Benben*', which is masculine in Old Egyptian, became feminine in Middle Egyptian, through confusion with the word '*Benbenet*', which signifies the top of a pyramid; *cf.* E. Edel, *Altägyptische Grammatik*, I, Rome, 1955, § 220. This seems to indicate that the idea of a pyramid was derived from the sacred Benben stone.

6 J. Spiegel, 'Das Auferstehungsritual der Unaspyramide', *Annales du Service des Antiquités d'Égypte*, LIII, 1955, 367 ff.

7 Pyramid Texts (ed. Sethe), §199. The lacuna in Sethe's edition is filled from Neith. I have rendered '*m*' as 'as' rather than 'from' before Atum and Khoprer.

8 Coffin Texts, II, 161*a*.

9 Pyramid Texts, §1466 ff. Literally 'O Guardian wherein is the mother of Pepi', but '*iry*', usually translated 'guardian' merely means

someone who acts for or is related to another. Here it signifies a male who replaces a female.

10 'The pure land' is the Primeval Mound.

11 Coffin Texts, II, 152f.

12 The masturbation motive may have originated in a legend about Min, the god of Koptos. *cf.* Kees, *op. cit.*, pp. 91 and 348.

13 The name written *D͵N* can be read 'Den', 'Wedimu' or 'Ny͵djert'. The latter—if it is tenable—means 'I belong to the Hand (Goddess).'

14 Coffin Texts, III, 334*j*. I have followed the Siut text, SI͵C.

15 The signs are not clear in either version. Perhaps 'fingers'? The text says 'Rê' where earlier scribes would have written 'Atum'.

16 *i.e.* 'my people' are not yet formed. The High God contains within himself the essence of all creatures that are to come hereafter. When created they are his people.

17 Lit. 'Mayet'—the personification of order; *cf.* C. L. Bleeker, *De Beteekenis van de egyptische Godin Maat*, Leiden, 1929. The early Egyptians rubbed noses as a sign of affection.

18 Pyramid Texts, §777–85. I have borrowed several suggestions from J. Spiegel, *Das Werden der altägyptischen Hochkultur*, Heidelberg, 1953, 176; and from J. Sainte Fare Garnot, *L'Hommage aux dieux*, Paris, 1954, 230 ff.

19 In the original. The reciter played the part of Geb.

20 The Kematef serpent is the original of Kneph, the supreme deity of some Gnostic sects.

21 Rochemonteix͵Chassinat, *Le temple d'Edfou*, I, 96; II, 76. I owe these references to Dr Erik Hornung.

22 Coffin Texts, IV, Spell 321, discussed by the present writer in *University of Birmingham Historical Journal*, V, 26 ff.

23 Cairo 28085. P. Lacau, *Sarcophages antérieurs au nouvel Empire*, Cairo, 1902, 220, 59.

24 A common phrase in the First Intermediate Period; *cf.* for example, R. Anthes, *Graffiti von Siut*, 20 (2).

25 Pyramid Texts, §229.

26 'With raised arm'—'*Ka'a*'—is the name of the last king of the First Dynasty.

27 Coffin Texts, Spell 154; Book of the Dead, 115; *cf.* K. Sethe, *Zeitschrift für Ägyptische Sprache*, LVIII, 1 ff.

28 The refrain of Spell 76 in the Coffin Texts.

29 Coffin Texts, V, 116*h*.

30 *ibid.*, II, Spell 79.

31 Coffin Texts from al Barsha, the cemetery of the ancient Hermopolis, use four strokes instead of the usual three to denote the plural.

32 Lacau, *op. cit.*, I, 220, 58.

33 Book of the Dead, 85, beginning.

34 *ibid.*, 15 (Ani, 18, 11).

35 Coffin Texts, Spell 223: 'I am the Double Lion' is restored from the later version in the Book of the Dead.

36 In the funerary symbolism the egg stands for the coffin from which the soul breaks out.

37 Pyramid Texts, §466 ff.

38 *ibid.*, §449 ff.

39 Coffin Texts, Spells 258, 260, 265 and 267.

40 H. Junker, *Oest. Akad. d. Wiss., Anzeiger*, XCI, 189.

41 Coffin Texts, IV, 239*b*.

42 *ibid.*, 79*b*.

43 Pyramid Texts, §1098 ff. I have based. this interpretation on K. Sethe, *Übersetzung und Kommentar zu den altägyptischen Pyramiden-texten*, IV, 368 ff.; *cf.* S. Schott, 'Die beiden Neunheiten als Ausdruck für Zähne und Lippen', *Z.A.S.*, LXXIV, 96 ff.

44 K. Sethe, *Dramatische Texte zu altägyptischen Mysterienspielen*, Leipzig, 1929; H. Junker, *Die Götterlehre von Memphis*, Berlin, 1940; J. Spiegel, *Das Werden der altägyptischen Hochkultur*, Chapter 12.

45 A. Heidel, *The Babylonian Genesis*, 2nd ed., Chicago, 1951, 18.

46 E. Dévaud, *Les maximes de Ptahhotep*, Fribourg, 1916, quoting lines 88, 116, 152 ff., 247 ff.

47 The name given at Memphis to the personification of the Primeval Mound.

48 or 'was satisfied'.

49 B. Grdseloff, *Annales du Service*, 1943, 290; *cf.* S. Morenz and F. Schubert, *Der Gott auf der Blume*, Berlin, 1953, *passim* and R. Anthes, *Z.A.S.*, LXXX, 81 ff.

50 Coffin Texts, IV, 197*c*—apparently a gloss.

51 Pyramid Texts, §264, following Anthes, *op. cit.*

CHAPTER II:

1 A. H. Gardiner, *The Admonitions of an Egyptian Sage*, Leipzig, 1909, 32.

2 M. Golenischeff, *Les papyrus hiératiques, nos. 1115, 1116A et 1116B*

de l'Ermitage Impérial à Saint-Pétersbourg, 1913, Pap. 1116A, l. 123 ff.

3 This can be either a rhetorical question or a reference to the chastise-ment of mankind.

4 Lit. 'knows the name'. As frequently in Egyptian, 'name' means 'true nature'. In Coffin Texts, I, 340d the Creator is described as 'His name is "None of the Gods know what moves him."'

5 E. Otto, 'Die Aetiologie des Grossen Katers in Heliopolis', *Z.A.S.*, LXXXI, 65.

6 E. Otto, *Der Vorwurf an Gott*, Hildesheim, 1951.

7 The so-called 'Dialogue of a man with his soul.' The section here quoted can be found most conveniently in Sethe, *Lesestücke*, Leipzig, 1934, 45.

8 Cairo, 28085. Lacau, *Sarcophages*, I, 220—the only text available to me.

9 *Ptahhotep*, I.507.

10 The so-called 'Cannibal Hymn' in the Pyramid Text presupposes a myth of this kind.

11 G. Posener, 'La légende de la mer insatiable', *Annuaire de l'Institut de Philologie et d'Histoire Orientales et Slaves*, XIII, Brussels, 1953, 461 ff.

12 K. Sethe, *Amun und die acht Urgötter von Hermopolis*, Berlin, 1929, 95.

13 Coffin Texts, IV, 147.

14 'Coil' means totality here, perhaps an echo of the belief that the High God has originated in serpent-form.

15 Coffin Texts, IV, Spell 325. The variants occur in coffins from Gebelein and Aswan (Eleventh Dynasty).

16 *ibid.*, Spell 307; Book of the Dead, 85.

17 Coffin Texts, IV, Spell 261; *cf.* Gardiner, *Transactions of the Society of Biblical Archaeology*, 1915, 253 ff.

18 The early versions from Spell 335 of the Coffin Texts. The texts of the New Kingdom differ widely from the earlier ones owing to the accre-tion of explanatory glosses which have been taken up into the text.

19 Early texts seem to indicate a sea or river battle. Maybe there was a myth that the primeval gods defeated water monsters from a boat.

20 Coffin Texts, I, 161 ff.

21 Lit. 'an area of land'.

22 Lit. 'two crawling ones'.

23 Inner coffin of Zepi (Louvre).

24 Coffin Texts, I, 320*d*.

25 A common expression, it refers to the blazing light of God at his first appearance.

26 An alternative version of this text is given in note 4 above.

27 Or 'all around me'.

28 Book of the Dead, 17.

29 Coffin Texts, IV, 140*d*.

30 *ibid.*, II, 240*e*ff.

31 *ibid.*, IV, 147*a*.

32 *ibid.*, II, 39*b*ff.

33 Some group of primeval deities, not yet determined.

34 Coffin Texts, V, Spell 554.

35 *ibid.*, IV, 181*c*ff.

36 The jackal was a wind spirit.

37 Hathor as the cow's head on a pole.

38 'Father' is not to be taken literally.

39 As Derchain has shown (*Chronique d'Égypte*, XXVII, 365), there are puns in this passage alluding to the cosmogony. These cannot be rendered in English.

40 There is no point in trying to find a definite location for Punt in these early religious texts. It is a distant southern country, the Egyptian Antipodes.

41 The 'year' consisted of 360 days. In addition, there were five days inserted between the end of the last month and New Year's Day. These were the birthdays of Osiris, Isis, Seth, Nephthys and one of the Horuses.

42 Bremner Rhind Papyrus (*Bibliotheca Aegyptiaca*, III, 26, 22ff); *cf.* R. O. Faulkner, *Journal of Egyptian Archaeology*, XXXII, 172.

43 'That place' means the world.

44 *i.e.* the sun.

45 Horus of Letopolis, a special form of Horus as the High God, who was blind when neither the sun nor the moon were visible.

46 The text has 'as Shu', etc. This refinement must mean something like 'I spat out and it was Shu.'

47 The Waters, the High God Atum, Shu and Tefnut—unless the text is corrupt, for one would have expected three, not four.

48 Horus means the High God here.

49 This seems to be an explanatory note.

50 Coffin Texts, IV, 173*f*ff.

51 Coffin Texts, IV, 98*b*ff.

52 But it does in Sumer, *cf.* E. Porada, *Mesopotamian Art in Cylinder Seals of the Pierpont Morgan Library*, New York, 1947, pl. 2.

53 Coffin Texts, IV, 98*g*ff.

54 Created as gods.

55 Coffin Texts, VI, 342*i*ff.

56 *ibid.*, VI, 388*j*ff.

CHAPTER III:

1 Z. Saad, *Royal Excavations at Helwan*, Cairo, 1952, pl. XIV, *b*.

2 J. Vandier, *La famine dans l'ancienne Égypte*, Paris, 1938, 83.

3 Pyramid Texts, §1039.

4 Coffin Texts, II, 104.

5 'Service of gifts'—in Egyptian theology the purpose of agriculture was to provide offerings at the altars of the gods and of the dead.

6 Pyramid Texts, §1195 ff.

7 Osiris is the son of the Earth God.

8 The word used—'*kbhw*'—denotes the flood waters as they are poured out over the land; *cf.* Erman-Grapow, *Wörterbuch der Ägyptischen Sprache*, V, 28 (2).

9 The 'Field of plenty' was originally the land which provided food for the royal palace (Cairo 1619, etc.) and was later used to describe paradise in material terms.

10 A. Moret, 'La légende d'Osiris à l'époque thébaine d'après l'hymne à Osiris du Louvre', *Bulletin de l'Institut français d'archéologie orientale du Caire*, 3, Cairo, 1931, 734.

11 A way of expressing well-being. When Si-renpet became governor of El Kab in the Twelfth Dynasty he was so pleased that 'he scratched the bellies of the stars . . . and danced among the planets' (Sethe, *Urkunden*, VII, 3).

12 Moret, *op. cit.*, 736.

13 *ibid.*, 740.

14 This statement is based on the discovery of a tumulus tomb of Osiris—if that is what it really is—at Medamud in Upper Egypt.

15 Translated in Chapter VI under the title 'The Great Quarrel'.

16 Book of the Dead, 175A.

17 Pyramid Texts, §258 ff.; *cf.* Ste. Fare Garnot, *L'Hommage*, 249 ff.

18 Pyramid Texts, §1004 ff.

19 *ibid.*, §581 ff.

20 *ibid.*, §205.

21 *ibid.*, §956 ff.; incorporating suggestions from Kees, *Lesebuch zur Religionsgeschichte*, 46 and Spiegel, *Werden*, 152 ff.

22 Pyramid Texts, §629.

23 Coffin Texts, IV, Spell 269. I have followed the early Sakkarah text except in two places where this is defective and the text has to be supplied from B. Mus. 6654.

24 H. Junker, *Giza*, XII, Vienna, 1955, 17.

CHAPTER IV:

1 For Osiris at Abydos, see H. Kees, *Unsterblichkeitsglaube . . . der alten Ägypter*, n.e. esp. 337 ff., H. W. Helck, *Archiv Orientalni*, XX, 72 ff. and L. G. Leeuwenberg, *Bulletin van der Vereeniging . . . tot antieke Beschaving*, Leiden, XXIX, 82 ff.

2 Coffin Texts, I, 197.

3 *ibid.*, 215e ff.

4 H. Kees, *Z.A.S.*, LXV, 65 ff. I have reversed lines 14 and 16 of Kees's text in translation to suit the English order of clauses.

5 Strictly, Henen-nesu is the general name for the city known to the Greeks as Heracleopolis; Naref is a suburb which contained the temple of Osiris.

6 E. Otto, 'Der Vorwurf an Gott', *Vorträge der orientalistischer Tagung in Marburg, 1950*, Hildesheim, 1951, 9.

7 Coffin Texts, 312. It has been treated by A. de Buck, *Journal of Egyptian Archaeology*, XXXV, 87 ff. and by E. Drioton, *Bibliotheca Orientalis*, X, 169 ff.

8 The Great Palace belongs to the god of the universe, so anyone who comes from it must be treated with respect.

CHAPTER V:

1 Coffin Texts, IV, 193*d*/*e*.

2 *ibid.*, IV, 276 ff.

3 *ibid.*, III, Spell 170, *cf.* Kees *Göttinger Totenbuchstudien*, Berlin, 1954, 19 ff.

4 G. Widengren, 'The Ascension of the Apostle and the Heavenly Book', *Uppsala Universitets Årsskrift*, 1950, 7.

5 Spells 451 and 351 in de Buck's edition. They form a connected text on the early Sakkarah coffin of Sitbastet.

6 *cf.* E. Drioton, 'La Religion égyptienne', *Histoire des religions*, ed. Brillant and Aigran, Paris, 1955, 88.

7 Coffin Texts, I, 21*d* (B-6-C) version.

8 Among primitives generally the dark interior of the earth contains the germ of everything that appears in the world and is also identified with the starry night sky. *cf.* K. Th. Preuss, *Die geistige Kultur der Naturvölker*, Berlin, 1932, 42. The best description of the various meanings of the '*Dat*' is Sethe, *Übersetzung und Kommentar zu den Pyramidentexten*, I, 49 ff.

9 Spell 336 contains a fragment of a myth about Sakhmet, the terrible goddess, who appeared first as a 'knot' (i.e. embryo) on top of the waters, and quickly grew up into a fiery monster who bestrode the world and brought the gods to subjection.

10 'City' hardly gives the correct sense of '*niwt*', which is charged with emotion in a way that is not paralleled by the word 'city'; '*niwt*' here means the numinous centre of the universe, the seat of God.

CHAPTER VI:

1 Pyramid Texts, §829*d/e*. See S. Schott, *Mythe und Mythenbildung*, Leipzig, 1945, 134.

2 In a sense the Primeval Waters are the 'Father' of Rê, but God as First Being is 'he who created himself'—an epithet usually applied to the Phoenix.

3 The personified Waters.

4 Up in the sky, the 'Great Palace'.

5 Rê asks the advice of Nun, the oldest, first.

6 Combining two myths of the origin of the sun—as creation of the waters envisaged as a single person, Nun, or as creation by the eight genii of the Hermopolis legend. *cf.* p. 54 ff.

7 The normal Egyptian oath.

8 This is based on a pun between '*shm*'—'to have control'—and Sakhmet, the terrible lioness and mistress of plague and slaughter.

9 Elephantine—in the extreme south of Egypt.

10 The High Priest at Heliopolis wore a side lock. See p. 54.

11 *i.e.* before he went on his tour of inspection.

12 Some town which had the reputation of producing the best-looking girls.

13 For Egyptian time cycles, see p. 141.

14 Son means 'grandson' here.

15 Probably the twilight. Coffin Text 227 describes Orion sailing in his boat over the *akhakh* of the sky. See Kees, *Untersuchungen*, XVII, 6.

16 Coffin Texts, V, 299*g* ff.

17 Lit. 'Catcher (sportsman?) of a phallus'—obviously an expletive.

18 Pyramid Texts, §681*d*/*e*.

19 A common phrase.

20 Is this another expletive?

21 Pyramid Texts, Spell 240. The 'desert' is the area of the non-human.

22 The site of Chemmis is a very controversial matter. *cf.* A. H. Gardiner, *J.E.A.*, XXX, 52 ff.

23 Pyramid Texts, §1214*b* ff.

24 *ibid.*, §1375—in the light of §1373, where the deceased is Horus as he sets out from Buto to claim his rightful inheritance.

25 Erman-Grapow, *Wörterbuch der Ägyptischen Sprache*, I, 15 (5).

26 Pyramid Texts, §1636*b*.

27 A. Klasens, *A Magical Statue Base*, Leiden, 1952. The argument that the text is essentially dramatic occurs in E. Drioton, *Le théâtre égyptien*, Cairo, 1942. Klasens disagrees.

28 I have tended to follow the Metternich Stela which is more restrained and seems to give a better text than the Leiden statue base.

29 [*sic*]. I do not understand this phase, despite Klasens' note on it in *A Magical Statue Base*, 98. It must mean 'not shining' or 'hidden'.

30 Metternich has 'death is destruction'. Leiden says 'death is their (the gods'?) destruction'. 'Death' must surely be that of Horus.

31 Osiris.

32 Can one just say, 'Horus will be as safe as the sun . . .'?

33 I have omitted the names of the seven scorpions, which do not aid the narrative.

34 The chief scorpion.

35 'Daughter' means a high-born woman of gentle birth.

36 I have omitted invocations to all the seven scorpions and a recapitulation of the opening section which is included in the spell.

37 The last two sentences seem to be misplaced—at least to modern taste.

38 A. Erman, *Zaubersprüche für Mutter und Kind*, Rs.2,2.

39 Papyrus Ebers, 69, 6.

40 A. H. Gardiner, *The Library of A. Chester Beatty; The Chester Beatty Papyri*, No. 1, Oxford, 1931. *cf.* J. Spiegel, *Die Erzählung vom*

Streite des Horus und Seth als Literaturwerk, Hamburg, 1937. Blackman, Wilson and Lefebvre have also contributed to the understanding of this difficult work.

41 Osiris is called Onnophris—*Wennofer*—in this text. For the meaning of this epithet see Gardiner, *Miscellanea Berolinensia*, 1952, 44 ff. In places I have used some brilliant suggestions by Wilson in Pritchard, *Ancient Near Eastern Texts*, 14 ff.

42 Some disorder seems to have crept into the text here.

43 Following Blackman, *J.E.A.*, XIX, 201.

44 Rê, Atum, Lord of All and Rê of the Horizon are all names for the High God.

45 Polite Egyptian for 'I'.

46 This looks as if it were added to suit the circumstances of the New Kingdom when Syrian goddesses were brought into the pantheon.

47 'Unweaned'?

48 Baba was a fertility god worshipped as a baboon or a white crown at Heracleopolis.

49 Hathor's name in Memphis.

50 For the sun's boat as the supreme court, see p. 71, *cf.* G. Nagel, *Bulletin de l'Institut français d'Archéologie orientale du Caire*, XXVIII.

51 An unknown locality.

52 So that the other gods should not see what he was doing. Seth is deceitful.

53 i.e. 'What more can you say?'

54 The celestial ferryman cannot be bribed.

55 'Brother'—relative.

56 Bronze only came into general use in Egypt in the New Kingdom.

57 Presumably the sun and moon—a trait borrowed from another myth.

58 'Stone' is a difficulty. Each of the contestants would have obeyed the instructions. Seth took the word in the literal sense, Horus caulked his boat with a material made from powdered 'stone'—at least either that or something like it.

59 230 feet.

60 Lit. 'on the outside'.

61 Perhaps mankind is divided into Egyptians and foreigners here.

62 Pyramid Texts, §1467, etc.

63 J. Spiegel. *Die Erzählung vom Streite des Horus und Seth als Literatur-werk*, Hamburg, 1937; especially 76 ff.

64 First recognized by E. Drioton, *Le théâtre égyptien*, Cairo, 1942

68 ff. *cf.* the later treatment by the same author in *Revue de l'Histoire du théâtre*, VI, 1954, 24 ff.

65 To an Egyptian this would have conveyed that the dragon will be opposed by the Great Goddess in her savage aspects.

66 These are obviously stage instructions.

67 *i.e.* at Seth's voice, which is the thunder.

68 Lit. *Aker*—a lion monster who dwelt in the interior of the earth. See p. 154f.

69 For the terrible goddess as the real opponent of Seth, see p. 223.

70 The universal taunt of the snake as a crawling creature. *cf.* Genesis, III, 14.

71 These sentences contain puns which cannot be rendered in another language.

72 Erman-Grapow, *op. cit.*, III, 107 (11).

73 i.e. Geb, the Earth God, who is represented in the pictures of the separation of Earth and Sky (see Fig. 6, p. 49) as lying down.

74 Coffin Text 148. *cf.* E. Drioton, *Le théâtre égyptien*, Cairo, 1942, 55 ff.

75 R. T. Rundle Clark, *University of Birmingham Historical Journal*, II, 1, 18ff.

76 '*swh.t*' means both 'egg' and 'embryo' in Egyptian.

77 i.e. the world.

78 The Great Magician is Seth. *cf.* Coffin Texts, II, 381*a*. This may be ironical.

79 Should this be given to Atum?

80 The text has become disarranged here. The 'Retreated One' is Atum and refers to the departure of the High God to the Sky—*cf.* Otto in *Z.A.S.*, LXXXI, 66.

81 A star?

CHAPTER VII:

1 O. G. S. Crawford, *The Eye Goddess*, London, 1957.

2 A full investigation of the Sacred Eye in Egypt has never been undertaken, but a beginning has now been made by Günter Rudnitsky: 'Die Aussage über das Auge des Horus', *Analecta Aegyptiaca*, V, Copenhagen, 1956.

3 There are other interpretations of the crouching falcon; it could have been a primitive, half articulated figurine or a mummified bird.

4 The eye is stylized in any case.

5 Sonnet 33.

6 God as he rose up on the Primeval Mound, or, as has been shown, perhaps the Mound itself. The coiling cobra is Rê's constant companion.

7 Perhaps, more accurately, it is the rising of the sun which makes them out of date—primeval or ancestral. See p. 87.

8 Lit. The *Hau nebut*—people who live, from the Egyptian point of view, in the far north, *cf.* J. Vercoutter, *Egyptiens et Prehellènes*, Paris, 1954, 37 ff.

9 Coffin Texts, Spell 335 (IV, 232 ff.), which was later expanded into Chapter 17 of the Book of the Dead.

10 The sky conceived as a cow.

11 Coffin Texts, III, 343.

12 Lacau, *Sarcophages antérieurs au nouvel Empire*, II, 29. For the 'Leonine One', see p. 145.

13 Pyramid Texts, Spell 220, *cf.* O. Firchow, *Grundzüge der Stylistik in den altägyptischen Pyramidentexten*, Berlin, 1954, 238.

14 H. Junker, 'Der Auszug der Hathor-Tefnut aus Nubien', *König. Preuss Akad. Berlin*, 1911. H. Junker, 'Die Onurislegende', *Denkschr. Wiener Akad.*, 59 (1), Vienna, 1917.

15 H. Kees, 'Bemerkungen zum Tieropfer der Ägypter und seiner Symbolik', *Gött. Nachr. Phil.-hist. Kl.* 1942, Nr. 2.

16 The animal rout as essentially foreign and the harbinger of Carnival needs investigation. It is one of the universal symbols.

17 Or above the sky vault.

18 This comment occurs as early as the Coffin Texts; Coffin Texts, IV, 219 f.

19 See the palette in the Metropolitan Museum, New York; illustrated by Ursula Schweitzer in *Das Wesen des Ka*, Hamburg, 1957, pl. Ia.

20 *Ptahhotep*, ed. Dévaud, l. 135 ff.

21 *Ptahhotep*, ed. Dévaud, l. 344.

22 This can be seen very clearly in the Horus name of Mycerinus of the Fourth Dynasty, which is written by a *Ka* sign, a bull and a male organ—'Generating Bull'?

23 Sethe, *Urkunden*, I, 189.

24 Pyramid Texts, §598.

25 *ibid.*, §1328.

26 *ibid.*, §610.

27 The *Tit* has been interpreted as symbolic of the blood of Isis when

she gave birth to Horus. This is derivative. The rubric to Book of the Dead 156 (see Nu, Brit. Mus. 10477, 27) shows it was regarded as a knot.

28 The best study of these inscriptions is J.-P. Lacau, 'Remarques sur les stèles fausses-portes de l'Horus Neteri-khet (Zoser) à Saqqarah', *Monuments Piot*, XLIX, 1957, 1–15.

29 Osiris normally wears the white crown of Upper Egypt. The *Atef* was originally a royal headgear, but it is already the distinguishing sign of triumphant Osiris in the Herakleopolitan Period; *cf.* Coffin Texts, Spell 313, esp. 11 ff.

30 Book of the Dead, Chapter 81, which is based on Pyramid Texts, Spell 250.

31 Medical Papyrus Hearst, 11, 13. See G. Posener, 'La Légende égyptienne de la mer insatiable', *Annuaire de l'Institut de Philosophie et d'Histoire Orientales et Slaves*, XIII, 1953, 461 ff.

32 Papyrus Ermitage, 1116A, *recto* l. 130 ff.

33 Pyramid Texts, §229.

34 *ibid.*, §434 ff. in the original first person.

35 K. Sethe, *Übersetzung und Kommentar zu den altägyptischen Pyramiden-texten*, I, 333.

36 E. Drioton, *Annales du Service des Antiquités d'Égypte*, XXXVIII, 240 ff.

37 Pyramid Texts, Spell 241.

38 *ibid.*, Spell 242. The last words are, literally, 'to whom he will be invisible'.

39 *ibid.*, §664.

40 *ibid.*, §668.

41 It forms part of the so-called 'Book of the Heavenly Cow'. Ch. Maystre, 'Le livre de la Vache du Ciel', *Bulletin de l'Institut français*, Cairo, 1941, 53 ff.

42 *i.e.* Before the separation of Earth and Sky, when Atum dwelt in the world.

43 *Hikê* is both the primeval Logos-Word and the god of magic.

44 Coffin Texts, I, 138/9 and 150.

45 *ibid.*

46 Herodotus, 11, 73.

47 A. Piankoff, 'The Theology of the New Kingdom in Ancient Egypt', *Antiquity and Survival*, I, The Hague 6, 488 ff.

48 They are not engaged in adoration because their palms are under the thumbs.

49 The sign might be read 'Neith' but it is more probably the marking on the expanded neck of the cobra and therefore stands for Ejo, the cobra goddess of *Dep*, part of the Delta city of Buto.

50 Book of the Dead, 36. *cf.* Budge, *Book of the Dead*, translation, London, 1956, 161. In rendering '*āpśait*' by 'grasshopper' I follow Erman-Grapow, *Wörterbuch*, I, 181, 19.

CHAPTER VIII:

1 The early portions come from Coffin Texts, IV, 228 ff. The later note is preserved in Chapter 17 of the Book of the Dead.

2 *cf.* The birth of Aphrodite Anadyomene from the blood of the phallus of Kronos.

3 See S. N. Kramer, *History begins at Sumer*, London, 1958.

4 H. Frankfort, *Cenotaph of Seti I at Abydos*, II, pl. 84–5. I follow Otto in *Das Verhältnis von Rite und Mythos im Ägyptischen*, Heidelberg, 1958, 19.

5 In Coffin Texts, VI.

INDEX

References to line drawings are indicated by page numbers in italic type